Processes of Constitutional Decisionmaking

2020 Supplement

2020 Supplement

Processes of Constitutional Decisionmaking

Cases and Materials

Seventh Edition

Prepared by Jack M. Balkin

Paul Brest
Professor of Law, Emeritus and Former Dean
Stanford Law School
and President, The William and Flora Hewlett Foundation

Sanford Levinson
W. St. John Garwood & W. St. John Garwood, Jr.
Centennial Chair in Law
University of Texas Law School

Jack M. Balkin
Knight Professor of Constitutional Law
and the First Amendment
Yale Law School

Akhil Reed Amar
Sterling Professor of Law and Political Science
Yale Law School

Reva B. Siegel
Nicholas deB. Katzenbach Professor of Law
Yale Law School

Published by Wolters Kluwer in New York.

Wolters Kluwer Legal & Regulatory U.S. serves customers worldwide with CCH, Aspen Publishers, and Kluwer Law International products. (www.WKLegaledu.com)

To contact Customer Service, e-mail customer.service@wolterskluwer.com, call 1-800-234-1660, fax 1-800-901-9075, or mail correspondence to:

    Wolters Kluwer
    Attn: Order Department
    PO Box 990
    Frederick, MD 21705

Printed in the United States of America.

1 2 3 4 5 6 7 8 9 0

ISBN 978-1-5438-2029-4

About Wolters Kluwer Legal & Regulatory U.S.

Wolters Kluwer Legal & Regulatory U.S. delivers expert content and solutions in the areas of law, corporate compliance, health compliance, reimbursement, and legal education. Its practical solutions help customers successfully navigate the demands of a changing environment to drive their daily activities, enhance decision quality and inspire confident outcomes.

Serving customers worldwide, its legal and regulatory portfolio includes products under the Aspen Publishers, CCH Incorporated, Kluwer Law International, ftwilliam.com, and MediRegs names. They are regarded as exceptional and trusted resources for general legal and practice-specific knowledge, compliance and risk management, dynamic workflow solutions, and expert commentary.

Contents

Processes of Constitutional Decisionmaking

2020 Supplement

Chapter 4

From Reconstruction to the New Deal: 1866-1934

Insert on p. 469 immediately before Note 1. The Idea of Police Power Jurisprudence:

JACOBSON v. MASSACHUSETTS
197 U.S. 11 (1905)

[A Massachusetts statute empowered local boards of health in cities and towns, "if necessary for the public health or safety," to "require . . . vaccination and revaccination of all the inhabitants thereof, and shall provide them with the means of free vaccination." Failure to comply would result in a five dollar fine. The statute made an exception for "children who present a certificate, signed by a registered physician, that they are unfit subjects for vaccination." In February 1902, the City of Cambridge, Massachusetts responded to an outbreak of smallpox by requiring smallpox vaccinations for those who had not been vaccinated since 1897. Vaccination would be available for free. Jacobson refused, and argued that the statute violated the Preamble to the Constitution, the Fourteenth Amendment, and "the spirit of the Constitution." After a jury trial, the court ordered him to pay the fine, and "ordered that he stand committed until the fine was paid."]

Mr. Justice HARLAN delivered the opinion of the court:

[A]lthough [the] preamble indicates the general purposes for which the people ordained and established the Constitution, it has never been regarded as the source of any substantive power conferred on the government of the United States, or on any of its departments. Such powers embrace only those expressly granted in the body of the Constitution, and such as may be implied from those so granted. Although, therefore, one of the declared objects of the Constitution was to secure the blessings of liberty to all under the sovereign jurisdiction and authority of the United States, no power can be exerted to that end by the United States, unless, apart from the preamble, it be found in some express delegation of power, or in some power to be properly implied therefrom. 1 Story, [Commentaries on the Constitution] § 462.

We also pass without discussion the suggestion that the above section of the statute is opposed to the spirit of the Constitution. Undoubtedly, as observed by Chief Justice Marshall, speaking for the court in *Sturges v. Crowninshield*, [17 U.S. (4 Wheat.) 122 (1819)], "the spirit of an instrument, especially of a constitution, is to be respected not less than its letter; yet the spirit is to be collected chiefly from its words." We have no need in this case to go beyond the plain, obvious meaning of the words in those provisions of the Constitution which, it is contended, must control our decision. . . .

[Defendant offered to prove] alleged injurious or dangerous effects of vaccination. [But] these so-called facts [are mere] matter[s] of opinion. The only "competent evidence" that could be presented to the court to prove these propositions was the testimony of experts, giving their opinions. [Even if defendant could produce medical experts to support his claims, a court] would have been obliged to consider the evidence in connection with facts of common knowledge, which the court will always regard in passing upon the constitutionality of a statute. . . .

[F]or nearly a century most of the members of the medical profession have regarded vaccination, repeated after intervals, as a preventive of smallpox; that, while they have recognized the possibility of injury to an individual from carelessness in the performance of it, or even in a conceivable case without carelessness, they generally have considered the risk of such an injury too small to be seriously weighed as against the benefits coming from the discreet and proper use of the preventive; and that not only the medical profession and the people generally have for a long time entertained these opinions, but legislatures and courts have acted upon them with general unanimity. If the defendant had been permitted to introduce such expert testimony as he had in support of these several propositions, it could not have changed the result. It would not have justified the court in holding that the legislature had transcended its power in enacting this statute on their judgment of what the welfare of the people demands. . . .

Is the statute . . . inconsistent with the liberty which the Constitution of the United States secures to every person against deprivation by the state?

The authority of the state to enact this statute is to be referred to what is commonly called the police power, — a power which the state did not surrender when becoming a member of the Union under the Constitution. Although this court has refrained from any attempt to define the limits of that power, yet it has distinctly recognized the authority of a state to enact quarantine laws and "health laws of every description;" indeed, all laws that relate to matters completely within its territory and which do not by their necessary operation affect the people of other states. According to settled principles, the police power of a state must be held to embrace, at least, such reasonable regulations established directly by legislative enactment as will protect the public health and the public safety. *Gibbons v. Ogden*. It is equally true that the state may invest local bodies called into existence for purposes of local administration with authority in some appropriate way to safeguard the public health and the public safety. . . .

The defendant insists that his liberty is invaded when the state subjects him to fine or imprisonment for neglecting or refusing to submit to vaccination; that a compulsory vaccination law is unreasonable, arbitrary, and oppressive, and, therefore, hostile to the inherent right of every freeman to care for his own body and health in such way as to him seems best; and that the execution of such a law against one who objects to vaccination, no matter for what reason, is nothing short of an assault upon his person. But the liberty secured by the Constitution of the United States to every person within its jurisdiction does not import an absolute right in each person to be, at all times and in all circumstances, wholly freed from restraint. There are manifold restraints to which every person is necessarily subject for the common good. On any other basis organized society could not exist with safety to its members. Society based on the rule that each one is a law unto himself would soon be confronted with disorder and anarchy. Real liberty for all could not exist under the operation of a principle which recognizes the right of each individual person to use his own, whether in respect of his person or his property, regardless of the injury that may be done to others. . . .

In *Crowley v. Christensen*, 137 U.S. 86, 89 [(1890), which upheld a California law banning the retail sale of liquor in the state], we said: "The possession and enjoyment of all rights are subject to such reasonable conditions as may be deemed by the governing authority of the country essential to the safety, health, peace, good order, and morals of the community. Even liberty itself, the greatest of all rights, is not unrestricted license to act according to one's own will. It is only freedom from restraint under conditions essential to the equal enjoyment of the same right by others. It is, then, liberty regulated by law." In the Constitution of Massachusetts adopted in 1780 it was laid down as a fundamental principle of the social compact that the whole people covenants with each citizen, and each citizen with the whole people, that all shall be governed by certain laws for "the common good," and that government is instituted "for the common good, for the protection, safety, prosperity, and happiness of the people, and not for the profit, honor, or private interests of any one man, family, or class of men." The good and welfare of the commonwealth, of which the legislature is primarily the judge, is the basis on which the police power rests in Massachusetts.

[T]he legislature of Massachusetts required the inhabitants of a city or town to be vaccinated only when, in the opinion of the board of health, that was necessary for the public health or the public safety. . . . To invest such a body with authority over such matters was not an unusual, nor an unreasonable or arbitrary, requirement. Upon the principle of self-defense, of paramount necessity, a community has the right to protect itself against an epidemic of disease which threatens the safety of its members. It is to be observed that when the regulation in question was adopted smallpox, according to the recitals in the regulation adopted by the board of health, was prevalent to some extent in the city of Cambridge, and the disease was increasing. . . . [I]f we are to attach, any value whatever to the knowledge which, it is safe to affirm, in common to all civilized peoples touching smallpox and the methods most usually employed to eradicate that disease, it cannot be adjudged that the present regulation of the board of health was not necessary in order to protect the public health and secure the public safety. . . . [T]he court would usurp the functions of another branch of government if it adjudged, as matter of law, that the mode adopted under the sanction of the state, to protect the people at large was arbitrary, and not justified by the necessities of the case. We say necessities of the case, because it might be that an acknowledged power of a local community to protect itself against an epidemic threatening the safety of all might be exercised in particular circumstances and in reference to particular persons in such an arbitrary, unreasonable manner, or might go so far beyond what was reasonably required for the safety of the public, as to authorize or compel the courts to interfere for the protection of such persons. . . .

[I]t was the duty of the constituted authorities primarily to keep in view the welfare, comfort, and safety of the many, and not permit the interests of the many to be subordinated to the wishes or convenience of the few. There is, of course, a sphere within which the individual may assert the supremacy of his own will, and rightfully dispute the authority of any human government, — especially of any free government existing under a written constitution, to interfere with the exercise of that will. But it is equally true that in every well-ordered society charged with the duty of conserving the safety of its members the rights of the individual in respect of his liberty may at times, under the pressure of great dangers, be subjected to such restraint, to be enforced by reasonable regulations, as the safety of the general public may demand. An American citizen arriving at an American port on a vessel in which, during the voyage, there had been cases of yellow fever or Asiatic cholera, he, although apparently free from disease himself, may yet, in some circumstances, be held in quarantine against his will on board of such vessel or in a quarantine station, until it be ascertained by inspection, conducted with due diligence, that the danger of the spread of the disease among the community at large has disappeared.

The liberty secured by the 14th Amendment, this court has said, consists, in part, in the right of a person "to live and work where he will" *Allgeyer v. Louisiana*, 165 U.S. 578 [(1897)], and yet he may be compelled, by force if need be, against his will and without regard to his personal wishes or his pecuniary interests, or even his religious or political convictions, to take his place in the ranks of the army of his country, and risk the chance of being shot down in its defense. It is not, therefore, true that the power of the public to guard itself against imminent danger depends in every case involving the control of one's body upon his willingness to submit to reasonable regulations established by the constituted authorities, under the sanction of the state, for the purpose of protecting the public collectively against such danger.

It is said, however, that the statute, as interpreted by the state court, although making an exception in favor of children certified by a registered physician to be unfit subjects for vaccination, makes no exception in case of adults in like condition. But this cannot be deemed a denial of the equal protection of the laws to adults; for the statute is applicable equally to all in like condition, and there are obviously reasons why regulations may be appropriate for adults which could not be safely applied to persons of tender years.

[Defendant pointed to] those of the medical profession who attach little or no value to vaccination as a means of preventing the spread of smallpox, or who think that vaccination causes other diseases of the body. What everybody knows the court must know, and therefore the state court judicially knew, as this court knows, that an opposite theory accords with the common belief, and is maintained by high medical authority. We must assume that, when the statute in question was passed, the legislature of Massachusetts was not unaware of these opposing theories, and was compelled, of necessity, to choose between them. It was not compelled to commit a matter involving the public health and safety to the final decision of a court or jury. It is no part of the function of a court or a jury to determine which one of two modes was likely to be the most effective for the protection of the public against disease. That was for the legislative department to determine in the light of all the information it had or could obtain. . . .

The state legislature proceeded upon the theory which recognized vaccination as at least an effective, if not the best-known, way in which to meet and suppress the evils of a smallpox epidemic that imperiled an entire population. . . . If there is any . . . power in the judiciary to review legislative action in respect of a matter affecting the general welfare, it can only be [according to] the rule that, if a statute purporting to have been enacted to protect the public health, the public morals, or the public safety, has no real or substantial relation to those objects, or is, beyond all question, a plain, palpable invasion of rights secured by the fundamental law, it is the duty of the courts to so adjudge, and thereby give effect to the Constitution. *Mugler v. Kansas*, 123 U.S. 623 [(1887) (state could limit sale of alcohol within the state)]; *Minnesota v. Barber*, 136 U.S. 313, 320 [(1890) (state could require health inspection before sale of meat);] *Atkin v. Kansas*, 191 U.S. 207, 223 [(1903) (state could restrict hours of state employees and employees of state contractors to eight hours a day to protect their health even if it could not restrict private employers in the same way)]. . . .

[I]n view of the methods employed to stamp out the disease of smallpox, [no one] can . . . confidently assert that the means prescribed by the state to that end has no real or substantial relation to the protection of the public health and the public safety. Such an assertion would not be consistent with the experience of this and other countries whose authorities have dealt with the disease of smallpox. [Justice Harlan discusses the history of smallpox regulation and scientific findings in Great Britain, Continental Europe, and Australia.] And the principle of vaccination as a means to prevent the spread of smallpox has been enforced in many states by statutes making the vaccination of children a condition of their right to enter or remain in public schools. . . .

The defendant offered to prove that vaccination "quite often" caused serious and permanent injury to the health of the person vaccinated; that the operation "occasionally" resulted in death; that it was "impossible" to tell "in any particular case" what the results of vaccination would be, or whether it would injure the health or result in death; that "quite often" one's blood is in a certain condition of impurity when it is not prudent or safe to vaccinate him; that there is no practical test by which to determine "with any degree of certainty" whether one's blood is in such condition of impurity as to render vaccination necessarily unsafe or dangerous; that vaccine matter is "quite often" impure and dangerous to be used, but whether impure or not cannot be ascertained by any known practical test; that the defendant refused to submit to vaccination for the reason that he had, "when a child," been caused great and extreme suffering for a long period by a disease produced by vaccination; and that he had witnessed a similar result of vaccination, not only in the case of his son, but in the cases of others.

[T]he legislature assumed that some children, by reason of their condition at the time, might not be fit subjects of vaccination; and it is suggested—and we will not say without reason—that such is the case with some adults. But the defendant did not offer to prove that, by reason of his then condition, he was in fact not a fit subject of vaccination at the time he was informed of the requirement of the regulation adopted by the board of health. . . . The matured opinions of medical men everywhere, and the experience of mankind, as all must know, negative the suggestion that it is not possible in any case to determine whether vaccination is safe. Was defendant exempted from the operation of the statute simply because of his dread of the same evil results experienced by him when a child, and which he had observed in the cases of his son and other children? Could he reasonably claim such an exemption because "quite often," or "occasionally," injury had resulted from vaccination, or because it was impossible, in the opinion of some, by any practical test, to determine with absolute certainty whether a particular person could be safely vaccinated?

[A]n affirmative answer to these questions would practically strip the legislative department of its function to care for the public health and the public safety when endangered by epidemics of disease. Such an answer would mean that compulsory vaccination could not, in any conceivable case, be legally enforced in a community, even at the command of the legislature, however widespread the epidemic of smallpox, and however deep and universal was the belief of the community and of its medical advisers that a system of general vaccination was vital to the safety of all.

We are not prepared to hold that a minority, residing or remaining in any city or town where smallpox is prevalent, and enjoying the general protection afforded by an organized local government, may thus defy the will of its constituted authorities, acting in good faith for all, under the legislative sanction of the state. If such be the privilege of a minority, then a like privilege would belong to each individual of the community, and the spectacle would be presented of the welfare and safety of an entire population being subordinated to the notions of a single individual who chooses to remain a part of that population. We are unwilling to hold it to be an element in the liberty secured by the Constitution of the United States that one person, or a minority of persons, residing in any community and enjoying the benefits of its local government, should have the power thus to dominate the majority when supported in their action by the authority of the state. . . . The safety and the health of the people of Massachusetts are, in the first instance, for that commonwealth to guard and protect. They are matters that do not ordinarily concern the national government. So far as they can be reached by any government, they depend, primarily, upon such action as the state, in its wisdom, may take; and we do not perceive that this legislation has invaded any right secured by the Federal Constitution.

[S]uppose the case of an adult who is embraced by the mere words of the act, but yet to subject whom to vaccination in a particular condition of his health or body would be cruel and inhuman in the last degree. We are not to be understood as holding that the statute was intended to be applied to such a case, or, if it was so intended, that the judiciary would not be competent to interfere and protect the health and life of the individual concerned. "All laws," this court has said, "should receive a sensible construction. General terms should be so limited in their application as not to lead to injustice, oppression, or an absurd consequence. It will always, therefore, be presumed that the legislature intended exceptions to its language which would avoid results of this character. The reason of the law in such cases should prevail over its letter." Until otherwise informed by the highest court of Massachusetts, we are not inclined to hold that the statute establishes the absolute rule that an adult must be vaccinated if it be apparent or can be shown with reasonable certainty that he is not at the time a fit subject of vaccination, or that vaccination, by reason of his then condition, would seriously impair his health, or probably cause his death. No such case is here presented. It is the cause of an adult who, for aught that appears, was himself in perfect health and a fit subject of vaccination, and yet, while remaining in the community, refused to obey the statute and the regulation adopted in execution of its provisions for the protection of the public health and the public safety, confessedly endangered by the presence of a dangerous disease. . . .

The judgment of the court below must be affirmed.

It is so ordered.

Mr. Justice BREWER and Mr. Justice PECKHAM dissent.

Discussion

1. Jacobson *and* Lochner. *Jacobson* was decided on February 20, 1905. *Lochner v. New York* was argued three days later, on February 23 and 24, 1905. It was decided on April 17, 1905. One of the cases Harlan cites in support of his argument, Atkin v. Kansas, 191 U.S. 207 (1903), upheld a maximum hour law for state workers and employees of state contractors, two years before *Lochner*. (In *Atkin*, Chief Justice Fuller and Justices Peckham and Brewer dissented without opinion).

2. *Public health, harm, and deference to government fact finding.* Is Harlan's approach consistent with Justice Peckham's decision in *Lochner v. New York*? Is it consistent with Harlan's own dissent in *Lochner*? How does Harlan describe the scope of police power in *Jacobson*? What degree of deference does he afford governments about contested matters of scientific fact, and about the relationship of means to ends?

3. Justice Peckham (along with Justice Brewer) dissented without opinion in *Jacobson*. What do you think his concerns were? (Note that Peckham and Brewer also dissented in Holden v. Hardy, 169 U.S. 366 (1898), which upheld maximum hour laws for people working in mines.) In *Lochner*, the question was whether the maximum hour law was really a health law or a disguised method of redistributing power or wealth from one class of persons to another. Are the same doubts present in *Jacobson*? Harlan argues that "[r]eal liberty for all could not exist under the operation of a principle which recognizes the right of each individual person to use his own, whether in respect of his person or his property, regardless of the injury that may be done to others." What do you think Peckham would say in response?

4. *Jacobson*, unlike *Lochner*, is still good law today, and courts in public health cases still cite its doctrine of deference to local governments and medical experts. To be sure, *Jacobson* reasons about these questions under then-existing doctrines of substantive due process and equal protection, and not under contemporary doctrines that generally require courts to exercise deference in ordinary economic and social legislation. Note also Justice Harlan's assertion that public health issues are primarily for state and local governments, and "do not ordinarily concern the national government." In 1905, the federal government was just beginning to legislate on health and safety issues. (The Pure Food and Drug Act, precursor of today's FDA, was passed in 1906.) After the New Deal and the growth of the administrative state, the federal government got more involved.

5. When *Jacobson* was decided in 1905, the Supreme Court had not yet applied the First Amendment to the states. Should the result have been different if, instead of arguing that the law violated his bodily integrity and his control over his own body, Jacobson argued that it was contrary to his religious beliefs? See *South Bay United Pentecostal Church v. Newsom*, discussed *infra*, Chapter 9.

6. How is the result in *Jacobson* affected by modern sexual autonomy cases like *Roe v. Wade*? Does that depend on what you think the proper basis for *Roe* is?

7. Note that the Massachusetts law fined people five dollars (around $150.00 in today's dollars) for refusing to be vaccinated. Why shouldn't the proper remedy for violation be compulsory vaccination rather than a fine? After all, if Jacobson paid the fine and caught smallpox later on, he might still infect other people. Does Harlan's opinion suggest that something more than a system of fines—for example, arresting people who refused to comply and forcing them to be vaccinated—would be constitutional?

8. At the end of the opinion, Harlan suggests that the case would be different if Jacobson could show that vaccination would endanger his health. The text of the Massachusetts statute only allowed exemption for children with certification from a doctor. Why does Harlan think that Jacobson would be exempted? Do you agree with Harlan's quick dismissal of Jacobson's equal protection argument?

9. *The Preamble and the "spirit of the Constitution."* Do you agree that the Preamble should play no role in Constitutional interpretation? Could you argue that the Preamble actually supports Massachusetts's position and not Jacobson's? What do you make of Harlan's arguments about the "spirit" of the Constitution? Are these arguments consistent with his arguments about how to interpret the Massachusetts statute at the end of the opinion, where he notes that "The reason of the law . . . should prevail over its letter"?

Part Two

Constitutional Adjudication
in the Modern World

Insert at the end of p. 540:

In Timbs v. Indiana, 139 S.Ct. 682 (2019), the Supreme Court applied the Excessive Fines Clause of the Eighth Amendment to the States. Timbs pleaded guilty to dealing in controlled substances. The State of Indiana brought a civil forfeiture action against Timbs' vehicle, arguing that it had been used to transport heroin. The value of the vehicle was four times as great as the maximum fine assessable against him for his drug conviction.

Writing for a unanimous Supreme Court, Justice Ginsburg argued that "the protection against excessive fines has been a constant shield throughout Anglo-American history: Exorbitant tolls undermine other constitutional liberties. Excessive fines can be used, for example, to retaliate against or chill the speech of political enemies. . . . Even absent a political motive, fines may be employed 'in a measure out of accord with the penal goals of retribution and deterrence,' for 'fines are a source of revenue,' while other forms of punishment 'cost a State money.' . . . This concern is scarcely hypothetical. See Brief for American Civil Liberties Union et al. as Amici Curiae 7 ("Perhaps because they are politically easier to impose than generally applicable taxes, state and local governments nationwide increasingly depend heavily on fines and fees as a source of general revenue.")." Thus, "[t]he historical and logical case for concluding that the Fourteenth Amendment incorporates the Excessive Fines Clause is overwhelming. Protection against excessive punitive economic sanctions secured by the Clause is, to repeat, both 'fundamental to our scheme of ordered liberty' and 'deeply rooted in this Nation's history and tradition.'"

Indiana argued that although the prohibition against excessive fines was traditional, the development of civil *in rem* forfeiture laws was a comparatively recent innovation and therefore "the Clause's specific application to such forfeitures is neither fundamental nor deeply rooted." The Court rejected this argument: "In considering whether the Fourteenth Amendment incorporates a protection contained in the Bill of Rights, we ask whether the right guaranteed—not each and every particular application of that right—is fundamental or deeply rooted." The Court had not asked, for example "whether the Free Speech Clause's application specifically to social media websites was fundamental or deeply rooted."

Justice Thomas concurred in the judgment, arguing that "the right to be free from excessive fines is one of the 'privileges or immunities of citizens of the United States' protected by the Fourteenth Amendment['s]" Privileges or Immunities Clause. Justice Gorsuch concurred, but added that "[a]s an original matter . . . the appropriate vehicle for incorporation may well be the Fourteenth Amendment's Privileges or Immunities Clause."

In Ramos v. Louisiana, 140 S.Ct. 1390 (2020), the Supreme Court applied the Sixth Amendment's requirement of unanimous jury verdicts for serious offenses to the states. In Apodaca v. Oregon, 406 U.S. 404 (1972), and Johnson v. Louisiana, 406 U.S. 356 (1972), four dissenting Justices held that the Sixth Amendment requires unanimous jury verdicts, and that this requirement applied to the states. Four Justices in the plurality held that unanimity was not required because its cost outweighed its benefits. Justice Powell, who held to a "two-track" theory of incorporation, cast the deciding vote. He argued that the history of the Sixth Amendment and subsequent precedents required unanimity. But he maintained that this guarantee was not fully applicable to the states, even though the Supreme Court, in Malloy v. Hogan, 378 U.S. 1 (1964), had rejected the two-track theory.

Justice Gorsuch wrote the majority opinion: "Wherever we might look to determine what the term 'trial by an impartial jury trial' meant at the time of the Sixth Amendment's adoption — whether it's the common law, state practices in the founding era, or opinions and treatises written soon afterward — the answer is unmistakable. A jury must reach a unanimous verdict in order to convict. The requirement of juror unanimity emerged in 14th century England and was soon accepted as a vital right protected by the common law. . . . It was against this backdrop that James Madison drafted and the States ratified the Sixth Amendment in 1791. By that time, unanimous verdicts had been required for about 400 years. If the term 'trial by an impartial jury' carried any meaning at all, it surely included a requirement as long and widely accepted as unanimity." Since the adoption of the Bill of Rights, "[t]his Court has, repeatedly and over many years, recognized that the Sixth Amendment requires unanimity. . . . In all, this Court has commented on the Sixth Amendment's unanimity requirement no fewer than 13 times over more than 120 years."

Most states, Justice Gorsuch explained, have required unanimous verdicts. Louisiana and Oregon's different rules originated in racism; in particular, a desire to dilute the effect of votes by black jurors in cases involving black criminal defendants. "[C]ourts in both Louisiana and Oregon have frankly acknowledged that race was a motivating factor in the adoption of their States' respective nonunanimity rules."

Given the weight of authority, the only remaining question was whether to abandon the result in *Apodaca*. A majority of Justices agreed, but came to the result in different ways. In one part of his opinion, Justice Gorsuch, joined by Justices Ginsburg and Breyer, held that *Apodaca*'s rule was not even binding precedent, since it reflected only Justice Powell's view.

In another part of his opinion, Justice Gorsuch, joined by Justices Ginsburg, Breyer, and Sotomayor, held that if *Apodaca* were a precedent, Oregon and Louisiana lacked sufficient reliance interests: "neither Louisiana nor Oregon claims anything like the prospective economic, regulatory, or social disruption litigants seeking to preserve precedent usually invoke. No one, it seems, has signed a contract, entered a marriage, purchased a home, or opened a business based on the expectation that, should a crime occur, at least the accused may be sent away by a 10-to-2 verdict. Nor does anyone suggest that nonunanimous verdicts have 'become part of our national culture.' It would be quite surprising if they had, given that nonunanimous verdicts are insufficient to convict in 48 States and federal court." It was true that "Louisiana and Oregon may need to retry defendants convicted of felonies by nonunanimous verdicts whose cases are still pending on direct appeal. . . . Those States credibly claim that the number of nonunanimous felony convictions still on direct appeal are somewhere in the hundreds, and retrying or plea bargaining these cases will surely impose a cost. But new rules of criminal procedures usually do, often affecting significant numbers of pending cases across the whole country."

Justices Sotomayor and Kavanaugh concurred in part. Each of their opinions agreed that *Apodaca* should be overruled and offered their own theories of how and when the Court should overturn previous precedents. Justice Sotomayor also emphasized the racial history of Louisiana and Oregon's rules. Justice Thomas concurred in the judgment, arguing that the case should have been decided under the Privileges or Immunities Clause.

Justice Alito, joined by Chief Justice Roberts and Justice Kagan, dissented: "I would not overrule *Apodaca*. Whatever one may think about the correctness of the decision, it has elicited enormous and entirely reasonable reliance. And before this Court decided to intervene, the decision appeared to have little practical importance going forward. Louisiana has now abolished non-unanimous verdicts, and Oregon seemed on the verge of doing the same until the Court intervened."

Chapter 6

Federalism, Separation of Powers, and National Security in the Modern Era

Add to the end of note 3 on p. 756:

In Allen v. Cooper, 140 S.Ct. 994 (2020), the Court applied *Florida Prepaid* to hold that Congress lacked authority to abrogate the states' sovereign immunity from copyright infringement suits in the Copyright Remedy Clarification Act of 1990. Justice Thomas concurred in part and in the judgment. Justice Breyer, joined by Justice Ginsburg, concurred in the judgment.

Insert on p. 824 immediately before Note: State Sovereign Immunity

MURPHY v. NATIONAL COLLEGIATE ATHLETIC ASSOCIATION
138 S.Ct. 1461 (2018)

[The Professional and Amateur Sports Protection Act (PASPA) makes it unlawful for a State or its subdivisions "to sponsor, operate, advertise, promote, license, or authorize by law or compact . . . a lottery, sweepstakes, or other betting, gambling, or wagering scheme based . . . on" competitive sporting events, 28 U.S.C. § 3702(1), and for "a person to sponsor, operate, advertise, or promote" those same gambling schemes if done "pursuant to the law or compact of a governmental entity," § 3702(2). But PASPA does not make sports gambling itself a federal crime. Instead, it allows the Attorney General, as well as professional and amateur sports organizations, to bring civil actions to enjoin violations.

"Grandfather" provisions allow existing forms of sports gambling to continue in four States. Another provision would have permitted New Jersey to set up a sports gambling scheme in Atlantic City within a year of PASPA's enactment. New Jersey did not take advantage of that option but later changed its mind, and passed a 2012 law legalizing sports gambling schemes in Atlantic City and at horseracing tracks. The NCAA and three major professional sports leagues successfully sued to enjoin New Jersey's new gambling law under PASPA.

In 2014, New Jersey passed a new law. Instead of affirmatively authorizing sports gambling schemes, the 2014 law simply repealed existing state-law provisions that prohibited sports gambling to the extent that they involved wagering on sporting events (1) by persons 21 years of age or older; (2) at a horseracing track or a casino or gambling house in Atlantic City; and (3) did not involve a New Jersey college team or a collegiate event taking place in the State of New Jersey. Once again, the NCAA and the sports leagues sued under PASPA. New Jersey defended on the ground that PAPSA violates the anti-commandeering principle of *New York v. United States*.]

Justice ALITO delivered the opinion of the Court.

II

Petitioners argue that the anti-authorization provision requires States to maintain their existing laws against sports gambling without alteration. . . . In our view, petitioners' interpretation is correct: When a State completely or partially repeals old laws banning sports gambling, it "authorize[s]" that activity. . . . The concept of state "authorization" makes sense only against a backdrop of prohibition or regulation. A State is not regarded as authorizing everything that it does not prohibit or regulate. No one would use the term in that way. For example, no one would say that a State "authorizes" its residents to brush their teeth or eat apples or sing in the shower. We commonly speak of state authorization only if the activity in question would otherwise be restricted. . . .

III

A

The anticommandeering doctrine may sound arcane, but it is simply the expression of a fundamental structural decision incorporated into the Constitution, *i.e.,* the decision to withhold from Congress the power to issue orders directly to the States. When the original States declared their independence, they claimed the powers inherent in sovereignty — in the words of the Declaration of Independence, the authority "to do all . . . Acts and Things which Independent States may of right do." The Constitution limited but did not abolish the sovereign powers of the States, which retained "a residuary and inviolable sovereignty.". . .

The Constitution limits state sovereignty in several ways. It directly prohibits the States from exercising some attributes of sovereignty. See, *e.g.,* Art. I, § 10. And the Constitution indirectly restricts the States by granting certain legislative powers to Congress, see Art. I, § 8, while providing in the Supremacy Clause that federal law is the "supreme Law of the Land . . . any Thing in the Constitution or Laws of any State to the Contrary notwithstanding," Art. VI, cl. 2. This means that when federal and state law conflict, federal law prevails and state law is preempted.

The legislative powers granted to Congress are sizable, but they are not unlimited. The Constitution confers on Congress not plenary legislative power but only certain enumerated powers. Therefore, all other legislative power is reserved for the States, as the Tenth Amendment confirms. And conspicuously absent from the list of powers given to Congress is the power to issue direct orders to the governments of the States. The anticommandeering doctrine simply represents the recognition of this limit on congressional authority. . . .

New York v. United States, 505 U.S. 144 (1992) . . . concerned a federal law that required a State, under certain circumstances, either to "take title" to low-level radioactive waste or to "regulat[e] according to the instructions of Congress." . . . Congress issued orders to either the legislative or executive branch of state government (depending on the branch authorized by state law to take the actions demanded). Either way, the Court held, the provision was unconstitutional because "the Constitution does not empower Congress to subject state governments to this type of instruction." . . . "We have always understood that even where Congress has the authority under the Constitution to pass laws requiring or prohibiting certain acts, it lacks the power directly to compel the States to require or prohibit those acts." "Congress may not simply 'commandee[r] the legislative processes of the States by directly compelling them to enact and enforce a federal regulatory program.'" "Where a federal interest is sufficiently strong to cause Congress to legislate, it must do so directly; it may not conscript state governments as its agents."

Five years after *New York*, the Court applied the same principles to a federal statute requiring state and local law enforcement officers to perform background checks and related tasks in connection with applications for handgun licenses. *Printz.* Holding this provision unconstitutional, the Court put the point succinctly: "The Federal Government" may not "command the States' officers, or those of their political subdivisions, to administer or enforce a federal regulatory program." This rule applies, *Printz* held, not only to state officers with policymaking responsibility but also to those assigned more mundane tasks.

B

Our opinions in *New York* and *Printz* explained why adherence to the anticommandeering principle is important. Without attempting a complete survey, we mention several reasons that are significant here.

First, the rule serves as "one of the Constitution's structural protections of liberty." *Printz.* "The Constitution does not protect the sovereignty of States for the benefit of the States or state governments as abstract political entities." *New York.* "To the contrary, the Constitution divides authority between federal and state governments for the protection of individuals." " '[A] healthy balance of power between the States and the Federal Government [reduces] the risk of tyranny and abuse from either front.'"

Second, the anticommandeering rule promotes political accountability. When Congress itself regulates, the responsibility for the benefits and burdens of the regulation is apparent. Voters who like or dislike the effects of the regulation know who to credit or blame. By contrast, if a State imposes regulations only because it has been commanded to do so by Congress, responsibility is blurred.

Third, the anticommandeering principle prevents Congress from shifting the costs of regulation to the States. If Congress enacts a law and requires enforcement by the Executive Branch, it must appropriate the funds needed to administer the program. It is pressured to weigh the expected benefits of the program against its costs. But if Congress can compel the States to enact and enforce its program, Congress need not engage in any such analysis.

IV

The PASPA provision at issue here—prohibiting state authorization of sports gambling—violates the anticommandeering rule. That provision unequivocally dictates what a state legislature may and may not do. . . . [S]tate legislatures are put under the direct control of Congress. It is as if federal officers were installed in state legislative chambers and were armed with the authority to stop legislators from voting on any offending proposals. A more direct affront to state sovereignty is not easy to imagine.

Neither respondents nor the United States contends that Congress can compel a State to enact legislation, but they say that prohibiting a State from enacting new laws is another matter. Noting that the laws challenged in *New York* and *Printz* "told states what they must do instead of what they must not do," respondents contend that commandeering occurs "only when Congress goes beyond precluding state action and affirmatively commands it."

This distinction is empty. It was a matter of happenstance that the laws challenged in *New York* and *Printz* commanded "affirmative" action as opposed to imposing a prohibition. The basic principle—that Congress cannot issue direct orders to state legislatures—applies in either event.

Here is an illustration. PASPA includes an exemption for States that permitted sports betting at the time of enactment, but suppose Congress did not adopt such an exemption. Suppose Congress ordered States with legalized sports betting to take the affirmative step of criminalizing that activity and ordered the remaining States to retain their laws prohibiting sports betting. There is no good reason why the former would intrude more deeply on state sovereignty than the latter.

B

Respondents and the United States [rely on] *South Carolina v. Baker*, 485 U.S. 505 (1988), [in which] the [challenged] federal law . . . removed the federal tax exemption for interest earned on state and local bonds unless they were issued in registered rather than bearer form. This law did not order the States to enact or maintain any existing laws. Rather, it simply had the indirect effect of pressuring States to increase the rate paid on their bearer bonds in order to make them competitive with other bonds paying taxable interest. . . . The anticommandeering doctrine does not apply when Congress evenhandedly regulates an activity in which both States and private actors engage.

That principle formed the basis for the Court's decision in *Reno v. Condon*, 528 U.S. 141 (2000), which [upheld] a federal law restricting the disclosure and dissemination of personal information provided in applications for driver's licenses. The law applied equally to state and private actors. It did not regulate the States' sovereign authority to "regulate their own citizens."

In *Hodel*, the federal law, which involved what has been called "cooperative federalism," by no means commandeered the state legislative process. Congress enacted a statute that comprehensively regulated surface coal mining and offered States the choice of "either implement[ing]" the federal program "or else yield[ing] to a federally administered regulatory program." Thus, the federal law *allowed* but did not *require* the States to implement a federal program. "States [were] not compelled to enforce the [federal] standards, to expend any state funds, or to participate in the federal regulatory program in any manner whatsoever." If a State did not "wish" to bear the burden of regulation, the "full regulatory burden [would] be borne by the Federal Government."

Finally, in *FERC v. Mississippi*, 456 U.S. 742 (1982), the federal law in question issued no command to a state legislature. Enacted to restrain the consumption of oil and natural gas, the federal law directed state utility regulatory commissions to consider, but not necessarily to adopt, federal " 'rate design' and regulatory standards." The Court held that this modest requirement did not infringe the States' sovereign powers, but the Court warned that it had "never . . . sanctioned explicitly a federal command to the States to promulgate and enforce laws and regulations." *FERC* was decided well before our decisions in *New York* and *Printz*, and PASPA, unlike the law in *FERC*, does far more than require States to *consider* Congress's preference that the legalization of sports gambling be halted. . . .

V

[Nor does] the anti-authorization prohibition . . . constitute[] a valid preemption provision. . . . [I]n order for the PASPA provision to preempt state law, it must satisfy two requirements. First, it must represent the exercise of a power conferred on Congress by the Constitution. . . . Second, since the Constitution "confers upon Congress the power to regulate individuals, not States," *New York*, the PASPA provision at issue must be best read as one that regulates private actors.

Our cases have identified three different types of preemption—"conflict," "express," and "field"—but all of them work in the same way: Congress enacts a law that imposes restrictions or confers rights on private actors; a state law confers rights or imposes restrictions that conflict with the federal law; and therefore the federal law takes precedence and the state law is preempted.

A recent example [of conflict preemption] is *Mutual Pharmaceutical Co. v. Bartlett*, 570 U.S. 472 (2013). In that case, a federal law enacted under the Commerce Clause regulated manufacturers of generic drugs, prohibiting them from altering either the composition or labeling approved by the Food and Drug Administration. A State's tort law, however, effectively required a manufacturer to supplement the warnings included in the FDA-approved label. We held that the state law was preempted because it imposed a duty that was inconsistent—*i.e.,* in conflict—with federal law.

"Express preemption" operates in essentially the same way, but this is often obscured by the language used by Congress in framing preemption provisions. [I]n *Morales v. Trans World Airlines, Inc.,* 504 U.S. 374 (1992) . . . [t]he Airline Deregulation Act of 1978 lifted prior federal regulations of airlines, and "[t]o ensure that the States would not undo federal deregulation with regulation of their own," the Act provided that "no State or political subdivision thereof . . . shall enact or enforce any law, rule, regulation, standard, or other provision having the force and effect of law relating to rates, routes, or services of any [covered] air carrier."

This language might appear to operate directly on the States, but it is a mistake to be confused by the way in which a preemption provision is phrased. . . . [I]f we look beyond the phrasing employed in the Airline Deregulation Act's preemption provision, it is clear that this provision operates just like any other federal law with preemptive effect. It confers on private entities (*i.e.,* covered carriers) a federal right to engage in certain conduct subject only to certain (federal) constraints.

"Field preemption" operates in the same way. Field preemption occurs when federal law occupies a "field" of regulation "so comprehensively that it has left no room for supplementary state legislation." In describing field preemption, we have sometimes used the same sort of shorthand employed by Congress in express preemption provisions. See, *e.g., Oneok, Inc. v. Learjet, Inc.,* 575 U.S. _____ (2015) ("Congress has forbidden the State to take action in the *field* that the federal statute pre-empts"). But in substance, field pre-emption does not involve congressional commands to the States. Instead, like all other forms of preemption, it concerns a clash between a constitutional exercise of Congress's legislative power and conflicting state law.

[I]n *Arizona v. United States,* 567 U.S. 387, [we explained that] federal statutes "provide a full set of standards governing alien registration," [and] we concluded that these laws "reflect[ ] a congressional decision to foreclose any state regulation in the area, even if it is parallel to federal standards." What this means is that the federal registration provisions not only impose federal registration obligations on aliens but also confer a federal right to be free from any other registration requirements.

In sum, regardless of the language sometimes used by Congress and this Court, every form of preemption is based on a federal law that regulates the conduct of private actors, not the States.

[I]t is clear that the PASPA provision prohibiting state authorization of sports gambling is not a preemption provision because there is no way in which this provision can be understood as a regulation of private actors. It certainly does not confer any federal rights on private actors interested in conducting sports gambling operations. (It does not give them a federal right to engage in sports gambling.) Nor does it impose any federal restrictions on private actors. . . . Thus, there is simply no way to understand the provision prohibiting state authorization as anything other than a direct command to the States. And that is exactly what the anticommandeering rule does not allow.

VI

[Justice Alito concluded that PASPA's prohibition of state licensing of sports gambling also violated the anticomandeering principle.] Just as Congress lacks the power to order a state legislature not to enact a law authorizing sports gambling, it may not order a state legislature to refrain from enacting a law licensing sports gambling.

Finally, Justice Alito concluded that the offending provision was not severable from the rest of PAPSA, so that the entire statute, which prohibited states and private parties from sponsoring, operating, or advertising, or promoting sports gambling schemes, was invalid.]

[A concurring opinion by Justice Thomas is omitted.]

[Justice Ginsburg dissented, joined by Justice Sotomayor and in part by Justice Breyer. She argued that the Court should not have struck down two features of PAPSA. The first bans States themselves (or their agencies) from "sponsor[ing], operat[ing], advertis[ing], [or] promot[ing]" sports-gambling schemes. The second stops private parties from "sponsor[ing], operat[ing], advertis[ing], or promot[ing]" sports-gambling schemes if state law authorizes them to do so. "Nothing in these . . . prohibitions commands States to do anything other than desist from conduct federal law proscribes." Justice Breyer agreed with the Court's constitutional analysis but agreed with Justice Ginsburg that parts of the statute should survive.]

Discussion

1. *Severability.* If the Court had struck down the ban on authorization of sports gambling schemes but not any other part of PAPSA, the federal ban on private parties "sponsor[ing], operat[ing], advertis[ing], or promot[ing]" sports-gambling schemes would have remained in place, and the NCAA and the sports leagues would still have been able to enforce it. Thus, the most important practical effect of *Murphy* was Justice Alito's severability holding—that if Congress had known that it could not constitutionally prohibit states from authorizing sports gambling schemes, Congress would not have wanted to leave the general federal ban on sports gambling in place. Do you agree?

2. *Ordering versus forbidding.* The Court argues that, from the standpoint of federalism, there is no difference between ordering a state to pass a particular regulation and forbidding it from passing a regulation. Consider Justice Alito's three justifications for the anticommandeering principle. Are they equally powerful in the context of forbidding a state from passing a law?

When the federal government forbids a state from passing a new law, does it shift additional enforcement costs to the state, or does it simply preserve the regulatory status quo? (What if regulatory costs increase over time? Should we say that the federal government is, in effect, shifting costs to the state?)

What about blurring of lines of responsibility? Does forbidding a state from passing a new law tend to confuse voters about who bears responsibility for the state's failure the law? For example, is it reasonable to think that PAPSA confused New Jersey's voters about the reason why the state hadn't legalized gambling? Why wouldn't New Jersey politicians have incentives to blame the federal government, making clear where the responsibility lay? On the other hand, are the incentives any different in a case in which the federal government requires New Jersey to pass a law? If not, this suggests that the confusion argument is not very strong in either the case of requiring or forbidding.

Perhaps preventing states from changing their laws eliminates a potential source of liberty. On the other hand, does PAPSA limit liberty more than if the federal government had simply directly prohibited gambling?

3. *Anticommandeering and preemption.* This last point suggests that *Murphy* may really be a requirement that federal government use direct regulation (and thus preemption) rather than forbidding states to pass new laws. As long as both states and private parties are prohibited from sponsoring gambling, Alito explains, there is no anticommandeering problem. Why do you think the federal government did not simply preempt state gambling laws and prohibit sports betting nationwide? One possibility is that a single federal rule would have made it more difficult politically to justify the grandfathering provisions for certain states. A second is that the federal government might have wanted to keep sports gambling illegal where bans existed but allow each state to decide on the appropriate penalties and methods of gambling regulation, keeping these questions (and prosecutions) within the state criminal justice system.

Note: Sanctuary Cities and Federalism

New federalism problems have arisen from the Trump Adminstration's attacks on "sanctuary cities." The term has no settled legal meaning. Key debates concern whether states and municipalities will cooperate with federal immigration officials in identifying, detaining, and delivering persons suspected of being undocumented aliens to federal officials.

An ICE detainer—or "immigration hold"—is an enforcement tool used by U.S. Immigration and Customs Enforcement (ICE). An ICE civil detainer request asks a local law enforcement agency to continue to hold an inmate who is in a local jail because of actual or suspected violations of state criminal laws for up to 48 hours after his or her scheduled release so that ICE can determine if it wants to take that individual into ICE custody.

Largely because of federalism doctrines such as *Printz v. United States*, ICE civil detainer requests are voluntary and local governments are not required to honor them. See also Morales v. Chadbourne, 793 F.3d 208, 215-217 (1st Cir. 2015) (holding that it is a violation of the Fourth Amendment for local jurisdictions to hold suspected or actual removable aliens in response to civil detainer requests because civil detainer requests are often not supported by an individualized determination of probable cause that a crime has been committed.) ICE does not reimburse local jurisdictions for the cost of detaining individuals in response to a civil detainer request and it does not indemnify local jurisdictions for the potential liability they could face for related Fourth Amendment violations.

A 1996 law, 8 U.S.C. § 1373, provides that a "State, or local government entity or official may not prohibit, or in any way restrict, any government entity or official from sending to, or receiving from, the Immigration and Naturalization Service information regarding the citizenship or immigration status, lawful or unlawful, of any individual." ICE is the successor of the Immigration and Naturalization Service. Is § 1373 consistent with the Tenth Amendment doctrines enunciated in *New York*, *Printz*, and *Murphy?* Could one read § 1373 narrowly to avoid constitutional problems?

As a presidential candidate, Donald Trump spoke out against sanctuary cities, and promised that he would end them. Shortly after taking office, on January 25, 2017, President Trump issued Executive Order No. 13768, "Enhancing Public Safety in the Interior of the United States." 82 Fed. Reg. 8799 (Jan. 25, 2017). Section 1 of the order reads, in part, "Sanctuary jurisdictions across the United States willfully violate Federal law in an attempt to shield aliens from removal from the United States." Section 2 states that the policy of the executive branch is to "[e]nsure that jurisdictions that fail to comply with applicable Federal law do not receive Federal funds, except as mandated by law."

Section 9(a) of the Executive Order restricts federal grants going to "sanctuary jurisdictions." It provides:

> In furtherance of this policy, the Attorney General and the Secretary [of Homeland Security], in their discretion and to the extent consistent with law, shall ensure that jurisdictions that willfully refuse to comply with 8 U.S.C. 1373 (sanctuary jurisdictions) are not eligible to receive Federal grants, except as deemed necessary for law enforcement purposes by the Attorney General or the Secretary. The Secretary has the authority to designate, in his discretion and to the extent consistent with law, a jurisdiction as a sanctuary jurisdiction. The Attorney General shall take appropriate enforcement action against any entity that violates 8 U.S.C. 1373, or which has in effect a statute, policy, or practice that prevents or hinders the enforcement of Federal law.

The Executive Order does not define "sanctuary jurisdiction" nor does it define what constitutes "willfully refus[ing] to comply with" § 1373. Section 1373, in turn, makes no mention of federal funds; it does not condition receipt of funds on compliance and it does not authorize withholding funds for violation.

Is the Executive Order consistent with the Constitution? Consider the following questions:

(1) Does the President have authority to withhold federal funds to enforce § 1373 if Congress has not explicitly authorized him to do so?

(2) Assuming that the President can condition receipt of federal funds on compliance with § 1373, is the resulting restriction on federal funds beyond federal powers under *South Dakota v. Dole* and *NFIB v. Sebelius?*

The Executive Order threatens to remove funding for all federal grants except funds "deemed necessary for law enforcement purposes." That means that the federal grants threatened concern those not deemed necessary for law enforcement purposes. Is there a sufficient nexus between the President's requirement and the funds that the President threatens to withhold? If there is a sufficient nexus, is the amount of federal funding (or the percentage of a state's or municipality's budget) withheld sufficiently large to be coercive under *Sebelius*?

For further discussion, see City and County of San Francisco v. Trump, 897 F.3d 1225 (9th Cir. 2018) (holding that the Executive Order was not authorized by Congress and therefore violated separation of powers); City of Seattle v. Trump, 250 F.Supp.3d 497 (W.D. Wash. 2017) (denying government motion to dismiss); City of Philadelphia v. Sessions, 280 F.Supp.3d 579 (E.D. Pa. 2018) (holding that the attempt to withhold federal grants was arbitrary and capricious and that § 1373 was unconstitutional under Murphy v. NCAA); see also United States v. California, 921 F.3d 865 (9th Cir. 2019) (upholding a California immigration law from a federal preemption challenge and invoking anti-commandeering principles); City of Los Angeles v. Barr, 929 F.3d 1163 (9th Cir. 2019) (upholding competitive grant program that awards extra points to applicants who agree to cooperate with federal officials on immigration enforcement).

Insert the following on p. 867 before subsection B:

TRUMP v. VANCE
2020 WL 3848062

CHIEF JUSTICE ROBERTS delivered the opinion of the Court.

In our judicial system, "the public has a right to every man's evidence." Since the earliest days of the Republic, "every man" has included the President of the United States. Beginning with Jefferson and carrying on through Clinton, Presidents have uniformly testified or produced documents in criminal proceedings when called upon by federal courts. This case involves — so far as we and the parties can tell — the first *state* criminal subpoena directed to a President. The President contends that the subpoena is unenforceable. We granted certiorari to decide whether Article II and the Supremacy Clause categorically preclude, or require a heightened standard for, the issuance of a state criminal subpoena to a sitting President.

I

In the summer of 2018, the New York County District Attorney's Office opened an investigation into what it opaquely describes as "business transactions involving multiple individuals whose conduct may have violated state law." A year later, the office — acting on behalf of a grand jury — served a subpoena *duces tecum* (essentially a request to produce evidence) on Mazars USA, LLP, the personal accounting firm of President Donald J. Trump. The subpoena directed Mazars to produce financial records relating to the President and business organizations affiliated with him, including "[t]ax returns and related schedules," from "2011 to the present."

The President, acting in his personal capacity, sued the district attorney and Mazars in Federal District Court to enjoin enforcement of the subpoena. He argued that, under Article II and the Supremacy Clause, a sitting President enjoys absolute immunity from state criminal process. He asked the court to issue a "declaratory judgment that the subpoena is invalid and unenforceable while the President is in office" and to permanently enjoin the district attorney "from taking any action to enforce the subpoena." Mazars, concluding that the dispute was between the President and the district attorney, took no position on the legal issues raised by the President. . . . [The District Court and the Second Circuit rejected the President's request for an injunction.] We granted certiorari.

II

In the summer of 1807, all eyes were on Richmond, Virginia. Aaron Burr, the former Vice President, was on trial for treason. Fallen from political grace after his fatal duel with Alexander Hamilton, and with a murder charge pending in New Jersey, Burr followed the path of many down-and-out Americans of his day—he headed West in search of new opportunity. But Burr was a man with outsized ambitions. Together with General James Wilkinson, the Governor of the Louisiana Territory, he hatched a plan to establish a new territory in Mexico, then controlled by Spain. Both men anticipated that war between the United States and Spain was imminent, and when it broke out they intended to invade Spanish territory at the head of a private army.

But while Burr was rallying allies to his cause, tensions with Spain eased and rumors began to swirl that Burr was conspiring to detach States by the Allegheny Mountains from the Union. Wary of being exposed as the principal co-conspirator, Wilkinson took steps to ensure that any blame would fall on Burr. He sent a series of letters to President Jefferson accusing Burr of plotting to attack New Orleans and revolutionize the Louisiana Territory.

Jefferson, who despised his former running mate Burr for trying to steal the 1800 presidential election from him, was predisposed to credit Wilkinson's version of events. The President sent a special message to Congress identifying Burr as the "prime mover" in a plot "against the peace and safety of the Union." According to Jefferson, Burr contemplated either the "severance of the Union" or an attack on Spanish territory. Jefferson acknowledged that his sources contained a "mixture of rumors, conjectures, and suspicions" but, citing Wilkinson's letters, he assured Congress that Burr's guilt was "beyond question."

The trial that followed was "the greatest spectacle in the short history of the republic," complete with a Founder-studded cast. People flocked to Richmond to watch, massing in tents and covered wagons along the banks of the James River, nearly doubling the town's population of 5,000. Burr's defense team included

Edmund Randolph and Luther Martin, both former delegates at the Constitutional Convention and renowned advocates. Chief Justice John Marshall, who had recently squared off with the Jefferson administration in *Marbury v. Madison*, 1 Cranch 137 (1803), presided as Circuit Justice for Virginia. Meanwhile Jefferson, intent on conviction, orchestrated the prosecution from afar, dedicating Cabinet meetings to the case, peppering the prosecutors with directions, and spending nearly $100,000 from the Treasury on the five-month proceedings.

In the lead-up to trial, Burr, taking aim at his accusers, moved for a subpoena *duces tecum* directed at Jefferson. The draft subpoena required the President to produce an October 21, 1806 letter from Wilkinson and accompanying documents, which Jefferson had referenced in his message to Congress. The prosecution opposed the request, arguing that a President could not be subjected to such a subpoena and that the letter might contain state secrets. Following four days of argument, Marshall announced his ruling to a packed chamber.

The President, Marshall declared, does not "stand exempt from the general provisions of the constitution" or, in particular, the Sixth Amendment's guarantee that those accused have compulsory process for obtaining witnesses for their defense. *United States v. Burr*, 25 F. Cas. 30, 33-34 (No. 14,692d) (CC Va. 1807). At common law the "single reservation" to the duty to testify in response to a subpoena was "the case of the king," whose "dignity" was seen as "incompatible" with appearing "under the process of the court." But, as Marshall explained, a king is born to power and can "do no wrong." The President, by contrast, is "of the people" and subject to the law. According to Marshall, the sole argument for exempting the President from testimonial obligations was that his "duties as chief magistrate demand his whole time for national objects." But, in Marshall's assessment, those demands were "not unremitting." And should the President's duties preclude his attendance at a particular time and place, a court could work that out upon return of the subpoena.

Marshall also rejected the prosecution's argument that the President was immune from a subpoena *duces tecum* because executive papers might contain state secrets. "A subpoena duces tecum," he said, "may issue to any person to whom an ordinary subpoena may issue." As he explained, no "fair construction" of the Constitution supported the conclusion that the right "to compel the attendance of witnesses[ ] does not extend" to requiring those witnesses to "bring[ ] with them such papers as may be material in the defence." And, as a matter of basic fairness, permitting such information to be withheld would "tarnish the reputation of the court." As for "the propriety of introducing any papers," that would "depend on the character of the paper, not on the character of the person who holds it." Marshall acknowledged that the papers sought by Burr could contain information "the disclosure of which would endanger the public safety," but stated that, again, such concerns would have "due consideration" upon the return of the subpoena.

While the arguments unfolded, Jefferson, who had received word of the motion, wrote to the prosecutor indicating that he would — subject to the prerogative to decide which executive communications should be withheld — "furnish on all occasions, whatever the purposes of justice may require." His "personal attendance," however, was out of the question, for it "would leave the nation without" the "sole branch which the constitution requires to be always in function."

Before Burr received the subpoenaed documents, Marshall rejected the prosecution's core legal theory for treason and Burr was accordingly acquitted. Jefferson, however, was not done. Committed to salvaging a conviction, he directed the prosecutors to proceed with a misdemeanor (yes, misdemeanor) charge for inciting war against Spain. Burr then renewed his request for Wilkinson's October 21 letter, which he later received a copy of, and subpoenaed a second letter, dated November 12, 1806, which the prosecutor claimed was privileged. Acknowledging that the President may withhold information to protect public safety, Marshall instructed that Jefferson should "state the particular reasons" for withholding the letter. *United States v. Burr*, 25 F. Cas. 187, 192 (No. 14,694) (CC Va. 1807). The court, paying "all proper respect" to those reasons, would then decide whether to compel disclosure. But that decision was averted when the misdemeanor trial was cut short after it became clear that the prosecution lacked the evidence to convict.

In the two centuries since the Burr trial, successive Presidents have accepted Marshall's ruling that the Chief Executive is subject to subpoena. In 1818, President Monroe received a subpoena to testify in a court-martial against one of his appointees. His Attorney General, William Wirt—who had served as a prosecutor during Burr's trial—advised Monroe that, per Marshall's ruling, a subpoena to testify may "be properly awarded to the President." Monroe offered to sit for a deposition and ultimately submitted answers to written interrogatories.

Following Monroe's lead, his successors have uniformly agreed to testify when called in criminal proceedings, provided they could do so at a time and place of their choosing. In 1875, President Grant submitted to a three-hour deposition in the criminal prosecution of a political appointee embroiled in a network of tax-evading whiskey distillers. A century later, President Ford's attempted assassin subpoenaed him to testify in her defense. See *United States v. Fromme*, 405 F. Supp. 578 (ED Cal. 1975). Ford obliged—from a safe distance—in the first videotaped deposition of a President. President Carter testified via the same means in the trial of two local officials who, while Carter was Governor of Georgia, had offered to contribute to his campaign in exchange for advance warning of any state gambling raids. Two years later, Carter gave videotaped testimony to a federal grand jury investigating whether a fugitive financier had entreated the White House to quash his extradition proceedings. President Clinton testified three times, twice via deposition pursuant to subpoenas in federal criminal trials of associates implicated during the Whitewater investigation, and once by video for a grand jury investigating possible perjury.

The bookend to Marshall's ruling came in 1974 when the question he never had to decide—whether to compel the disclosure of official communications over the objection of the President—came to a head. That spring, the Special Prosecutor appointed to investigate the break-in of the Democratic National Committee Headquarters at the Watergate complex filed an indictment charging seven defendants associated with President Nixon and naming Nixon as an unindicted co-conspirator. As the case moved toward trial, the Special Prosecutor secured a subpoena *duces tecum* directing Nixon to produce, among other things, tape recordings of Oval Office meetings. Nixon moved to quash the subpoena, claiming that the Constitution provides an absolute privilege of confidentiality to all presidential communications. This Court rejected that argument in *United States v. Nixon*, 418 U.S. 683 (1974), a decision we later described as "unequivocally and emphatically endors[ing] Marshall's" holding that Presidents are subject to subpoena. *Clinton v. Jones*, 520 U.S. 681, 704 (1997).

The *Nixon* Court readily acknowledged the importance of preserving the confidentiality of communications "between high Government officials and those who advise and assist them." . . . But, like Marshall two centuries prior, the Court recognized the countervailing interests at stake. Invoking the common law maxim that "the public has a right to every man's evidence," the Court observed that the public interest in fair and accurate judicial proceedings is at its height in the criminal setting, where our common commitment to justice demands that "guilt shall not escape" nor "innocence suffer." Because these dual aims would be "defeated if judgments" were "founded on a partial or speculative presentation of the facts," the *Nixon* Court recognized that it was "imperative" that "compulsory process be available for the production of evidence needed either by the prosecution or the defense."

The Court thus concluded that the President's "generalized assertion of privilege must yield to the demonstrated, specific need for evidence in a pending criminal trial." Two weeks later, President Nixon dutifully released the tapes.

III

The history surveyed above all involved *federal* criminal proceedings. Here we are confronted for the first time with a subpoena issued to the President by a local grand jury operating under the supervision of a *state* court. . . . While the subpoena was directed to the President's accounting firm, the parties agree that the papers at issue belong to the President and that Mazars is merely the custodian. Thus, for purposes of immunity, it is functionally a subpoena issued to the President. [relocated footnote—eds.]

[The] President. . . . argues that the Supremacy Clause gives a sitting President absolute immunity from state criminal subpoenas because compliance with those subpoenas would categorically impair a President's performance of his Article II functions. The Solicitor General . . . urges us to resolve this case by holding that a state grand jury subpoena for a sitting President's personal records must, at the very least, "satisfy a heightened standard of need," which the Solicitor General contends was not met here.

A

We begin with the question of absolute immunity. No one doubts that Article II guarantees the independence of the Executive Branch. As the head of that branch, the President "occupies a unique position in the constitutional scheme." *Nixon v. Fitzgerald*, 457 U.S. 731, 749 (1982). His duties . . . come with protections that safeguard the President's ability to perform his vital functions. See, *e.g.*, *ibid.* (concluding that the President enjoys "absolute immunity from damages liability predicated on his official acts"); *Nixon*, 418 U.S., at 708 (recognizing that presidential communications are presumptively privileged).

In addition, the Constitution guarantees "the entire independence of the General Government from any control by the respective States." *Farmers and Mechanics Sav. Bank of Minneapolis v. Minnesota*, 232 U.S. 516, 521 (1914). . . .

Marshall's ruling in *Burr*, entrenched by 200 years of practice and our decision in *Nixon*, confirms that *federal* criminal subpoenas do not "rise to the level of constitutionally forbidden impairment of the Executive's ability to perform its constitutionally mandated functions." *Clinton*. But the President, joined in part by the Solicitor General, argues that *state* criminal subpoenas pose a unique threat of impairment and thus demand greater protection. To be clear, the President does not contend here that *this* subpoena, in particular, is impermissibly burdensome. Instead he makes a *categorical* argument about the burdens generally associated with state criminal subpoenas, focusing on three: diversion, stigma, and harassment. . . .

1

The President's primary contention, which the Solicitor General supports, is that complying with state criminal subpoenas would necessarily divert the Chief Executive from his duties. He grounds that concern in *Nixon v. Fitzgerald*, which recognized a President's "absolute immunity from damages liability predicated on his official acts." . . . Indeed, we expressly rejected immunity based on distraction alone 15 years later in *Clinton v. Jones* . . . [when] President Clinton argued that the risk of being "distracted by the need to participate in litigation" entitled a sitting President to absolute immunity from civil liability, not just for official acts, as in *Fitzgerald*, but for private conduct as well. We disagreed with that rationale, explaining that the "dominant concern" in *Fitzgerald* was not mere distraction but the distortion of the Executive's "decisionmaking process" with respect to official acts that would stem from "worry as to the possibility of damages." The Court recognized that Presidents constantly face myriad demands on their attention, "some private, some political, and some as a result of official duty." But, the Court concluded, "[w]hile such distractions may be vexing to those subjected to them, they do not ordinarily implicate constitutional . . . concerns."

The same is true of criminal subpoenas. Just as a "properly managed" civil suit is generally "unlikely to occupy any substantial amount of" a President's time or attention, two centuries of experience confirm that a properly tailored criminal subpoena will not normally hamper the performance of the President's constitutional duties. If anything, we expect that in the mine run of cases, where a President is subpoenaed during a proceeding targeting someone else, as Jefferson was, the burden on a President will ordinarily be lighter than the burden of defending against a civil suit.

The President, however, believes the district attorney is investigating him and his businesses. In such a situation, he contends, the "toll that criminal process . . . exacts from the President is even heavier" than the distraction at issue in *Fitzgerald* and *Clinton*, because "criminal litigation" poses unique burdens on the President's time and will generate a "considerable if not overwhelming degree of mental preoccupation."

But the President is not seeking immunity from the diversion occasioned by the prospect of future criminal *liability*. Instead he concedes — consistent with the position of the Department of Justice — that state grand juries are free to investigate a sitting President with an eye toward charging him after the completion of his term. . . . The President's objection therefore must be limited to the *additional* distraction caused by the subpoena itself. But that argument runs up against the 200 years of precedent establishing that Presidents, and their official communications, are subject to judicial process, see *Burr*, even when the President is under investigation, see *Nixon*.

2

The President next claims that the stigma of being subpoenaed will undermine his leadership at home and abroad. Notably, the Solicitor General does not endorse this argument, perhaps because we have twice denied absolute immunity claims by Presidents in cases involving allegations of serious misconduct. See *Clinton*; *Nixon*. But even if a tarnished reputation were a cognizable impairment, there is nothing inherently stigmatizing about a President performing "the citizen's normal duty of . . . furnishing information relevant" to a criminal investigation. *Branzburg v. Hayes*, 408 U.S. 665, 691 (1972). Nor can we accept that the risk of association with persons or activities under criminal investigation can absolve a President of such an important public duty. Prior Presidents have weathered these associations in federal cases, and there is no reason to think any attendant notoriety is necessarily greater in state court proceedings.

To be sure, the consequences for a President's public standing will likely increase if he is the one under investigation. But, again, the President concedes that such investigations are permitted under Article II and the Supremacy Clause, and receipt of a subpoena would not seem to categorically magnify the harm to the President's reputation.

Additionally, while the current suit has cast the Mazars subpoena into the spotlight, longstanding rules of grand jury secrecy aim to prevent the very stigma the President anticipates. . . . [T]hose who make unauthorized disclosures regarding a grand jury subpoena do so at their peril. See, *e.g.*, N.Y. Penal Law Ann. § 215.70 (West 2010) (designating unlawful grand jury disclosure as a felony).

3

Finally, the President and the Solicitor General warn that subjecting Presidents to state criminal subpoenas will make them "easily identifiable target[s]" for harassment. *Fitzgerald.* But we rejected a nearly identical argument in *Clinton*, where then-President Clinton argued that permitting civil liability for unofficial acts would "generate a large volume of politically motivated harassing and frivolous litigation." The President and the Solicitor General nevertheless argue that state criminal subpoenas pose a heightened risk and could undermine the President's ability to "deal fearlessly and impartially" with the States. They caution that, while federal prosecutors are accountable to and removable by the President, the 2,300 district attorneys in this country are responsive to local constituencies, local interests, and local prejudices, and might "use criminal process to register their dissatisfaction with" the President. What is more, we are told, the state courts supervising local grand juries may not exhibit the same respect that federal courts show to the President as a coordinate branch of Government.

We recognize, as does the district attorney, that harassing subpoenas could, under certain circumstances, threaten the independence or effectiveness of the Executive. Even so, in *Clinton* we found that the risk of harassment was not "serious" because federal courts have the tools to deter and, where necessary, dismiss vexatious civil suits. And, while we cannot ignore the possibility that state prosecutors may have political motivations, here again the law already seeks to protect against the predicted abuse.

First, grand juries are prohibited from engaging in "arbitrary fishing expeditions" and initiating investigations "out of malice or an intent to harass." . . . These protections, as the district attorney himself puts it, "apply with special force to a President, in light of the office's unique position as the head of the Executive Branch." And, in the event of such harassment, a President would be entitled to the protection of federal courts. The policy against federal interference in state criminal proceedings, while strong, allows "intervention in those cases where the District Court properly finds that the state proceeding is motivated by a desire to harass or is conducted in bad faith." *Huffman v. Pursue, Ltd.*, 420 U.S. 592, 611 (1975).

Second, contrary to Justice Alito's characterization, our holding does not allow States to "run roughshod over the functioning of [the Executive B]ranch." The Supremacy Clause prohibits state judges and prosecutors from interfering with a President's official duties. See, *e.g., Tennessee v. Davis*, 100 U.S. 257, 263 (1880) ("No State government can . . . obstruct [the] authorized officers" of the Federal Government.). Any effort to manipulate a President's policy decisions or to "retaliat[e]" against a President for official acts through issuance of a subpoena, would thus be an unconstitutional attempt to "influence" a superior sovereign "exempt" from such obstacles, see *McCulloch*. We generally "assume[ ] that state courts and prosecutors will observe constitutional limitations." *Dombrowski v. Pfister*, 380 U.S. 479, 484 (1965). Failing that, federal law allows a President to challenge any allegedly unconstitutional influence in a federal forum, as the President has done here. . . .

Given these safeguards and the Court's precedents, we cannot conclude that absolute immunity is necessary or appropriate under Article II or the Supremacy Clause. Our dissenting colleagues agree. Justice Thomas reaches the same conclusion based on the original understanding of the Constitution reflected in Marshall's decision in *Burr*. And Justice Alito, also persuaded by *Burr*, "agree[s]" that "not all" state criminal subpoenas for a President's records "should be barred." On that point the Court is unanimous.

B

We next consider whether a state grand jury subpoena seeking a President's private papers must satisfy a heightened need standard. The Solicitor General would require a threshold showing that the evidence sought is "critical" for "specific charging decisions" and that the subpoena is a "last resort," meaning the evidence is "not available from any other source" and is needed "now, rather than at the end of the President's term." . . .

We disagree, for three reasons. First, such a heightened standard would extend protection designed for official documents to the President's private papers. As the Solicitor General and Justice Alito acknowledge, their proposed test is derived from executive privilege cases that trace back to *Burr*. There, Marshall explained that if Jefferson invoked presidential privilege over executive communications, the court would not "proceed against the president as against an ordinary individual" but would instead require an affidavit from the defense that "would clearly show the paper to be essential to the justice of the case." *Burr*. The Solicitor General and Justice Alito would have us apply a similar standard to a President's personal papers. But this argument does not account for the relevant passage from *Burr*: "If there be a paper in the possession of the executive, which is *not of an official nature*, he must stand, as respects that paper, in nearly the same situation with any other individual." (emphasis added). And it is only "nearly" — and not "entirely" — because the President retains the right to assert privilege over documents that, while ostensibly private, "partake of the character of an official paper."

Second, neither the Solicitor General nor Justice Alito has established that heightened protection against state subpoenas is necessary for the Executive to fulfill his Article II functions. Beyond the risk of harassment, which we addressed above, the only justification they offer for the heightened standard is protecting Presidents from "unwarranted burdens." In effect, they argue that even if federal subpoenas to a President are warranted whenever evidence is material, state subpoenas are warranted "only when [the] evidence is essential." But that double standard has no basis in law. For if the state subpoena is not issued to manipulate, the documents themselves are not protected, and the Executive is not impaired, then nothing in Article II or the Supremacy Clause supports holding state subpoenas to a higher standard than their federal counterparts.

Finally, in the absence of a need to protect the Executive, the public interest in fair and effective law enforcement cuts in favor of comprehensive access to evidence. Requiring a state grand jury to meet a heightened standard of need would hobble the grand jury's ability to acquire "all information that might possibly bear on its investigation." And, even assuming the evidence withheld under that standard were preserved until the conclusion of a President's term, in the interim the State would be deprived of investigative leads that the evidence might yield, allowing memories to fade and documents to disappear. This could frustrate the identification, investigation, and indictment of third parties (for whom applicable statutes of limitations might lapse). More troubling, it could prejudice the innocent by depriving the grand jury of *exculpatory* evidence.

Rejecting a heightened need standard does not leave Presidents with "no real protection." To start, a President may avail himself of the same protections available to every other citizen. These include the right to challenge the subpoena on any grounds permitted by state law, which usually include bad faith and undue burden or breadth. . . . And, as in federal court, "[t]he high respect that is owed to the office of the Chief Executive . . . should inform the conduct of the entire proceeding, including the timing and scope of discovery." *Clinton.* . . .

Furthermore, although the Constitution does not entitle the Executive to absolute immunity or a heightened standard, he is not "relegate[d]" only to the challenges available to private citizens. A President can raise subpoena-specific constitutional challenges, in either a state or federal forum. As previously noted, he can challenge the subpoena as an attempt to influence the performance of his official duties, in violation of the Supremacy Clause. This avenue protects against local political machinations "interposed as an obstacle to the effective operation of a federal constitutional power."

In addition, the Executive can — as the district attorney concedes — argue that compliance with a particular subpoena would impede his constitutional duties. . . . As a result, "once the President sets forth and explains a conflict between judicial proceeding and public duties," or shows that an order or subpoena would "significantly interfere with his efforts to carry out" those duties, "the matter changes." At that point, a court should use its inherent authority to quash or modify the subpoena, if necessary to ensure that such "interference with the President's duties would not occur." . . .

The daylight between our opinion and Justice Thomas's "dissent" is not as great as that label might suggest. We agree that Presidents are neither absolutely immune from state criminal subpoenas nor insulated by a heightened need standard. We agree that Presidents may challenge specific subpoenas as impeding their Article II functions. And, although we affirm while Justice Thomas would vacate, we agree that this case will be remanded to the District Court. [relocated footnote — eds.]

* * *

Two hundred years ago, a great jurist of our Court established that no citizen, not even the President, is categorically above the common duty to produce evidence when called upon in a criminal proceeding. We reaffirm that principle today and hold that the President is neither absolutely immune from state criminal subpoenas seeking his private papers nor entitled to a heightened standard of need. . . . The arguments presented here and in the Court of Appeals were limited to absolute immunity and heightened need. The Court of Appeals, however, has directed that the case be returned to the District Court, where the President may raise further arguments as appropriate.

We affirm the judgment of the Court of Appeals and remand the case for further proceedings consistent with this opinion.

It is so ordered.

Justice KAVANAUGH, with whom Justice GORSUCH joins, concurring in the judgment.

The Court today unanimously concludes that a President does not possess absolute immunity from a state criminal subpoena, but also unanimously agrees that this case should be remanded to the District Court, where the President may raise constitutional and legal objections to the subpoena as appropriate. I agree with those two conclusions. . . .

In our system of government, as this Court has often stated, no one is above the law. That principle applies, of course, to a President. At the same time, in light of Article II of the Constitution, this Court has repeatedly declared—and the Court indicates again today—that a court may not proceed against a President as it would against an ordinary litigant. . . .

The question here, then, is how to balance the State's interests and the Article II interests. The longstanding precedent that has applied to federal criminal subpoenas for official, privileged Executive Branch information is *United States v. Nixon*, 418 U.S. 683 (1974). That landmark case requires that a prosecutor establish a "demonstrated, specific need" for the President's information. . . . [This] is a tried-and-true test that accommodates both the interests of the criminal process and the Article II interests of the Presidency. The *Nixon* standard ensures that a prosecutor's interest in subpoenaed information is sufficiently important to justify an intrusion on the Article II interests of the Presidency. The *Nixon* standard also reduces the risk of subjecting a President to unwarranted burdens, because it provides that a prosecutor may obtain a President's information only in certain defined circumstances. . . .

A state criminal subpoena to a President raises Article II and Supremacy Clause issues because of the potential for a state prosecutor to use the criminal process and issue subpoenas in a way that interferes with the President's duties, through harassment or diversion. Cf. *Nixon v. Fitzgerald*, 457 U.S. 731, 751-753 (1982). . . .

Because this case again entails a clash between the interests of the criminal process and the Article II interests of the Presidency, I would apply the longstanding *Nixon* "demonstrated, specific need" standard to this case. The majority opinion does not apply the *Nixon* standard. . . . That said, the majority opinion appropriately takes account of some important concerns that also animate *Nixon* and the Constitution's balance of powers. The majority opinion explains that a state prosecutor may not issue a subpoena for a President's personal information out of bad faith, malice, or an intent to harass a President; as a result of prosecutorial impropriety; to seek information that is not relevant to an investigation; that is overly broad or unduly burdensome; to manipulate, influence, or retaliate against a President's official acts or policy decisions; or in a way that would impede, conflict with, or interfere with a President's official duties. All nine Members of the Court agree, moreover, that a President may raise objections to a state criminal subpoena not just in state court but also in federal court. . . . As I see it, the standards identified by the majority opinion should be considered, in this context, Article II requirements, not just statutory or state-law requirements. [relocated footnote—eds.] . . . And the majority opinion indicates that, in light of the "high respect that is owed to the office of the Chief Executive," courts "should be particularly meticulous" in assessing a subpoena for a President's personal records.

In the end, much may depend on how the majority opinion's various standards are applied in future years and decades. It will take future cases to determine precisely how much difference exists between (i) the various standards articulated by the majority opinion, (ii) the overarching *Nixon* "demonstrated, specific need" standard that I would adopt, and (iii) Justice Thomas's and Justice Alito's other proposed standards. In any event, in my view, lower courts in cases of this sort involving a President will almost invariably have to begin by delving into why the State wants the information; why and how much the State needs the information, including whether the State could obtain the information elsewhere; and whether compliance with the subpoena would unduly burden or interfere with a President's official duties. . . .

Justice THOMAS, dissenting.

. . . I agree with the majority that the President is not entitled to absolute immunity from *issuance* of the subpoena. But he may be entitled to relief against its *enforcement*. I therefore agree with the President that the proper course is to vacate and remand. If the President can show that "his duties as chief magistrate demand his whole time for national objects," *United States v. Burr*, 25 F. Cas. 30, 34 (No. 14,692d) (CC Va. 1807) (Marshall, C. J.), he is entitled to relief from enforcement of the subpoena. . . .

I agree with the majority that the President does not have absolute immunity from the issuance of a grand jury subpoena. Unlike the majority, however, I do not reach this conclusion based on a primarily functionalist analysis. Instead, I reach it based on the text of the Constitution, which, as understood by the ratifying public and incorporated into an early circuit opinion by Chief Justice Marshall, does not support the President's claim of absolute immunity. . . . I do not address the continuing validity of *Nixon v. Fitzgerald*, 457 U.S. 731 (1982), which no party asks us to revisit. [relocated footnote—eds.]

The text of the Constitution explicitly addresses the privileges of some federal officials, but it does not afford the President absolute immunity. Members of Congress are "privileged from Arrest during their Attendance at the Session of their respective Houses, and in going to and returning from the same," except for "Treason, Felony and Breach of the Peace." Art. I, § 6, cl. 1. The Constitution further specifies that, "for any Speech or Debate in either House, they shall not be questioned in any other Place." *Ibid.* By contrast, the text of the Constitution contains no explicit grant of absolute immunity from legal process for the President. As a Federalist essayist noted during ratification, the President's "person is not so much protected as that of a member of the House of Representatives" because he is subject to the issuance of judicial process "like any other man in the ordinary course of law." An American Citizen I (Sept. 26, 1787), in 2 Documentary History of the Ratification of the Constitution 141 (M. Jansen ed. 1976) (emphasis deleted).

Prominent defenders of the Constitution confirmed the lack of absolute Presidential immunity. James Wilson, a signer of the Constitution and future Justice of this Court, explained to his fellow Pennsylvanians that "far from being above the laws, [the President] is amenable to them in his private character as a citizen, and in his public character by *impeachment*." 2 Debates on the Constitution 480 (J. Elliot ed. 1891) (emphasis in original). James Iredell, another future Justice, observed in the North Carolina ratifying convention that "[i]f [the President] commits any crime, he is punishable by the laws of his country." 4 *id.*, at 109. A fellow North Carolinian similarly argued that, "[w]ere it possible to suppose that the President should give wrong instructions to his deputies, . . . citizens . . . would have redress in the ordinary courts of common law."

The sole authority that the President cites from the drafting or ratification process is The Federalist No. 69, but it provides him no real support. Alexander Hamilton stated that "[t]he President of the United States would be liable to be impeached, tried, and upon conviction of treason, bribery, or other high crimes or misdemeanors, removed from office; and would afterwards be liable to prosecution and punishment in the ordinary course of law." The Federalist No. 69. Hamilton did not say that the President was temporarily immune from judicial process. Moreover, he made this comment to reassure readers that the President was "amenable to personal punishment and disgrace." For the President, this is at best ambiguous evidence that cannot overcome the clear evidence discussed above.

The President further relies on a private letter written by President Jefferson. In the letter, Jefferson worried that the Executive would lose his independence "if he were subject to the *commands* of the [judiciary], & to imprisonment for disobedience; if the several courts could bandy him from pillar to post, keep him constantly trudging from north to south & east to west, and withdraw him entirely from his constitutional duties." 10 Works of Thomas Jefferson 404 n. (P. Ford ed. 1905) (emphasis in original). But President Jefferson never squarely argued for absolute immunity. And, the concern Jefferson had about demands on the President's time is addressed by the standard that Chief Justice Marshall articulated in *Burr*.

The President also quotes the views of Vice President John Adams and then-Senator Oliver Ellsworth in 1789. The record of the conversation we have from a fellow Senator's diary is brief. Adams or Ellsworth (or perhaps both) stated that "you could only impeach [the President], and no other process whatever lay against him." Journal of William Maclay 167 (E. Maclay ed. 1890). The only reason given was that it would "stop the whole machine of Government."

Senator Philip Schuyler joined the conversation and gave his own reason: " 'I think the President [is] a kind of sacred person.' " Schuyler's theory clearly has no basis in the Constitution, and the view held by Adams and Ellsworth seems to be grounds for relief from enforcement rather than a basis for absolute immunity from issuance of a subpoena. . . .

[In *Burr*,] Chief Justice Marshall pre-emptively rejected any notion of absolute immunity, despite the fact that the Government did not so much as suggest it in court. He distinguished the President from the British monarch, who did have immunity, calling it an "essentia[l] . . . difference" in our system that the President "is elected from the mass of the people, and, on the expiration of the time for which he is elected, returns to the mass of the people again." Thus, the President was more like a state governor or a member of the British cabinet than a king. Chief Justice Marshall found no authority suggesting that these officials were immune from judicial process. . . .

In addition to contesting the issuance of the subpoena, the President also seeks injunctive and declaratory relief against its enforcement. The majority recognizes that the President can seek relief from enforcement, but it does not vacate and remand for the lower courts to address this question. I would do so and instruct them to apply the standard articulated by Chief Justice Marshall in *Burr*: If the President is unable to comply because of his official duties, then he is entitled to injunctive and declaratory relief.

In *Burr*, after explaining that the President was not absolutely immune from issuance of a subpoena, Chief Justice Marshall proceeded to explain that the President might be excused from the enforcement of one. As he put it, "[t]he guard, furnished to this high officer, to protect him from being harassed by vexatious and unnecessary subpoenas, is to be looked for in the conduct of a court *after those subpoenas have issued*; not in any circumstance which is to precede their being issued." 25 F. Cas., at 34 (emphasis added). Chief Justice Marshall set out the pertinent standard: To avoid enforcement of the subpoena, the President must "sho[w]" that "his duties as chief magistrate demand his whole time for national objects." . . .

Although *Burr* involved a federal subpoena, the same principle applies to a state subpoena. The ability of the President to discharge his duties until his term expires or he is removed from office by the Senate is "integral to the structure of the Constitution." . . . Accordingly, a federal court may provide injunctive and declaratory relief to stay enforcement of a state subpoena when the President meets the *Burr* standard. . . .

[T]he demands on the President's time and the importance of his tasks are extraordinary, and the office of the President cannot be delegated to subordinates. A subpoena imposes both demands on the President's limited time and a mental burden, even when the President is not directly engaged in complying. This understanding of the Presidency should guide courts in deciding whether to enforce a subpoena for the President's documents.

Courts must also recognize their own limitations. When the President asserts that matters of foreign affairs or national defense preclude his compliance with a subpoena, the Judiciary will rarely have a basis for rejecting that assertion. Judges "simply lack the relevant information and expertise to second-guess determinations made by the President based on information properly withheld."

"[E]ven if the courts could compel the Executive to produce the necessary information" to understand the demands on his time, decisions about that information "are simply not amenable to judicial determination because '[t]hey are delicate, complex, and involve large elements of prophecy.'" The President has at his disposal enormous amounts of classified intelligence regarding the Government's concerns around the globe. His decisionmaking is further informed by experience in matters of foreign affairs, national defense, and intelligence that judges almost always will not have. And his decisionmaking takes into account the full spectrum of the Government's operations, not just the matters directly related to a particular case. Even with perfect information, courts lack the institutional competence to engage in a searching review of the President's reasons for not complying with a subpoena. . . .

The President and the Solicitor General argue that the grand jury must make a showing of heightened need. I agree with the majority's decision not to adopt this standard, but for different reasons. The constitutional question in this case is whether the President is able to perform the duties of his office, whereas a heightened need standard addresses a logically independent issue. Under a heightened-need standard, a grand jury with only the usual need for particular information would be refused it when the President is perfectly able to comply, while a grand jury with a heightened need would be entitled to it even if compliance would place undue obligations on the President. This result makes little sense and lacks any basis in the original understanding of the Constitution. I would leave questions of the grand jury's need to state law. [relocated footnote — eds.] . . .

I would vacate and remand to allow the District Court to determine whether enforcement of this subpoena should be enjoined because the President's "duties as chief magistrate demand his whole time for national objects." Accordingly, I respectfully dissent.

Justice ALITO, dissenting.

This case is almost certain to be portrayed as a case about the current President and the current political situation, but the case has a much deeper significance. While the decision will of course have a direct effect on President Trump, what the Court holds today will also affect all future Presidents — which is to say, it will affect the Presidency, and that is a matter of great and lasting importance to the Nation.

The event that precipitated this case is unprecedented. Respondent Vance, an elected state prosecutor, launched a criminal investigation of a sitting President and obtained a grand jury subpoena for his records. The specific question before us — whether the subpoena may be enforced — cannot be answered adequately without considering the broader question that frames it: whether the Constitution imposes restrictions on a State's deployment of its criminal law enforcement powers against a sitting President. If the Constitution sets no such limits, then a local prosecutor may prosecute a sitting President. And if that is allowed, it follows *a fortiori* that the subpoena at issue can be enforced. On the other hand, if the Constitution does not permit a State to prosecute a sitting President, the next logical question is whether the Constitution restrains any other prosecutorial or investigative weapons. . . .

These are important questions that go to the very structure of the Government created by the Constitution. In evaluating these questions, two important structural features must be taken into account.

The first is the nature and role of the Presidency. . . . [B]ecause "[t]he President is the only person who alone composes a branch of government . . . , there is not always a clear line between his personal and official affairs." *Trump v. Mazars USA, LLP.* As a result, the law's treatment of the person who serves as President can have an important effect on the institution, and the institution of the Presidency plays an indispensable role in our constitutional system. . . .

"Constitutionally speaking, the President never sleeps. The President must be ready, at a moment's notice, to do whatever it takes to preserve, protect, and defend the Constitution and the American people." Amar & Katyal, Executive Privileges and Immunities: The Nixon and Clinton Cases, 108 Harv. L. Rev. 701, 713 (1995). Without a President who is able at all times to carry out the responsibilities of the office, our constitutional system could not operate, and the country would be at risk. That is why the Twenty-fifth Amendment created a mechanism for temporarily transferring the responsibilities of the office to the Vice President if the President is incapacitated for even a brief time. The Amendment has been explicitly invoked on only two occasions, each time for a period of about two hours. This mechanism reflects an appreciation that the Nation cannot be safely left without a functioning President for even a brief time. . . .

The second structural feature is the relationship between the Federal Government and the States. . . . The Constitution permitted the States to retain many of the sovereign powers that they previously possessed, but it gave the Federal Government powers that were deemed essential for the Nation's well-being and, indeed, its survival. And it provided for the Federal Government to be independent of and, within its allotted sphere, supreme over the States. Art. VI, cl. 2. Accordingly, a State may not block or interfere with the lawful work of the National Government. . . .

[T]wo centuries of case law prohibit the States from taxing, regulating, or otherwise interfering with the lawful work of federal agencies, instrumentalities, and officers. The Court premised these cases on the principle that "the activities of the Federal Government are free from regulation by any State. No other adjustment of competing enactments or legal principles is possible." *Mayo v. United States*, 319 U.S. 441, 445 (1943) (footnote omitted). . . .

In *McCulloch*, Maryland's sovereign taxing power had to yield, and in a similar way, a State's sovereign power to enforce its criminal laws must accommodate the indispensable role that the Constitution assigns to the Presidency. This must be the rule with respect to a state prosecution of a sitting President. Both the structure of the Government established by the Constitution and the Constitution's provisions on the impeachment and removal of a President make it clear that the prosecution of a sitting President is out of the question. It has been aptly said that the President is the "sole indispensable man in government," and subjecting a sitting President to criminal prosecution would severely hamper his ability to carry out the vital responsibilities that the Constitution puts in his hands. . . .

The constitutional provisions on impeachment provide further support for the rule that a President may not be prosecuted while in office. . . . After providing that the judgment cannot impose any punishment beyond removal from the Presidency and disqualification from holding any other federal office, the Constitution states that "the Party convicted shall nevertheless be liable and subject to Indictment, Trial, Judgment, and Punishment, according to Law." Art. I, § 3, cl. 7. The plain implication is that criminal prosecution, like removal from the Presidency and disqualification from other offices, is a consequence that can come about only after the Senate's judgment, not during or prior to the Senate trial. . . .

While the prosecution of a sitting President provides the most dramatic example of a clash between the indispensable work of the Presidency and a State's exercise of its criminal law enforcement powers, other examples are easy to imagine. Suppose state officers obtained and sought to execute a search warrant for a sitting President's private quarters in the White House. Suppose a state court authorized surveillance of a telephone that a sitting President was known to use. Or suppose that a sitting President was subpoenaed to testify before a state grand jury and, as is generally the rule, no Presidential aides, even those carrying the so-called "nuclear football," were permitted to enter the grand jury room. What these examples illustrate is a principle that this Court has recognized: legal proceedings involving a sitting President must take the responsibilities and demands of the office into account. See *Clinton v. Jones*, 520 U.S. 681, 707 (1997).

It is not enough to recite sayings like "no man is above the law" and "the public has a right to every man's evidence." These sayings are true—and important—but they beg the question. . . . the nature of the office demands in some instances that the application of laws be adjusted at least until the person's term in office ends.

I now come to the specific investigative weapon at issue in the case before us—a subpoena for a sitting President's records. This weapon is less intrusive in an immediate sense than those mentioned above. Since the records are held by, and the subpoena was issued to, a third party, compliance would not require much work on the President's part. And after all, this is just one subpoena.

But we should heed the "great jurist," who rejected a similar argument in *McCulloch*. If we say that a subpoena to a third party is insufficient to undermine a President's performance of his duties, what about a subpoena served on the President himself? Surely in that case, the President could turn over the work of gathering the requested documents to attorneys or others recruited to perform the task. And if one subpoena is permitted, what about two? Or three? Or ten? Drawing a line based on such factors would involve the same sort of "perplexing inquiry, so unfit for the judicial department" that Marshall rejected in *McCulloch*.

The Court faced a similar issue when it considered whether a President can be sued for an allegedly unlawful act committed in the performance of official duties. See *Nixon v. Fitzgerald*, 457 U.S. 731 (1982). We did not ask whether the particular suit before us would have interfered with the carrying out of Presidential duties. (It could not have had that effect because President Nixon had already left office.)

Instead, we adopted a rule for all such suits, and we should take a similar approach here. The rule should take into account both the effect of subpoenas on the functioning of the Presidency and the risk that they will be used for harassment.

I turn first to the question of the effect of a state grand jury subpoena for a President's records. When the issuance of such a subpoena is part of an investigation that regards the President as a "target" or "subject," the subpoena can easily impair a President's "energetic performance of [his] constitutional duties." Few individuals will simply brush off an indication that they may be within a prosecutor's crosshairs. Few will put the matter out of their minds and go about their work unaffected. For many, the prospect of prosecution will be the first and last thing on their minds every day.

Respondent asserts that his office has never characterized President Trump as a "target" of the investigation, but by the same token, respondent has never said that the President is not a "target." [relocated footnote — eds.]

We have come to expect our Presidents to shoulder burdens that very few people could bear, but it is unrealistic to think that the prospect of possible criminal prosecution will not interfere with the performance of the duties of the office. . . .

There are more than 2,300 local prosecutors and district attorneys in the country. Many local prosecutors are elected, and many prosecutors have ambitions for higher elected office. . . . If a sitting President is intensely unpopular in a particular district — and that is a common condition — targeting the President may be an alluring and effective electoral strategy. But it is a strategy that would undermine our constitutional structure.

The Framers understood the importance of protecting the Presidency from interference by the States. . . . [T]o prevent a State from compromising a President's independence, the Convention adopted a provision barring a President from receiving an "Emolument" from any State, U.S. Const., Art. II, § 1, cl. 7.

Two centuries later, the Court's decision in *Clinton* reflected a similar concern. The Court held that a sitting President could be sued in federal court, but the Court took pains to reserve judgment on the question whether "a comparable claim might succeed in a state tribunal." 520 U.S., at 691. "[A]ny direct control by a state court over the President," the Court observed, might raise concerns about "protecting federal officials from possible local prejudice."

In light of the above, a subpoena like the one now before us should not be enforced unless it meets a test that takes into account the need to prevent interference with a President's discharge of the responsibilities of the office. I agree with the Court that not all such subpoenas should be barred. There may be situations in which there is an urgent and critical need for the subpoenaed information. The situation in the Burr trial, where the documents at issue were sought by a criminal defendant to defend against a charge of treason, is a good example. But in a case like the one at hand, a subpoena should not be allowed unless a heightened standard is met.

Prior cases involving Presidential subpoenas have always applied special, heightened standards. In the Burr trial, Chief Justice Marshall was careful to note that "in no case of this kind would a court be required to proceed against the president as against an ordinary individual," and he held that the subpoena to President Jefferson was permissible only because the prosecutor had shown that the materials sought were "essential to the justice of the [pending criminal] case." *United States v. Burr.*

In *United States v. Nixon,* 418 U.S. 683 (1974), where the Watergate Special Prosecutor subpoenaed tape recordings and documents under the control of President Nixon, this Court refused to quash the subpoena because there was a "demonstrated, specific need for [the] evidence in a pending criminal trial." In an earlier Watergate-related case where a Senate Committee subpoenaed President Nixon's White House tapes, the D.C. Circuit refused to order their production because the Committee had failed to show that "the subpoenaed evidence [wa] s demonstrably critical to the responsible fulfillment of the Committee's functions." *Senate Select Committee on Presidential Campaign Activities v. Nixon,* 498 F. 2d 725, 731 (1974). Later, when an independent counsel investigating a Cabinet officer wanted to enforce a federal grand jury subpoena for privileged materials held by the White House counsel, the D.C. Circuit explained that enforcement demanded a " 'demonstrated, specific need'" for the materials sought. *In re Sealed Case,* 121 F. 3d 729, 736 (1997) (*per curiam*).

The important point is not that the subpoena in this case should necessarily be governed by the particular tests used in these cases, most of which involved official records that were claimed to be privileged. Rather, the point is that we should not treat this subpoena like an ordinary grand jury subpoena and should not relegate a President to the meager defenses that are available when an ordinary grand jury subpoena is challenged. But that, at bottom, is the effect of the Court's decision.

The Presidency deserves greater protection. Thus, in a case like this one, a prosecutor should be required (1) to provide at least a general description of the possible offenses that are under investigation, (2) to outline how the subpoenaed records relate to those offenses, and (3) to explain why it is important that the records be produced and why it is necessary for production to occur while the President is still in office.

In the present case, the district attorney made a brief proffer, but important questions were left hanging. It would not be unduly burdensome to insist on answers before enforcing the subpoena.

One obvious question concerns the scope of the subpoena. The subpoena issued by the grand jury is largely a copy of the subpoenas issued by Committees of the House of Representatives, and it would be quite a coincidence if the records relevant to an investigation of possible violations of New York criminal law just so happened to be almost identical to the records thought by congressional Committees to be useful in considering federal legislation. It is therefore appropriate to ask the district attorney to explain the need for the various items that the subpoena covers.

The district attorney should also explain why it is important that the information in question be obtained from the President's records rather than another source. And the district attorney should set out why he finds it necessary that the records be produced now as opposed to when the President leaves office. At argument, respondent's counsel told us that his office's concern is the expiration of the statute of limitations, but there are potential solutions to that problem. Even if New York law does not automatically suspend the statute of limitations for prosecuting a President until he leaves office, it may be possible to eliminate the problem by waiver. And if the prosecutor's statute-of-limitations concerns relate to parties other than the President, he should be required to spell that out.

There may be other good reasons why immediate enforcement is important, such as the risk that evidence or important leads will be lost, but if a prosecutor believes that immediate enforcement is needed for such a reason, the prosecutor should be required to provide a reasonably specific explanation why that is so and why alternative means, such as measures to preserve evidence and prevent spoliation, would not suffice. . . .

Unlike this rule, which would not undermine any legitimate state interests, the opinion of the Court provides no real protection for the Presidency. The Court discounts the risk of harassment and assumes that state prosecutors will observe constitutional limitations, and I also assume that the great majority of state prosecutors will carry out their responsibilities responsibly. But for the reasons noted, there is a very real risk that some will not. . . . For all practical purposes, the Court's decision places a sitting President in the same unenviable position as any other person whose records are subpoenaed by a grand jury. . . .

The Court's decision threatens to impair the functioning of the Presidency and provides no real protection against the use of the subpoena power by the Nation's 2,300+ local prosecutors. Respect for the structure of Government created by the Constitution demands greater protection for an institution that is vital to the Nation's safety and well-being.

I therefore respectfully dissent.

Discussion

1. *Running out the clock.* Throughout his candidacy for president, and his first term in office, Donald Trump has resisted providing access to his tax returns. The reasons why remain mysterious, but his conduct — so different from other modern presidential candidates — repeatedly generated suspicions among his political opponents that he has something to hide.

Even though the Supreme Court announced that the President was not immune from state subpoenas, the Court sent the case back to the New York courts with instructions to consider any subpoena-specific challenges Trump might have. That means that litigation over the grand jury subpoena will continue, probably until well after the 2020 elections. The practical effect of *Trump v. Vance*, therefore, is that Trump will be able to run for president twice without ever having to reveal what is in his tax returns. To this extent, and despite the Court's rebuke of his claims of absolute immunity, the case must be seen as a short-term win for Trump.

In the long run, however, the New York prosecutors will probably be able to inspect Trump's tax returns, either in his second term as president, or, if he loses the 2020 election, when he becomes a private citizen. Nevertheless, because of the rules concerning grand jury secrecy in New York, Trump's tax returns still may not be revealed to the public even if he loses later on. From this perspective, too, *Vance v. Trump* is less of a defeat for Trump than it might first have appeared. But it will have repercussions for future presidents.

2. *Federalism and unpopular presidents*. In one sense, *Vance* follows straightforwardly from the logic of *United States v. Nixon*. The two most important differences are, first, that the material being requested was not subject to executive privilege—which made the prosecutor's claim even stronger. The second difference, however, is that *Nixon* did not involve a state criminal prosecution. As Justices Alito and Thomas note, there are many state and local prosecutors who might want to make trouble for a president who is unpopular in their part of the country.

How much should this matter? Presidents Bush and Obama were very unpopular in different parts of the country, and yet neither faced a state grand jury subpoena. On the other hand, President Clinton did have to testify before a federal grand jury, but that is because he was caught lying in a deposition in the Paula Jones sexual harassment case.

Is Trump's situation *sui generis* because there was long-standing concern about his illegal activities before he became president, and Americans are very unlikely to elect such a person again? Or, in our highly polarized age, does *Vance* mean that, from now on, every president will be under criminal investigation by some local or state prosecutor?

3. *The* Nixon *standard*. Justices Kavanaugh and Gorsuch argue that even though the material is not privileged, the New York prosecutor should have to meet the "demonstrated, specific need" standard of *United States v. Nixon*. This would help deter ambitious and politically motivated prosecutors from fishing expeditions. How difficult would it be for the prosecutor to meet that standard? To what extent does that question turn on whether Trump himself is actually a target of the investigation?

4. *Not enough time for television and golf.* Justice Thomas argues that the central question is not whether the prosecutor can demonstrate a specific need. Rather, it is whether "enforcement of this subpoena should be enjoined because the President's 'duties as chief magistrate demand his whole time for national objects.'"

To understand what this test means in practice, we need to know if a court should consider whether presidents in general must devote all their time to the serious duties of the presidency, or whether President Trump himself *actually* does. If the question is the former, then Thomas's test will rarely be met, because, as Thomas explains, the president continually has to process intelligence and consider threats around the globe: "[T]he demands on the President's time and the importance of his tasks are extraordinary, and the office of the President cannot be delegated to subordinates." As Justice Alito puts it, "Constitutionally speaking, the President never sleeps."

On the other hand, if the test is whether Trump himself is too busy to respond to a subpoena, the answer is probably no. News accounts and books written by former administration officials report that President Trump pays little attention to policy, refuses briefings, and spends much of his time watching television and playing golf. Nevertheless, the Justice Department could argue that, regardless of what this president actually does, his duties require round the clock attention and so the subpoena is too burdensome. How should a court apply Thomas's test? Should courts investigate President Trump's *actual* schedule and *actual* behavior — which might be viewed as unduly intrusive — or should they accept the Justice Department's assurances that his "duties as chief magistrate demand his whole time for national objects"?

Note: Congressional Oversight in the Trump Presidency

In January 2019, Democrats gained control of the House of Representatives. Under the previous Republican majority, there was relatively little oversight or investigation into President Trump's many scandals. Democrats signaled that they were ready to make up for lost time. They began to issue multiple requests for documents and testimony.

President Trump offered a characteristically aggressive response: " 'We're fighting all the subpoenas,' Mr. Trump told reporters outside the White House. 'These aren't, like, impartial people. The Democrats are trying to win 2020.' "[1]

Thus began a series of controversies in which House Democrats requested material and testimony, and the White House refused. We can divide the controversies into two basic sets of issues.

1. *Assertions of executive privilege and categorical "immunity" with respect to Administration documents and the testimony of Administration officials.* President Trump has repeatedly asserted executive privilege with respect to document requests from Congress, including with respect to documents previously made available to Special Counsel Robert Mueller (who was part of the Executive Branch).

President Trump has also repeatedly refused to allow current and former Administration officials to testify before Congress. Executive privilege allows the President to prevent senior advisors who work with and advise him every day from disclosing their conversations and interactions with him. In order to

---

1. Charlie Savage, Trump Vows Stonewall of 'All' House Subpoenas, Setting Up Fight Over Powers, N.Y. Times, April 24, 2019, https://www.nytimes.com/2019/04/24/us/politics/donald-trump-subpoenas.html.

protect that privilege, the executive branch has historically asserted testimonial immunity with respect to the President's close advisors who regularly meet with and advise him. Moreover, it has also asserted this immunity with respect to former officials. These claims of testimonial immunity have been executive branch positions in both Democratic and Republican Administrations.

However, the President does not have effective control over former officials, and it is up to them to decide whether to testify, and, if so, whether to assert the privilege (or a form of "immunity" from testimony).[2] They may do so out of their loyalty to the President for whom they served, in order to protect the institution of the Presidency, because of their ethical obligations as attorneys, or for other political or personal reasons.

The only judicial decision squarely on point rejects the Executive branch's position on testimonial immunity. In Comm. on Judiciary, U.S. House of Representatives v. Miers, 558 F.Supp.2d 53, 100-02 (D.D.C. 2008), the district court rejected absolute immunity for former senior presidential advisors. The case involved Harriet Miers, who at that time was a former White House Counsel to President George W. Bush. The district court agreed that immunity might be appropriate in cases "where national security or foreign affairs form the basis for the Executive's assertion of privilege." Senior advisors could also "assert executive privilege in response to any specific questions posed by the Committee." The district court, however, rejected a general immunity from having to testify:

> There are powerful reasons supporting the rejection of absolute immunity as asserted by the Executive here. If the Court held otherwise, the presumptive presidential privilege could be transformed into an absolute privilege and Congress's legitimate interest in inquiry could be easily thwarted. . . . [I]f the Executive's absolute immunity argument were to prevail, Congress could be left with no recourse to obtain information that is plainly not subject to any colorable claim of executive privilege. . . . Clear precedent and persuasive policy reasons confirm that the Executive cannot be the judge of its own privilege . . . Ms. Miers is not excused from compliance with the Committee's subpoena by virtue of a claim of executive privilege that may ultimately be made. Instead, she must appear before the Committee to provide testimony, and invoke executive privilege where appropriate.

The Executive Branch has not accepted the *Miers* decision as a correct statement of the law.

President Trump has also asserted the privilege beyond the smaller circle of senior advisors who interact with and advise the President every day.[3] In addition,

---

2. See Marty Lederman, What Is a Private Citizen to Do (When Caught in the Middle of an Interbranch Dispute)?, Balkinization, July 11, 2007, https://balkin.blogspot.com/2007/07/whatis-private-citizen-to-do-when.html.

3. See, e.g., Jacqueline Thomsen, White House sought to assert executive privilege in Kobach interview on census citizenship question, Cummings says, The Hill, June 7, 2019, https://thehill.com/regulation/court-battles/447510-white-house-sought-to-assert-executive-privilege-in-kobach-interview; Ryan Goodman & John T. Nelson, Annie Donaldson Is Not the President's "Alter Ego," Just Security, June 24, 2019, https://www.justsecurity.org/64681/annie-donaldson-is-not-the-presidents-alter-ego/.

the Trump Administration has been asserting a prophylactic claim of executive privilege with respect to large classes of documents.[4]

Beyond the central precedent of *United States v. Nixon*, which held that executive privilege must yield to "the fundamental demands of due process of law in the fair administration of justice," there is very little case law on the scope of executive privilege. (See *Miers, supra.*) A large number of opinions have been produced not by the courts but by the Justice Department's Office of Legal Counsel, and therefore are understandably sympathetic to the position of the President. Whatever one thinks the actual scope of executive privilege should be, the President has institutional incentives to claim a far broader privilege in conflicts with Congress and the courts.

One reason for the lack of case law is the practical problem of enforcement. Congress can issue a subpoena for documents or testimony. But if the President asserts executive privilege, Congress's options are limited.

First, Congress can vote (or threaten to vote) government officials in contempt for failing to appear, or for refusing to produce requested documents. For example, a Republican-controlled House held Attorney General Eric Holder in criminal and civil contempt in 2012 in a dispute over document production in the House's investigation of the Fast and Furious scandal involving the Bureau of Alcohol, Tobacco, and Firearms. The contempt citation, however, was practically ineffective: the document production issues were not resolved until the spring of 2019, long after President Obama left office.

That is because Congress has few ways of enforcing its orders. Congress has inherent powers to enforce its orders through contempt proceedings, arrest and imprisonment, but it has chosen not to use them for close to a century. See McGrain v. Daugherty, 273 U.S. 135 (1927) (upholding Congress's power to arrest and detain a witness in a Congressional investigation of antitrust policy.); Anderson v. Dunn, 19 U.S. (6 Wheat.) 204 (1821) (holding that Congress has the power to punish for contempt). Because Congress does not use its own contempt powers, Congress has to rely on criminal or civil proceedings.

Criminal proceedings require Congress to refer a matter to a U.S. Attorney. But the U.S. Attorney works for the Justice Department, which is part of the Executive Branch. The usual policy of the Justice Department is to refuse to bring criminal contempt proceedings against a member of the Executive Branch who is relying upon a claim of privilege or immunity that the President and DOJ have approved. For example, after the House held Attorney General Eric Holder in contempt in 2012, the Justice Department refused to prosecute.

That leaves civil proceedings. Congress can go to federal court to enforce its orders. But court proceedings generally take a great deal of time — sometimes many years. By the time the appeals process is exhausted, the Administration may be out of office — or Congress held by a different party.

---

4. See Jonathan Shaub, The Prophylactic Executive Privilege, Lawfare, June 14, 2019, https://www.lawfareblog.com/prophylactic-executive-privilege.

As a result, most disputes over executive privilege are resolved by negotiations between the two branches, which usually come to some sort of accommodation. Because Congress and the President regularly need to cooperate on many topics and at many levels, there are reasons for each to accommodate the other. Each also has its own balance of considerations. The Executive branch has to balance concerns about bad publicity (i.e., that it is hiding something illegal or embarrassing), and about the possibility of congressional payback in other contexts, against the Executive branch's interests in protecting the confidentiality of its operations over the long run. Conversely, Congress has to balance its desire for information against its own concerns about bad publicity, as well as the possibility that negotiations will break down and Congress must go to the courts and face a protracted struggle.

In the Trump Administration, the Executive Branch has somewhat fewer incentives for cooperation than usual. There is very little that Trump wants from a Democratic House and little to gain politically from cooperating with them. Accordingly, President Trump has made fairly broad assertions of privilege and attempted to delay resolution of disputes with Congress, cooperating only when necessary. By acting intransigently on multiple fronts, he may be able to wear down Congress. Even if many of his claims of executive privilege and testimonial immunity are overblown, they simply add to Congress's work in having to deal with them.

To be sure, Congress can threaten to impeach the President for his refusals. It can also begin impeachment proceedings and use them to investigate the President. There is a plausible argument that executive privilege must yield, or that its scope is far narrower, when Congress is investigating articles of impeachment. Otherwise, the President would truly be beyond investigation and accountability.

As a matter of fact, the House of Representatives did impeach Donald Trump in December 2019. One of the two counts was for obstructing Congress in its investigations of the President. But the result of the impeachment showed how hollow the threat of impeachment actually was against a determined President. President Trump was quickly acquitted by a Senate controlled by members of his own party. The President now knows that no matter how uncooperative he is, he cannot be removed as long as he has forty-one votes in the Senate, and he can use the fact that he was impeached to show his supporters that he is being unfairly treated by the other party. Under these conditions, why should he cooperate?

Following the 2019 impeachment, Congress's options to obtain compliance for oversight requests have become quite limited. For example, the House can try to leverage things that the President wants or needs from House Democrats. But because the Republican Party controls the Senate, the House has no control over executive branch appointments and judgeships.

Although disputes and bargaining between the branches have been commonplace. President Trump's blanket assertion that he will fight *all* congressional requests for documents and testimony is unprecedented in American history. What role should norms and conventions play in characterizing what is happening? In restraining the political branches?[5] What should the other participants do if one of the participants refuses to accept their understanding of the existing norms?

Suppose you think that Trump's position is inconsistent with existing norms and conventions about how the two parties should bargain in disputes about Congressional oversight. Will norm-breaking have any long term effects, or do you predict that things will snap back to normal in the next presidency?

2. *Documents from third parties and third party witnesses unconnected to the Administration.* Congress has also sought documents from third parties who are not former senior advisors to the President. Executive privilege generally does not apply in these cases. Nevertheless, the Trump Administration sought to block Congress from reviewing them. This litigation eventually reached the Supreme Court in the spring of 2020.

TRUMP v. MAZARS USA, LLP
2020 WL 3848061

CHIEF JUSTICE ROBERTS delivered the opinion of the Court.

Over the course of five days in April 2019, three committees of the U.S. House of Representatives issued four subpoenas seeking information about the finances of President Donald J. Trump, his children, and affiliated businesses. We have held that the House has authority under the Constitution to issue subpoenas to assist it in carrying out its legislative responsibilities. . . .

[The House Committee on Financial Services issued a subpoena to Deutsche Bank seeking any document related to account activity, due diligence, foreign transactions, business statements, debt schedules, statements of net worth, tax returns, and suspicious activity identified by Deutsche Bank. It issued a second subpoena to Capital One for similar information. The Permanent Select Committee on Intelligence issued a subpoena to Deutsche Bank that mirrored the subpoena issued by the Financial Services Committee. And the House Committee on Oversight and Reform issued a subpoena to the President's personal accounting firm, Mazars USA, LLP, demanding information related to the President and several affiliated businesses. Although each of the committees sought overlapping sets of financial documents, each supplied different justifications for the requests, explaining that the information would help guide legislative reform in areas ranging from money laundering and terrorism to foreign involvement in U.S. elections.]

The House asserts that the financial information sought here — encompassing a decade's worth of transactions by the President and his family — will help guide legislative reform in areas ranging from money laundering and terrorism

---

5. On the role of norms in executive branch practice, see Daphna Renan, Presidential Norms and Article II, 131 Harv. L. Rev. 2187 (2018). On the role of norms more generally in sustaining the rule of law, see Tara Leigh Grove, The Origins (and Fragility) of Judicial Independence, 71 Vand. L. Rev. 465 (2018).

to foreign involvement in U.S. elections. The President contends that the House lacked a valid legislative aim and instead sought these records to harass him, expose personal matters, and conduct law enforcement activities beyond its authority. The question presented is whether the subpoenas exceed the authority of the House under the Constitution. . . .

II

[H]istorically, disputes over congressional demands for presidential documents have not ended up in court. Instead, they have been hashed out in the "hurly-burly, the give-and-take of the political process between the legislative and the executive."

That practice began with George Washington and the early Congress. In 1792, a House committee requested Executive Branch documents pertaining to General St. Clair's campaign against the Indians in the Northwest Territory, which had concluded in an utter rout of federal forces when they were caught by surprise near the present-day border between Ohio and Indiana. See T. Taylor, Grand Inquest: The Story of Congressional Investigations 19-23 (1955). Since this was the first such request from Congress, President Washington called a Cabinet meeting, wishing to take care that his response "be rightly conducted" because it could "become a precedent."

The meeting, attended by the likes of Alexander Hamilton, Thomas Jefferson, Edmund Randolph, and Henry Knox, ended with the Cabinet of "one mind": The House had authority to "institute inquiries" and "call for papers" but the President could "exercise a discretion" over disclosures, "communicat[ing] such papers as the public good would permit" and "refus[ing]" the rest. President Washington then dispatched Jefferson to speak to individual congressmen and "bring them by persuasion into the right channel." The discussions were apparently fruitful, as the House later narrowed its request and the documents were supplied without recourse to the courts. See 3 Annals of Cong. 536 (1792).

Jefferson, once he became President, followed Washington's precedent. . . . Ever since, congressional demands for the President's information have been resolved by the political branches without involving this Court. . . . Congress and the President maintained this tradition of negotiation and compromise — without the involvement of this Court — until the present dispute. Indeed, from President Washington until now, we have never considered a dispute over a congressional subpoena for the President's records. And, according to the parties, the appellate courts have addressed such a subpoena only once, when a Senate committee sub-poenaed President Nixon during the Watergate scandal. *Senate Select Committee on Presidential Campaign Activities v. Nixon*, 498 F.2d 725 (CADC 1974) (en banc). In that case, the court refused to enforce the subpoena, and the Senate did not seek review by this Court. . . .

This dispute therefore represents a significant departure from historical prac-tice. Although the parties agree that this particular controversy is justiciable, we recognize that it is the first of its kind to reach this Court; that disputes of this sort can raise important issues concerning relations between the branches; that related disputes involving congressional efforts to seek official Executive Branch information recur on a regular basis, including in the context of deeply partisan controversy; and that Congress and the Executive have nonetheless managed for over two centuries to resolve such disputes among themselves without the benefit of guidance from us. Such longstanding practice " 'is a consideration of great weight' " in cases concerning "the allocation of power between [the] two elected branches of Government," and it imposes on us a duty of care to ensure that we not needlessly disturb "the compromises and working arrangements that [those] branches . . . themselves have reached." *NLRB v. Noel Canning*, 573 U.S. 513, 524-526 (2014). . . .

Congress has no enumerated constitutional power to conduct investigations or issue subpoenas, but we have held that each House has power "to secure needed information" in order to legislate. *McGrain v. Daugherty*, 273 U.S. 135, 161 (1927). This "power of inquiry — with process to enforce it — is an essential and appropriate auxiliary to the legislative function." Without information, Congress would be shooting in the dark, unable to legislate "wisely or effectively." The congressional power to obtain information is "broad" and "indispensable." *Watkins v. United States*, 354 U.S. 178, 187, 215 (1957). It encompasses inquiries into the administration of existing laws, studies of proposed laws, and "surveys of defects in our social, economic or political system for the purpose of enabling the Congress to remedy them."

Because this power is "justified solely as an adjunct to the legislative process," it is subject to several limitations. Most importantly, a congressional subpoena is valid only if it is "related to, and in furtherance of, a legitimate task of the Congress." The subpoena must serve a "valid legislative purpose," *Quinn v. United States*, 349 U.S. 155, 161 (1955); it must "concern[ ] a subject on which legislation 'could be had,' " *Eastland v. United States Servicemen's Fund*, 421 U.S. 491, 506 (1975) (quoting *McGrain*).

Furthermore, Congress may not issue a subpoena for the purpose of "law enforcement," because "those powers are assigned under our Constitution to the Executive and the Judiciary." *Quinn*. Thus Congress may not use subpoenas to "try" someone "before [a] committee for any crime or wrongdoing." *McGrain*. Congress has no " 'general' power to inquire into private affairs and compel disclosures," and "there is no congressional power to expose for the sake of exposure," *Watkins*. "Investigations conducted solely for the personal aggrandizement of the investigators or to 'punish' those investigated are indefensible."

Finally, recipients of legislative subpoenas retain their constitutional rights throughout the course of an investigation. And recipients have long been understood to retain common law and constitutional privileges with respect to certain materials, such as attorney-client communications and governmental communications protected by executive privilege.

The President contends, as does the Solicitor General appearing on behalf of the United States, that the usual rules for congressional subpoenas do not govern here because the President's papers are at issue. They argue for a more demanding standard based in large part on cases involving the Nixon tapes — recordings of conversations between President Nixon and close advisers discussing the break-in at the Democratic National Committee's headquarters at the Watergate complex. The tapes were subpoenaed by a Senate committee and the Special Prosecutor investigating the break-in, prompting President Nixon to invoke executive privilege and leading to two cases addressing the showing necessary to require the President to comply with the subpoenas. See *Nixon*; *Senate Select Committee*. . . .

Quoting *Nixon*, the President asserts that the House must establish a "demonstrated, specific need" for the financial information, just as the Watergate special prosecutor was required to do in order to obtain the tapes. And drawing on *Senate Select Committee* — the D. C. Circuit case refusing to enforce the Senate subpoena for the tapes — the President and the Solicitor General argue that the House must show that the financial information is "demonstrably critical" to its legislative purpose.

We disagree that these demanding standards apply here. Unlike the cases before us, *Nixon* and *Senate Select Committee* involved Oval Office communications over which the President asserted executive privilege. That privilege safeguards the public interest in candid, confidential deliberations within the Executive Branch; it is "fundamental to the operation of Government." *Nixon*. As a result, information subject to executive privilege deserves "the greatest protection consistent with the fair administration of justice." We decline to transplant that protection root and branch to cases involving nonprivileged, private information, which by definition does not implicate sensitive Executive Branch deliberations.

The standards proposed by the President and the Solicitor General — if applied outside the context of privileged information — would risk seriously impeding Congress in carrying out its responsibilities. The President and the Solicitor General would apply the same exacting standards to *all* subpoenas for the President's information, without recognizing distinctions between privileged and nonprivileged information, between official and personal information, or between various legislative objectives. Such a categorical approach would represent a significant departure from the longstanding way of doing business between the branches, giving short shrift to Congress's important interests in conducting inquiries to obtain the information it needs to legislate effectively. . . .

Legislative inquiries might involve the President in appropriate cases; as noted, Congress's responsibilities extend to "every affair of government." *Ibid.* (internal quotation marks omitted). Because the President's approach does not take adequate account of these significant congressional interests, we do not adopt it.

The House meanwhile would have us ignore that these suits involve the President. Invoking our precedents concerning investigations that did not target the President's papers, the House urges us to uphold its subpoenas because they "relate[ ] to a valid legislative purpose" or "concern[ ] a subject on which legislation could be had." That approach is appropriate, the House argues, because the cases before us are not "momentous separation-of-powers disputes." . . .

The House's approach fails to take adequate account of the significant separation of powers issues raised by congressional subpoenas for the President's information. Congress and the President have an ongoing institutional relationship as the "opposite and rival" political branches established by the Constitution. As a result, congressional subpoenas directed at the President differ markedly from congressional subpoenas we have previously reviewed, and they bear little resemblance to criminal subpoenas issued to the President in the course of a specific investigation. Unlike those subpoenas, congressional subpoenas for the President's information unavoidably pit the political branches against one another.

Far from accounting for separation of powers concerns, the House's approach aggravates them by leaving essentially no limits on the congressional power to subpoena the President's personal records. Any personal paper possessed by a President could potentially "relate to" a conceivable subject of legislation, for Congress has broad legislative powers that touch a vast number of subjects. The President's financial records could relate to economic reform, medical records to health reform, school transcripts to education reform, and so on. . . . Without limits on its subpoena powers, Congress could "exert an imperious controul" over the Executive Branch and aggrandize itself at the President's expense, just as the Framers feared. The Federalist No. 71 (A. Hamilton); No. 48 (J. Madison); *Bowsher v. Synar*, 478 U.S. 714, 721-722, 727 (1986). And a limitless subpoena power would transform the "established practice" of the political branches. *Noel Canning*. Instead of negotiating over information requests, Congress could simply walk away from the bargaining table and compel compliance in court.

The House and the courts below suggest that these separation of powers concerns are not fully implicated by the particular subpoenas here, but we disagree. We would have to be "blind" not to see what "[a]ll others can see and understand": that the subpoenas do not represent a run-of-the-mill legislative effort but rather a clash between rival branches of government over records of intense political interest for all involved.

The interbranch conflict here does not vanish simply because the subpoenas seek personal papers or because the President sued in his personal capacity. The President is the only person who alone composes a branch of government. As a result, there is not always a clear line between his personal and official affairs. "The interest of the man" is often "connected with the constitutional rights of the place." The Federalist No. 51. Given the close connection between the Office of the President and its occupant, congressional demands for the President's papers can implicate the relationship between the branches regardless whether those papers are personal or official. Either way, a demand may aim to harass the President or render him "complaisan[t] to the humors of the Legislature." [The Federalist] No. 71. In fact, a subpoena for personal papers may pose a heightened risk of such impermissible purposes, precisely because of the documents' personal nature and their less evident connection to a legislative task. No one can say that the controversy here is less significant to the relationship between the branches simply because it involves personal papers. Quite the opposite. That appears to be what makes the matter of such great consequence to the President and Congress.

In addition, separation of powers concerns are no less palpable here simply because the subpoenas were issued to third parties. Congressional demands for the President's information present an interbranch conflict no matter where the information is held—it is, after all, the President's information. Were it otherwise, Congress could sidestep constitutional requirements any time a President's information is entrusted to a third party—as occurs with rapidly increasing frequency. Indeed, Congress could declare open season on the President's information held by schools, archives, internet service providers, e-mail clients, and financial institutions. The Constitution does not tolerate such ready evasion; it "deals with substance, not shadows." *Cummings v. Missouri*, 4 Wall. 277, 325 (1867).

Congressional subpoenas for the President's personal information implicate weighty concerns regarding the separation of powers. Neither side, however, identifies an approach that accounts for these concerns. . . . A balanced approach is necessary, one that takes a "considerable impression" from "the practice of the government," *McCulloch* v. *Maryland*, and "resist[s]" the "pressure inherent within each of the separate Branches to exceed the outer limits of its power," *INS v. Chadha*, 462 U.S. 919, 951 (1983). We therefore conclude that, in assessing whether a subpoena directed at the President's personal information is "related to, and in furtherance of, a legitimate task of the Congress," courts must perform a careful analysis that takes adequate account of the separation of powers principles at stake, including both the significant legislative interests of Congress and the "unique position" of the President, *Clinton*. . . .

First, courts should carefully assess whether the asserted legislative purpose warrants the significant step of involving the President and his papers. "'[O]ccasion[s] for constitutional confrontation between the two branches' should be avoided whenever possible." Congress may not rely on the President's information if other sources could reasonably provide Congress the information it needs in light of its particular legislative objective. The President's unique constitutional position means that Congress may not look to him as a "case study" for general legislation.

Unlike in criminal proceedings, where "[t]he very integrity of the judicial system" would be undermined without "full disclosure of all the facts," *Nixon*, efforts to craft legislation involve predictive policy judgments that are "not hamper[ed] . . . in quite the same way" when every scrap of potentially relevant evidence is not available. . . .

Second, to narrow the scope of possible conflict between the branches, courts should insist on a subpoena no broader than reasonably necessary to support Congress's legislative objective. The specificity of the subpoena's request "serves as an important safeguard against unnecessary intrusion into the operation of the Office of the President."

Third, courts should be attentive to the nature of the evidence offered by Congress to establish that a subpoena advances a valid legislative purpose. The more detailed and substantial the evidence of Congress's legislative purpose, the better. That is particularly true when Congress contemplates legislation that raises sensitive constitutional issues, such as legislation concerning the Presidency. . . .

Fourth, courts should be careful to assess the burdens imposed on the President by a subpoena. We have held that burdens on the President's time and attention stemming from judicial process and litigation, without more, generally do not cross constitutional lines. See *Vance*; *Clinton*. But burdens imposed by a congressional subpoena should be carefully scrutinized, for they stem from a rival political branch that has an ongoing relationship with the President and incentives to use subpoenas for institutional advantage.

Other considerations may be pertinent as well; one case every two centuries does not afford enough experience for an exhaustive list.

When Congress seeks information "needed for intelligent legislative action," it "unquestionably" remains "the duty of *all* citizens to cooperate." Congressional subpoenas for information from the President, however, implicate special concerns regarding the separation of powers. The courts below did not take adequate account of those concerns. The judgments of the Courts of Appeals for the D.C. Circuit and the Second Circuit are vacated, and the cases are remanded for further proceedings consistent with this opinion.

It is so ordered.

Justice THOMAS, dissenting.

. . . I would hold that Congress has no power to issue a legislative subpoena for private, nonofficial documents — whether they belong to the President or not. Congress may be able to obtain these documents as part of an investigation of the President, but to do so, it must proceed under the impeachment power. Accordingly, I would reverse the judgments of the Courts of Appeals. . . .

The scope of [Congress's] implied powers is very limited. The Constitution does not sweep in powers "of inferior importance, merely because they are inferior." *McCulloch*. . . . At the time of the founding, the power to subpoena private, nonofficial documents was not included by necessary implication in any of Congress' legislative powers. This understanding persisted for decades and is consistent with the Court's first decision addressing legislative subpoenas, *Kilbourn v. Thompson*, 103 U.S. 168 (1881). The test that this Court created in *McGrain v. Daugherty*, 273 U.S. 135 (1927), and the majority's variation on that standard today, are without support as applied to private, nonofficial documents. . . . I express no opinion about the constitutionality of legislative subpoenas for other kinds of evidence. [relocated footnote — eds.]

The Committees argue that Congress wields the same investigatory powers that the British Parliament did at the time of the founding. But this claim overlooks one of the fundamental differences between our Government and the British Government: Parliament was supreme. Congress is not. . . . [I]n a system in which Congress is not supreme, the individual protections in the Bill of Rights, such as the prohibition on unreasonable searches and seizures, meaningfully constrain Congress' power to compel documents from private citizens. . . .

The subpoenas in these cases also cannot be justified based on the practices of 18th-century American legislatures. . . . [N]one of the examples from 18th-century colonial and state history support a power to issue a legislative subpoena for private, nonofficial documents.

Given that Congress has no exact precursor in England or colonial America, founding-era congressional practice is especially informative about the scope of implied legislative powers. Thus, it is highly probative that no founding-era Congress issued a subpoena for private, nonofficial documents. . . . Congress began issuing them by the end of the 1830s. However, the practice remained controversial in Congress and this Court throughout the first century of the Republic. . . .

When this Court first addressed a legislative subpoena, it refused to uphold it. After casting doubt on legislative subpoenas generally, the Court in *Kilbourn v. Thompson*, held that the subpoena at issue was unlawful because it sought to investigate private conduct. . . . The Court did not reach a conclusion on the . . . theory that a legislative subpoena power was necessary for Congress to carry out its legislative duties. But it observed that, based on British judicial opinions, not "much aid [is] given to the doctrine, that this power exists as one necessary to enable either House of Congress to exercise successfully their function of legislation." . . .

The Court instead based its decision on the fact that the subpoena at issue "ma[de] inquiry into the private affairs of the citizen." Such a power, the Court reasoned, "is judicial and not legislative," and "no judicial power is vested in the Congress or either branch of it, save in the cases" of punishing Members, compelling Members' attendance, judging elections and qualifications, and impeachment and trial. . . .

Nearly half a century later, in *McGrain v. Daugherty*, the Court reached the question reserved in *Kilbourn* — whether Congress has the power to issue legislative subpoenas. It rejected *Kilbourn*'s reasoning and upheld the power to issue legislative subpoenas as long as they were relevant to a legislative power. Although *McGrain* involved oral testimony, the Court has since extended this test to subpoenas for private documents. The Committees rely on *McGrain*, but this line of cases misunderstands both the original meaning of Article I and the historical practice underlying it. . . .

The opinion in *McGrain* lacks any foundation in text or history with respect to subpoenas for private, nonofficial documents. It fails to recognize that Congress, unlike Parliament, is not supreme. It does not cite any specific precedent for issuing legislative subpoenas for private documents from 18th-century colonial or state practice. And it identifies no founding-era legislative subpoenas for private documents.

Since *McGrain*, the Court has pared back Congress' authority to compel testimony and documents. It has held that certain convictions of witnesses for contempt of Congress violated the Fifth Amendment. See *Watkins v. United States*,

354 U.S. 178 (1957) (Due Process Clause); *Quinn v. United States*, 349 U.S. 155 (1955) (Self-Incrimination Clause); see also *Barenblatt v. United States*, 360 U.S. 109, 153-154 (1959) (Black, J., dissenting). It has also affirmed the reversal of a conviction on the ground that the Committee lacked authority to issue the subpoena. See *United States v. Rumely*, 345 U.S. 41 (1953). And today, it creates a new four-part, nonexhaustive test for cases involving the President. Rather than continue our trend of trying to compensate for *McGrain*, I would simply decline to apply it in these cases because it is readily apparent that the Committees have no constitutional authority to subpoena private, nonofficial documents. . . .

If the Committees wish to investigate alleged wrongdoing by the President and obtain documents from him, the Constitution provides Congress with a special mechanism for doing so: impeachment. . . . I express no view on whether there are any limitations on the impeachment power that would prevent the House from subpoenaing the documents at issue. [relocated footnote — eds.]

Justice ALITO, dissenting.

Justice Thomas makes a valuable argument about the constitutionality of congressional subpoenas for a President's personal documents. In these cases, however, I would assume for the sake of argument that such subpoenas are not categorically barred. Nevertheless, legislative subpoenas for a President's personal documents are inherently suspicious. Such documents are seldom of any special value in considering potential legislation, and subpoenas for such documents can easily be used for improper non-legislative purposes. Accordingly, courts must be very sensitive to separation of powers issues when they are asked to approve the enforcement of such subpoenas.

In many cases, disputes about subpoenas for Presidential documents are fought without judicial involvement. If Congress attempts to obtain such documents by subpoenaing a President directly, those two heavyweight institutions can use their considerable weapons to settle the matter. But when Congress issues such a subpoena to a third party, Congress must surely appreciate that the Judiciary may be pulled into the dispute, and Congress should not expect that the courts will allow the subpoena to be enforced without seriously examining its legitimacy.

Whenever such a subpoena comes before a court, Congress should be required to make more than a perfunctory showing that it is seeking the documents for a legitimate legislative purpose and not for the purpose of exposing supposed Presidential wrongdoing. The House can inquire about possible Presidential wrongdoing pursuant to its impeachment power, but the Committees do not defend these subpoenas as ancillary to that power.

Instead, they claim that the subpoenas were issued to gather information that is relevant to legislative issues, but there is disturbing evidence of an improper law enforcement purpose. In addition, the sheer volume of documents sought calls out for explanation.

The Court recognizes that the decisions below did not give adequate consideration to separation of powers concerns. Therefore, after setting out a non-exhaustive list of considerations for the lower courts to take into account, the Court vacates the judgments of the Courts of Appeals and sends the cases back for reconsideration. I agree that the lower courts erred and that these cases must be remanded, but I do not think that the considerations outlined by the Court can be properly satisfied unless the House is required to show more than it has put forward to date.

Specifically, the House should provide a description of the type of legislation being considered, and while great specificity is not necessary, the description should be sufficient to permit a court to assess whether the particular records sought are of any special importance. The House should also spell out its constitutional authority to enact the type of legislation that it is contemplating, and it should justify the scope of the subpoenas in relation to the articulated legislative needs. In addition, it should explain why the subpoenaed information, as opposed to information available from other sources, is needed. Unless the House is required to make a showing along these lines, I would hold that enforcement of the subpoenas cannot be ordered. Because I find the terms of the Court's remand inadequate, I must respectfully dissent.

Discussion

1. *Catch me if you can.* As in *Trump v. Vance*, the result in *Trump v. Mazars* allows President Trump to run out the clock on congressional investigations into his finances. The litigation will continue well into his second term if he wins. If he loses, Congress may well drop the investigation.

2. *Why can't we all just get along?* The Court notes that it has never been asked to pass on a subpoena like this before, and that is because the political branches usually negotiate the issue. But one reason why Congress negotiates the issue is because, as discussed earlier in this note, Congress has few practical alternatives. Recourse to the courts takes time, and therefore normally favors the party that wants to delay, which is usually the President.

Mazars does little to disturb this arrangement. Its new four-part test is complicated, highly fact-specific, and requires a balancing of interests. Therefore it can't easily be applied in a clear-cut fashion by lower courts. For that reason, it will, if anything, protract litigation rather than speed it up. In essence, the Supreme Court is saying to Congress and the President: We are annoyed that things got this far. Work things out on your own next time, because if you don't, and come back to the courts, the resolution is going to take a very long time, because the criteria we have just announced are very fact-specific.

Of course, the way the Court has resolved the controversy means that if succeeding presidents are as intransigent as President Trump has proven to be, they too will have little to fear from the courts. They will usually be able to run out the clock, as he has done in this case. And that means that Congress will have to find other forms of leverage.

3. *Mixed results for Congress.* There are still other reasons to think that *Mazars* is not a major victory for Congressional oversight. When the litigation

began, the baseline was *Watkins*, which held that courts would generally defer to Congress. It is true that the Court rejected President Trump's most aggressive claims. But the four-factor test moves things away from deference to Congress and toward greater protection for the President. In addition, the Justice Department (and the OLC) now get to develop the Court's new four-factor test in litigation. They will do what they can to push the doctrinal development of the *Mazars* test in the direction of presidential power, and in the long run, they may well succeed.

4. *Using the President as a "case study."* Before *Mazars*, it was generally recognized that Congress's ability to investigate had to relate to potential legislation it might pass. But in practice, this was not much of a limitation. Congress can pass laws on virtually any subject. (What it cannot do through the commerce power, for example, it can do through the spending power, and so on.) Moreover, because Congress has the power, under Article V, to propose new constitutional amendments, it can presumably hold hearings for the purpose of considering a new amendment to the Constitution that would increase its existing powers.

In *Mazars*, the Court makes clear that "Congress may not rely on the President's information if other sources could reasonably provide Congress the information it needs in light of its particular legislative objective. The President's unique constitutional position means that Congress may not look to him as a 'case study' for general legislation." So, if Congress wants to investigate international money laundering, it can't use President Trump's financial records from Mazars and Deutsche Bank as a convenient way to study the more general problem.

Suppose that Congress suspects that the President himself has engaged in illegal money laundering, which puts him a compromising position with respect to a foreign power. After *Mazars*, how should it articulate the purposes of its investigation? Must it declare that it is considering impeaching the President, or can it stop short of that?

5. *Presidential harassment.* The Court is clearly worried about the possibility that Congress will harass the President with investigations to score political points. But in *Trump v. Vance*, the Court does not seem particularly worried that state and local prosecutors — a far larger number of independent actors — will use the criminal process to harass the President. What explains the difference between the two situations?

6. *Litigation about the President's tax returns. Mazars* does not resolve all of the disputes between the President and Congress. One that is still ongoing concerns disclosure of the President's tax returns.

In defiance of long-standing political conventions, President Trump famously refused to disclose his tax returns during the 2016 campaign, offering various excuses for why he was not yet able to do so. After the election, he announced that he would not release them. His refusal to make his tax returns public infuriated his political opponents, who sought various ways to discover what was in them.

Federal law treats federal tax returns as confidential, and the Treasury Department generally may not disclose them to the public or to other parties.

26 U.S.C. §§ 6103(a), 7213(a). However, there are exceptions for authorized disclosures. One such disclosure appears in 26 U.S.C. § 6103(f)(1), which provides that "Upon written request from the chairman of the Committee on Ways and Means of the House of Representatives, the chairman of the Committee on Finance of the Senate, or the chairman of the Joint Committee on Taxation, the Secretary [of the Treasury] shall furnish such committee with any return or return information specified in such request, except that any return or return information which can be associated with, or otherwise identify, directly or indirectly, a particular taxpayer shall be furnished to such committee only when sitting in closed executive session unless such taxpayer otherwise consents in writing to such disclosure." Subsection (f)(4)(A) authorizes the House Ways and Means Committee and the Senate Finance Committee—unlike other committees—to share such information with the full House or Senate, thereby effectively making it public.

On April 3, 2019, the Chairman of the House Committee on Ways and Means, Representative Richard Neal, requested the last six years of President Trump's individual tax returns, and those of eight associated business entities, as well as the audit histories and work papers associated with each return. Chairman Neal explained the reason for his request as follows:

> Consistent with its authority, the Committee is considering legislative proposals and conducting oversight related to our Federal tax laws, including, but not limited to, the extent to which the IRS audits and enforces the Federal tax laws against a President. Under the Internal Revenue Manual, individual income tax returns of a President are subject to mandatory examination, but this practice is IRS policy and not codified in the Federal tax laws. It is necessary for the Committee to determine the scope of any such examination and whether it includes a review of underlying business activities required to be reported on the individual income tax return.

Treasury Secretary Steven Mnuchin refused to release the returns, and on June 13, 2019, the Office of Legal Counsel issued an opinion.[6] The OLC opinion argued that

> The text of section 6103(f). . . . does not require the Committee to state any purpose for its request. But Congress could not constitutionally confer upon the Committee the right to compel the Executive Branch to disclose confidential information without a legitimate legislative purpose. Under the facts and circumstances, the Secretary of the Treasury reasonably and correctly concluded that the Committee's asserted interest in reviewing the Internal Revenue Service's audits of presidential returns was pretextual and that its true aim was to make the President's tax returns public, which is not a legitimate legislative purpose.
>
> . . .
>
> During the prior Congress, Chairman Neal, who was then the Committee's Ranking Member, repeatedly urged the Committee to invoke section 6103(f) to make the President's tax returns "available to the public," declaring that

---

6. Congressional Committee's Request for the President's Tax Returns Under 26 U.S.C. § 6103(f), Office of Legal Counsel (June 13, 2019), https://www.justice.gov/olc/file/1173756/download.

"Committee Democrats remain steadfast in [their] pursuit to have [President Trump's] individual tax returns disclosed to the public." . . . Before the midterm elections, Chairman Neal (as well as other members of his party) promised that, if they won a majority in the House, then the Chairman would wield his authority to demand the President's tax returns.

. . .

While the Executive Branch should accord due deference and respect to a committee's request, the Committee's stated purpose in the April 3 letter blinks reality. It is pretextual. No one could reasonably believe that the Committee seeks six years of President Trump's tax returns because of a newly discovered interest in legislating on the presidential-audit process. The Committee's request reflects the next assay in a long-standing political battle over the President's tax returns. Consistent with their long-held views, Chairman Neal and other majority members have invoked the Committee's authority to obtain and publish these returns. Recognizing that the Committee may not pursue exposure for exposure's sake, however, the Committee has devised an alternative reason for the request.

. . . When faced with a congressional request for confidential taxpayer information, must the Secretary close his eyes and blindly accept a pretextual justification for that request? Or must the Secretary implement the statute in a manner faithful to constitutional limitations? We believe that the Executive's duty to "take Care that the Laws be faithfully executed," U.S. Const. art. II, § 3, permits only one answer. Where, as here, there is reason to doubt the Committee's asserted legislative purpose, Treasury may examine the objective fit between that purpose and the information sought, as well as any other evidence that may bear upon the Committee's true objective. In doing so, Treasury acts as part of a politically accountable branch with a constitutional duty to resist legislative intrusions upon executive power and therefore does not act under the same institutional constraints as the Judiciary. Here, because the Committee lacked a legitimate legislative purpose, its request did not qualify for the statutory exception to taxpayer confidentiality, and the law required Treasury to deny that request.

In its opinion, the OLC claimed that the real reasons for the request are to discover and expose to the public Trump's potential financial conflicts of interest and ties to foreign nations, and, in particular, to assess what "the Russians have on Donald Trump politically, personally, [and] financially" and to "help the American people better understand the extent of Trump's financial ties to Putin's Russia" (quoting House members).

The House of Representatives brought suit to enforce its subpoena and the matter is now in the district court. How should the court decide the case after *Mazars*? Does the existence of a federal statute make any difference to *Mazars'* four-factor test?

Insert on p. 903, immediately before *National Labor Relations Board v. Noel Canning*:

FINANCIAL OVERSIGHT AND MANAGEMENT BOARD FOR PUERTO RICO V. AURELIUS INVESTMENT, LLC, 140 S.Ct. 1649 (2020): In 2016, in response to a fiscal crisis in Puerto Rico, Congress used its power under the Territories Clause of Article IV § 3, cl. 2, to enact the Puerto Rico Oversight, Management, and Economic Stability Act (PROMESA). PROMESA created a seven-member Financial Oversight and Management Board, whose job was to promote financial stability for the island. After the Board began bankruptcy proceedings to restructure Puerto Rico's debt, a hedge fund (which had bought up Puerto Rico's debt) and a labor union sued to stop the bankruptcy proceeding. They argued that the members of the Oversight Board, who had been selected by President Obama, should also have been confirmed by the Senate. They pointed to the Constitution's Appointments Clause, which says that the President "shall nominate, and by and with the Advice and Consent of the Senate, shall appoint . . . all . . . Officers of the United States. . . ." Art. II, § 2, cl. 2.

The Supreme Court, in an opinion by Justice Breyer, held that PROMESA's method for selecting the Oversight Board was constitutional: "when Congress creates local offices using [its powers over the federal territories under Article IV, § 3, cl. 2, and over the District of Columbia under Article I, § 8, cl. 17], the officers exercise power of the local government, not the Federal Government. . . . Longstanding practice indicates that a federal law's creation of an office in this context does not automatically make its holder an "Officer of the United States."

Rather, Congress has often used these two provisions to create local offices filled in ways other than those specified in the Appointments Clause. The Appointments Clause restricts the appointment of "Officers of the United States" who exercise the power of the federal government in federal territories and the District of Columbia. But, Justice Breyer concluded, "the Appointments Clause . . . *does not* restrict the appointment of local officers that Congress vests with primarily local duties under Article IV, § 3, or Article I, § 8, cl. 17." In this case, Congress provided that the Board is "an entity within the territorial government" and "shall not be considered a department, agency, establishment, or instrumentality of the Federal Government." It "also gave the Board a structure, a set of duties, and related powers all of which are consistent with this statement." Hence the Board's members were local officers with "primarily local powers and duties."

Justice Thomas concurred in the judgment: "Territorial officials performing duties created under Article IV of the Constitution are not federal officers within the original meaning of the phrase 'Officers of the United States.' . . . Because the Board's members perform duties pursuant to Article IV, they do not qualify as 'Officers of the United States.'"

Justice Sotomayor also concurred in the judgment: "These cases raise serious questions about when, if ever, the Federal Government may constitutionally exercise authority to establish territorial officers in a Territory like Puerto Rico, where Congress seemingly ceded that authority long ago to Puerto Rico itself. The 1950s compact between the Federal Government and Puerto Rico undoubtedly carried ramifications for Puerto Rico's status under federal and international law; the same may be true of the Appointments Clause analysis here." The whole point of "Public Law 600's compact between Puerto Rico and the Federal Government seemed to be that the people of Puerto Rico may choose their own territorial officers, rather than have such officers foisted on the Territory by the Federal Government." Hence "the result of these cases seems anomalous. The Board members, tasked with determining the financial fate of a self-governing Territory, exist in a twilight zone of accountability, neither selected by Puerto Rico itself nor subject to the strictures of the Appointments Clause." Justice Sotomayor concluded: "I am skeptical that the Constitution countenances this freewheeling exercise of control over a population that the Federal Government has explicitly agreed to recognize as operating under a government of their own choosing, pursuant to a constitution of their own choosing. Surely our Founders, having labored to attain such recognition of self-determination, would not view that same recognition with respect to Puerto Rico as a mere act of grace. Nevertheless, because these issues are not properly presented in these cases, I reluctantly concur in the judgment."

* * *

SEILA LAW LLC v. CONSUMER FINANCIAL PROTECTION BUREAU
2020 WL 3492641

CHIEF JUSTICE ROBERTS delivered the opinion of the Court with respect to Parts I, II, and III.

I

In the summer of 2007, then-Professor Elizabeth Warren called for the creation of a new, independent federal agency focused on regulating consumer financial products. Professor Warren believed the financial products marketed to ordinary American households — credit cards, student loans, mortgages, and the like — had grown increasingly unsafe due to a "regulatory jumble" that paid too much attention to banks and too little to consumers. To remedy the lack of "coherent, consumer-oriented" financial regulation, she proposed "concentrat[ing] the review of financial products in a single location" — an independent agency modeled after the multimember Consumer Product Safety Commission.

That proposal soon met its moment. Within months of Professor Warren's writing, the subprime mortgage market collapsed, precipitating a financial crisis that wiped out over $10 trillion in American household wealth and cost millions of Americans their jobs, their retirements, and their homes. In the aftermath, the Obama administration embraced Professor Warren's recommendation. Through the Treasury Department, the administration encouraged Congress to establish an agency with a mandate to ensure that "consumer protection regulations" in the financial sector "are written fairly and enforced vigorously." Like Professor Warren, the administration envisioned a traditional independent agency, run by a multimember board with a "diverse set of viewpoints and experiences."

In 2010, Congress acted on these proposals and created the Consumer Financial Protection Bureau (CFPB) as an independent financial regulator within the Federal Reserve System. Dodd-Frank Wall Street Reform and Consumer Protection Act (Dodd-Frank), 124 Stat. 1376. Congress tasked the CFPB with "implement[ing]" and "enforc[ing]" a large body of financial consumer protection laws to "ensur[e] that all consumers have access to markets for consumer financial products and services and that markets for consumer financial products and services are fair, transparent, and competitive." 12 U.S.C. § 5511(a). Congress transferred the administration of 18 existing federal statutes to the CFPB, including the Fair Credit Reporting Act, the Fair Debt Collection Practices Act, and the Truth in Lending Act. In addition, Congress enacted a new prohibition on "any unfair, deceptive, or abusive act or practice" by certain participants in the consumer-finance sector. Congress authorized the CFPB to implement that broad standard (and the 18 pre-existing statutes placed under the agency's purview) through binding regulations.

Congress also vested the CFPB with potent enforcement powers. The agency has the authority to conduct investigations, issue subpoenas and civil investigative demands, initiate administrative adjudications, and prosecute civil actions in federal court. To remedy violations of federal consumer financial law, the CFPB may seek restitution, disgorgement, and injunctive relief, as well as civil penalties of up to $1,000,000 (inflation adjusted) for each day that a violation occurs. . . .

The CFPB's rulemaking and enforcement powers are coupled with extensive adjudicatory authority. The agency may conduct administrative proceedings to "ensure or enforce compliance with" the statutes and regulations it administers. When the CFPB acts as an adjudicator, it has "jurisdiction to grant any appropriate legal or equitable relief." . . .

Congress's design for the CFPB differed from the proposals of Professor Warren and the Obama administration in one critical respect. Rather than create a traditional independent agency headed by a multimember board or commission, Congress elected to place the CFPB under the leadership of a single Director. The CFPB Director is appointed by the President with the advice and consent of the Senate. The Director serves for a term of five years, during which the President may remove the Director from office only for "inefficiency, neglect of duty, or malfeasance in office."

Unlike most other agencies, the CFPB does not rely on the annual appropriations process for funding. Instead, the CFPB receives funding directly from the Federal Reserve, which is itself funded outside the appropriations process through bank assessments. Each year, the CFPB requests an amount that the Director deems "reasonably necessary to carry out" the agency's duties, and the Federal Reserve grants that request so long as it does not exceed 12% of the total operating expenses of the Federal Reserve (inflation adjusted). In recent years, the CFPB's annual budget has exceeded half a billion dollars.

Seila Law LLC is a California-based law firm that provides debt-related legal services to clients. In 2017, the CFPB issued a civil investigative demand to Seila Law to determine whether the firm had "engag[ed] in unlawful acts or practices in the advertising, marketing, or sale of debt relief services." . . . The demand (essentially a subpoena) directed Seila Law to produce information and documents related to its business practices . . . [When Seila Law refused, the CFPB sought to enforce its demand in federal court. Seila Law defended on the ground that] the agency's leadership by a single Director removable only for cause violated the separation of powers. [Both the District Court and the Ninth Circuit rejected the argument and ordered Seila Law to comply]. . . .

We granted certiorari to address the constitutionality of the CFPB's structure. We also requested argument on an additional question: whether, if the CFPB's structure violates the separation of powers, the CFPB Director's removal protection can be severed from the rest of the Dodd-Frank Act. . . .

III

We hold that the CFPB's leadership by a single individual removable only for inefficiency, neglect, or malfeasance violates the separation of powers.

A

Article II provides that "[t]he executive Power shall be vested in a President," who must "take Care that the Laws be faithfully executed." Art. II, § 1, cl. 1; *id.*, § 3. The entire "executive Power" belongs to the President alone. But because it would be "impossib[le]" for "one man" to "perform all the great business of the State," the Constitution assumes that lesser executive officers will "assist the supreme Magistrate in discharging the duties of his trust." 30 Writings of George Washington 334 (J. Fitzpatrick ed. 1939).

These lesser officers must remain accountable to the President, whose authority they wield. As Madison explained, "[I]f any power whatsoever is in its nature Executive, it is the power of appointing, overseeing, and controlling those who execute the laws." 1 Annals of Cong. 463 (1789). That power, in turn, generally includes the ability to remove executive officials, for it is "only the authority that can remove" such officials that they "must fear and, in the performance of [their] functions, obey." *Bowsher* [*v. Synar*, 478 U.S. 714, 726 (1986)].

The President's removal power has long been confirmed by history and precedent. It "was discussed extensively in Congress when the first executive departments were created" in 1789. *Free Enterprise Fund* [*v. Public Company Accounting Oversight Bd.*, 561 U.S. 477, 492 (2010)]. "The view that 'prevailed, as most consonant to the text of the Constitution' and 'to the requisite responsibility and harmony in the Executive Department,' was that the executive power included a power to oversee executive officers through removal." *Ibid.* (quoting Letter from James Madison to Thomas Jefferson (June 30, 1789), 16 Documentary History of the First Federal Congress 893 (2004)). The First Congress's recognition of the President's removal power in 1789 "provides contemporaneous and weighty evidence of the Constitution's meaning," and has long been the "settled and well understood construction of the Constitution," *Ex parte Hennen*, 13 Pet. 230, 259 (1839).

The Court recognized the President's prerogative to remove executive officials in *Myers v. United States*, 272 U.S. 52 (1926). Chief Justice Taft, writing for the Court, conducted an exhaustive examination of the First Congress's determination in 1789, the views of the Framers and their contemporaries, historical practice, and our precedents up until that point. He concluded that Article II "grants to the President" the "general administrative control of those executing the laws, including the power of appointment *and removal* of executive officers." (emphasis added). Just as the President's "selection of administrative officers is essential to the execution of the laws by him, so must be his power of removing those for whom he cannot continue to be responsible." "[T]o hold otherwise," the Court reasoned, "would make it impossible for the President . . . to take care that the laws be faithfully executed."

We recently reiterated the President's general removal power in *Free Enterprise Fund*. "Since 1789," we recapped, "the Constitution has been understood to empower the President to keep these officers accountable — by removing them from office, if necessary." Although we had previously sustained congressional limits on that power in certain circumstances, we declined to extend those limits to "a new situation not yet encountered by the Court" — an official insulated by *two* layers of for-cause removal protection. In the face of that novel impediment to the President's oversight of the Executive Branch, we adhered to the general rule that the President possesses "the authority to remove those who assist him in carrying out his duties."

Free Enterprise Fund left in place two exceptions to the President's unrestricted removal power. First, in *Humphrey's Executor* [*v. United States*, 295 U.S. 602 (1935)], decided less than a decade after *Myers*, the Court upheld a statute that protected the Commissioners of the FTC from removal except for "inefficiency, neglect of duty, or malfeasance in office." In reaching that conclusion, the Court stressed that Congress's ability to impose such removal restrictions "will depend upon the character of the office."

Because the Court limited its holding "to officers of the kind here under consideration," the contours of the *Humphrey's Executor* exception depend upon the characteristics of the agency before the Court. Rightly or wrongly, the Court viewed the FTC (as it existed in 1935) as exercising "no part of the executive power." Instead, it was "an administrative body" that performed "specified duties as a legislative or as a judicial aid." It acted "as a legislative agency" in "making investigations and reports" to Congress and "as an agency of the judiciary" in making recommendations to courts as a master in chancery. "To the extent that [the FTC] exercise[d] any executive *function*[,] as distinguished from executive *power* in the constitutional sense," it did so only in the discharge of its "quasi-legislative or quasi-judicial powers." *Ibid.* (emphasis added).

The Court's conclusion that the FTC did not exercise executive power has not withstood the test of time. As we observed in *Morrison v. Olson*, 487 U.S.

654 (1988), "[I]t is hard to dispute that the powers of the FTC at the time of *Humphrey's Executor* would at the present time be considered 'executive,' at least to some degree." See also *Arlington v. FCC*, 569 U.S. 290, 305, n. 4 (2013) (even though the activities of administrative agencies "take 'legislative' and 'judicial' forms," "they are exercises of—indeed, under our constitutional structure they *must be* exercises of—the 'executive Power.'" [relocated footnote—eds.]

[In *Humphrey's Executor*] [t]he Court identified several organizational features that helped explain its characterization of the FTC as non-executive. Composed of five members—no more than three from the same political party—the Board was designed to be "non-partisan" and to "act with entire impartiality."

The FTC's duties were "neither political nor executive," but instead called for "the trained judgment of a body of experts" "informed by experience." And the Commissioners' staggered, seven-year terms enabled the agency to accumulate technical expertise and avoid a "complete change" in leadership "at any one time."

In short, *Humphrey's Executor* permitted Congress to give for-cause removal protections to a multimember body of experts, balanced along partisan lines, that performed legislative and judicial functions and was said not to exercise any executive power. Consistent with that understanding, the Court later applied "[t]he philosophy of *Humphrey's Executor*" to uphold for-cause removal protections for the members of the War Claims Commission—a three-member "adjudicatory body" tasked with resolving claims for compensation arising from World War II. *Wiener v. United States*, 357 U.S. 349, 356 (1958).

While recognizing an exception for multimember bodies with "quasi-judicial" or "quasi-legislative" functions, *Humphrey's Executor* reaffirmed the core holding of *Myers* that the President has "unrestrictable power . . . to remove purely executive officers." 295 U.S., at 632. The Court acknowledged that between purely executive officers on the one hand, and officers that closely resembled the FTC Commissioners on the other, there existed "a field of doubt" that the Court left "for future consideration."

We have recognized a second exception for *inferior* officers in two cases, *United States v. Perkins* and *Morrison v. Olson*. Article II distinguishes between two kinds of officers—principal officers (who must be appointed by the President with the advice and consent of the Senate) and inferior officers (whose appointment Congress may vest in the President, courts, or heads of Departments). § 2, cl. 2. While "[o]ur cases have not set forth an exclusive criterion for distinguishing between principal and inferior officers," we have in the past examined factors such as the nature, scope, and duration of an officer's duties. *Edmond v. United States*, 520 U.S. 651, 661 (1997). More recently, we have focused on whether the officer's work is "directed and supervised" by a principal officer. *Id.* [relocated footnote—eds.]

In *Perkins*, we upheld tenure protections for a naval cadet-engineer. And, in *Morrison*, we upheld a provision granting good-cause tenure protection to an independent counsel appointed to investigate and prosecute particular alleged crimes by high-ranking Government officials. Backing away from the reliance in

Humphrey's Executor on the concepts of "quasi-legislative" and "quasi-judicial" power, we viewed the ultimate question as whether a removal restriction is of "such a nature that [it] impede[s] the President's ability to perform his constitutional duty." Although the independent counsel was a single person and performed "law enforcement functions that typically have been undertaken by officials within the Executive Branch," we concluded that the removal protections did not unduly interfere with the functioning of the Executive Branch because "the independent counsel [was] an inferior officer under the Appointments Clause, with limited jurisdiction and tenure and lacking policymaking or significant administrative authority."

These two exceptions — one for multimember expert agencies that do not wield substantial executive power, and one for inferior officers with limited duties and no policymaking or administrative authority — "represent what up to now have been the outermost constitutional limits of permissible congressional restrictions on the President's removal power."

B

Neither *Humphrey's Executor* nor *Morrison* resolves whether the CFPB Director's insulation from removal is constitutional. Start with *Humphrey's Executor.* Unlike the New Deal-era FTC upheld there, the CFPB is led by a single Director who cannot be described as a "body of experts" and cannot be considered "non-partisan" in the same sense as a group of officials drawn from both sides of the aisle. Moreover, while the staggered terms of the FTC Commissioners prevented complete turnovers in agency leadership and guaranteed that there would always be some Commissioners who had accrued significant expertise, the CFPB's single-Director structure and five-year term guarantee abrupt shifts in agency leadership and with it the loss of accumulated expertise.

In addition, the CFPB Director is hardly a mere legislative or judicial aid. Instead of making reports and recommendations to Congress, as the 1935 FTC did, the Director possesses the authority to promulgate binding rules fleshing out 19 federal statutes, including a broad prohibition on unfair and deceptive practices in a major segment of the U.S. economy. And instead of submitting recommended dispositions to an Article III court, the Director may unilaterally issue final decisions awarding legal and equitable relief in administrative adjudications. Finally, the Director's enforcement authority includes the power to seek daunting monetary penalties against private parties on behalf of the United States in federal court — a quintessentially executive power not considered in *Humphrey's Executor.*

The logic of *Morrison* also does not apply. Everyone agrees the CFPB Director is not an inferior officer, and her duties are far from limited. Unlike the independent counsel, who lacked policymaking or administrative authority, the Director has the sole responsibility to administer 19 separate consumer-protection statutes that cover everything from credit cards and car payments to mortgages and student loans. It is true that the independent counsel in *Morrison* was empowered to initiate criminal investigations and prosecutions, and in that respect wielded core executive power. But that power, while significant, was trained inward to high-ranking Governmental actors identified by others, and was confined to a specified matter in which the Department of Justice had a potential conflict of interest. By contrast, the CFPB Director has the authority to bring the coercive power of the state to bear on millions of private citizens and businesses, imposing even billion-dollar penalties through administrative adjudications and civil actions.

In light of these differences, the constitutionality of the CFPB Director's insulation from removal cannot be settled by *Humphrey's Executor* or *Morrison* alone.

C

The question instead is whether to extend those precedents to the "new situation" before us, namely an independent agency led by a single Director and vested with significant executive power. We decline to do so. Such an agency has no basis in history and no place in our constitutional structure.

[A]n agency with a structure like that of the CFPB is almost wholly unprecedented. After years of litigating the agency's constitutionality, the Courts of Appeals, parties, and *amici* have identified "only a handful of isolated" incidents in which Congress has provided good-cause tenure to principal officers who wield power alone rather than as members of a board or commission.

First, the CFPB's defenders point to the Comptroller of the Currency, who enjoyed removal protection for *one year* during the Civil War. That example has rightly been dismissed as an aberration. It was "adopted without discussion" during the heat of the Civil War and abandoned before it could be "tested by executive or judicial inquiry." *Myers*. Second, the supporters of the CFPB point to the Office of the Special Counsel (OSC), which has been headed by a single officer since 1978. But this first enduring single-leader office, created nearly 200 years after the Constitution was ratified, drew a contemporaneous constitutional objection from the Office of Legal Counsel under President Carter and a subsequent veto on constitutional grounds by President Reagan . . . An Act similar to the one vetoed by President Reagan was eventually signed by President George H. W. Bush after extensive negotiations and compromises with Congress. . . . The OSC should not be confused with the independent counsel in *Morrison* or the special counsel recently appointed to investigate allegations related to the 2016 Presidential election. Despite sharing similar titles, those individuals have no relationship to the OSC. [relocated footnotes — eds.] . . . In any event, the OSC exercises only limited jurisdiction to enforce certain rules governing Federal Government employers and employees. It does not bind private parties at all or wield regulatory authority comparable to the CFPB.

Third, the CFPB's defenders note that the Social Security Administration (SSA) has been run by a single Administrator since 1994. That example, too, is comparatively recent and controversial. President Clinton questioned the constitutionality of the SSA's new single-Director structure upon signing it into law. In addition, unlike the CFPB, the SSA lacks the authority to bring enforcement actions against private parties. Its role is largely limited to adjudicating claims for Social Security benefits.

The only remaining example is the Federal Housing Finance Agency (FHFA), created in 2008 to assume responsibility for Fannie Mae and Freddie Mac. That agency is essentially a companion of the CFPB, established in response to the same financial crisis. It regulates primarily Government-sponsored enterprises, not purely private actors. And its single-Director structure is a source of ongoing controversy. Indeed, it was recently held unconstitutional by the Fifth Circuit, sitting en banc. See *Collins v. Mnuchin*, 938 F.3d 553, 587-588 (2019).

With the exception of the one-year blip for the Comptroller of the Currency, these isolated examples are modern and contested. And they do not involve regulatory or enforcement authority remotely comparable to that exercised by the CFPB. The CFPB's single-Director structure is an innovation with no foothold in history or tradition. . . . The dissent categorizes the CFPB as one of many "financial regulators" that have historically enjoyed some insulation from the President. But even assuming financial institutions like the Second Bank and the Federal Reserve can claim a special historical status, the CFPB is in an entirely different league. It acts as a mini legislature, prosecutor, and court, responsible for creating substantive rules for a wide swath of industries, prosecuting violations, and levying knee-buckling penalties against private citizens. And, of course, it is the only agency of its kind run by a single Director. [relocated footnote — eds.]

In addition to being a historical anomaly, the CFPB's single-Director configuration is incompatible with our constitutional structure. Aside from the sole exception of the Presidency, that structure scrupulously avoids concentrating power in the hands of any single individual.

"The Framers recognized that, in the long term, structural protections against abuse of power were critical to preserving liberty." *Bowsher*. Their solution to governmental power and its perils was simple: divide it. To prevent the "gradual concentration" of power in the same hands, they enabled "[a]mbition . . . to counteract ambition" at every turn. The Federalist No. 51 (J. Madison). At the highest level, they "split the atom of sovereignty" itself into one Federal Government and the States. They then divided the "powers of the new Federal Government into three defined categories, Legislative, Executive, and Judicial." *Chadha*.

They did not stop there. Most prominently, the Framers bifurcated the federal legislative power into two Chambers: the House of Representatives and the Senate, each composed of multiple Members and Senators. Art. I, §§ 2, 3.

The Executive Branch is a stark departure from all this division. The Framers viewed the legislative power as a special threat to individual liberty, so they divided that power to ensure that "differences of opinion" and the "jarrings of parties" would "promote deliberation and circumspection" and "check excesses in the majority." See The Federalist No. 70 (A. Hamilton); see also *id.*, No. 51. By contrast, the Framers thought it necessary to secure the authority of the Executive so that he could carry out his unique responsibilities. See *id.*, No. 70. As Madison put it, while "the weight of the legislative authority requires that it should be . . . divided, the weakness of the executive may require, on the other hand, that it should be fortified." *Id.*, No. 51.

The Framers deemed an energetic executive essential to "the protection of the community against foreign attacks," "the steady administration of the laws," "the protection of property," and "the security of liberty." *Id.*, No. 70. Accordingly, they chose not to bog the Executive down with the "habitual feebleness and dila-toriness" that comes with a "diversity of views and opinions." *Id.* Instead, they gave the Executive the "[d]ecision, activity, secrecy, and dispatch" that "charac-terise the proceedings of one man." *Id.*

To justify and check *that* authority—unique in our constitutional struc-ture—the Framers made the President the most democratic and politically accountable official in Government. Only the President (along with the Vice President) is elected by the entire Nation. And the President's political account-ability is enhanced by the solitary nature of the Executive Branch, which pro-vides "a single object for the jealousy and watchfulness of the people." *Id.* The President "cannot delegate ultimate responsibility or the active obligation to supervise that goes with it," because Article II "makes a single President respon-sible for the actions of the Executive Branch."

The resulting constitutional strategy is straightforward: divide power every-where except for the Presidency, and render the President directly accountable to the people through regular elections. In that scheme, individual executive offi-cials will still wield significant authority, but that authority remains subject to the ongoing supervision and control of the elected President. Through the President's oversight, "the chain of dependence [is] preserved," so that "the lowest officers, the middle grade, and the highest" all "depend, as they ought, on the President, and the President on the community." 1 Annals of Cong. 499 (J. Madison).

The CFPB's single-Director structure contravenes this carefully calibrated system by vesting significant governmental power in the hands of a single indi-vidual accountable to no one. The Director is neither elected by the people nor meaningfully controlled (through the threat of removal) by someone who is. The Director does not even depend on Congress for annual appropriations. See The Federalist No. 58 (J. Madison) (describing the "power over the purse" as the "most compleat and effectual weapon" in representing the interests of the people). Yet the Director may *unilaterally*, without meaningful supervision, issue final regulations, oversee adjudications, set enforcement priorities, initiate prosecutions, and determine what penalties to impose on private parties. With no colleagues to persuade, and no boss or electorate looking over her shoulder, the Director may dictate and enforce policy for a vital segment of the economy affecting millions of Americans.

The CFPB Director's insulation from removal by an accountable President is enough to render the agency's structure unconstitutional. But several other features of the CFPB combine to make the Director's removal protection even more problematic. In addition to lacking the most direct method of presidential control—removal at will—the agency's unique structure also forecloses certain indirect methods of Presidential control.

Because the CFPB is headed by a single Director with a five-year term, some Presidents may not have any opportunity to shape its leadership and thereby influence its activities. A President elected in 2020 would likely not appoint a CFPB Director until 2023, and a President elected in 2028 may *never* appoint one. That means an unlucky President might get elected on a consumer-protection platform and enter office only to find herself saddled with a holdover Director from a competing political party who is dead set *against* that agenda. To make matters worse, the agency's single-Director structure means the President will not have the opportunity to appoint any other leaders — such as a chair or fellow members of a Commission or Board — who can serve as a check on the Director's authority and help bring the agency in line with the President's preferred policies.

The CFPB's receipt of funds outside the appropriations process further aggravates the agency's threat to Presidential control. The President normally has the opportunity to recommend or veto spending bills that affect the operation of administrative agencies. And, for the past century, the President has annually submitted a proposed budget to Congress for approval. Presidents frequently use these budgetary tools "to influence the policies of independent agencies." But no similar opportunity exists for the President to influence the CFPB Director. Instead, the Director receives over $500 million per year to fund the agency's chosen priorities. And the Director receives that money from the Federal Reserve, which is itself funded outside of the annual appropriations process. This financial freedom makes it even more likely that the agency will "slip from the Executive's control, and thus from that of the people."

Amicus raises three principal arguments in the agency's defense. At the outset, *amicus* questions the textual basis for the removal power and highlights statements from Madison, Hamilton, and Chief Justice Marshall expressing "heterodox" views on the subject. But those concerns are misplaced. It is true that "there is no 'removal clause' in the Constitution," but neither is there a "separation of powers clause" or a "federalism clause." These foundational doctrines are instead evident from the Constitution's vesting of certain powers in certain bodies. As we have explained many times before, the President's removal power stems from Article II's vesting of the "executive Power" in the President. *Free Enterprise Fund*, (quoting Art. II, § 1, cl. 1). As for the opinions of Madison, Hamilton, and Chief Justice Marshall, we have already considered the statements cited by *amicus* and discounted them in light of their context (Madison), the fact they reflect initial impressions later abandoned by the speaker (Hamilton), or their subsequent rejection as ill-considered dicta (Chief Justice Marshall).

Next, *amicus* offers a grand theory of our removal precedents that, if accepted, could leave room for an agency like the CFPB — and many other innovative intrusions on Article II. According to *amicus*, *Humphrey's Executor* and *Morrison* establish a general rule that Congress may impose "modest" restrictions on the President's removal power, with only two limited exceptions. Congress may not reserve a role *for itself* in individual removal decisions (as it attempted to do in *Myers* and *Bowsher*). And it may not eliminate the President's removal power altogether (as it effectively did in *Free Enterprise Fund*). Outside those two situations, *amicus* argues, Congress is generally free to constrain the President's removal power.

But text, first principles, the First Congress's decision in 1789, *Myers*, and *Free Enterprise Fund* all establish that the President's removal power is the rule, not the exception. While we do not revisit *Humphrey's Executor* or any other precedent today, we decline to elevate it into a freestanding invitation for Congress to impose additional restrictions on the President's removal authority. . . .

[T]he dissent would endorse whatever "the times demand, so long as the President retains the ability to carry out his constitutional functions." But that amorphous test provides no real limiting principle. The "clearest" (and only) "example" the dissent can muster for what may be prohibited is a for-cause removal restriction placed on the President's "close military or diplomatic advisers." But that carveout makes no logical or constitutional sense. In the dissent's view, for-cause removal restrictions are permissible because they guarantee the President "meaningful control" over his subordinates. If that is the theory, then what is the harm in giving the President the same "meaningful control" over his close advisers? The dissent claims to see a constitutional distinction between the President's "own constitutional duties in foreign relations and war" and his duty to execute laws passed by Congress. But the same Article that establishes the President's foreign relations and war duties expressly entrusts him to take care that the laws be faithfully executed. And, from the perspective of the governed, it is far from clear that the President's core and traditional powers present greater cause for concern than peripheral and modern ones. If anything, "[t]he growth of the Executive Branch, which now wields vast power and touches almost every aspect of daily life, *heightens* the concern that it may slip from the Executive's control, and thus from that of the people." *Free Enterprise Fund* (emphasis added). [relocated footnote — eds.]

Finally, *amicus* contends that if we identify a constitutional problem with the CFPB's structure, we should avoid it by broadly construing the statutory grounds for removing the CFPB Director from office. The Dodd-Frank Act provides that the Director may be removed for "inefficiency, neglect of duty, or malfeasance in office." In *amicus*' view, that language could be interpreted to reserve substantial discretion to the President.

We are not persuaded. For one, *Humphrey's Executor* implicitly rejected an interpretation that would leave the President free to remove an officer based on disagreements about agency policy. In addition, while both *amicus* and the House of Representatives invite us to adopt whatever construction would cure the constitutional problem, they have not advanced any workable standard derived from the statutory language. *Amicus* suggests that the proper standard might permit removals based on *general* policy disagreements, but not *specific* ones; the House suggests that the permissible bases for removal might vary depending on the context and the Presidential power involved. They do not attempt to root either of those standards in the statutory text. Further, although nearly identical language governs the removal of some two-dozen multimember independent agencies, *amicus* suggests that the standard should vary from agency to agency, morphing as necessary to avoid constitutional doubt. We decline to embrace such an uncertain and elastic approach to the text.

Amicus and the House also fail to engage with the Dodd-Frank Act as a whole, which makes plain that the CFPB is an "independent bureau." Neither *amicus* nor the House explains how the CFPB would be "independent" if its head were required to implement the President's policies upon pain of removal. The Constitution might of course compel the agency to be dependent on the President notwithstanding Congress's contrary intent, but that result cannot fairly be inferred from the statute Congress enacted.

Constitutional avoidance is not a license to rewrite Congress's work to say whatever the Constitution needs it to say in a given situation. Without a proffered interpretation that is rooted in the statutory text and structure, and would avoid the constitutional violation we have identified, we take Congress at its word that it meant to impose a meaningful restriction on the President's removal authority.

The dissent, for its part, largely reprises points that the Court has already considered and rejected: It notes the lack of an express removal provision, invokes Congress's general power to create and define executive offices, highlights isolated statements from individual Framers, downplays the decision of 1789, minimizes *Myers*, brainstorms methods of Presidential control short of removal, touts the need for creative congressional responses to technological and economic change, and celebrates a pragmatic, flexible approach to American governance.

If these arguments sound familiar, it's because they are. They were raised by the dissent in *Free Enterprise Fund*. The answers to these repeated concerns (beyond those we have already covered) are the same today as they were ten years ago. Today, as then, Congress's "plenary control over the salary, duties, and even existence of executive offices" makes "Presidential oversight" *more* critical—not less—as the "[o]nly" tool to "counter [Congress's] influence." Today, as then, the various "bureaucratic minutiae" a President might use to corral agency personnel is no substitute for at will removal. And today, as always, the urge to meet new technological and societal problems with novel governmental structures must be tempered by constitutional restraints that are not known—and were not chosen—for their efficiency or flexibility.

As we explained in *Free Enterprise Fund*, "One can have a government that functions without being ruled by functionaries, and a government that benefits from expertise without being ruled by experts." While "[n]o one doubts Congress's power to create a vast and varied federal bureaucracy," the expansion of that bureaucracy into new territories the Framers could scarcely have imagined only sharpens our duty to ensure that the Executive Branch is overseen by a President accountable to the people.

IV

Having concluded that the CFPB's leadership by a single independent Director violates the separation of powers, we now turn to the appropriate remedy. We directed the parties to brief and argue whether the Director's removal protection was severable from the other provisions of the Dodd-Frank Act that establish the CFPB. If so, then the CFPB may continue to exist and operate notwithstanding Congress's unconstitutional attempt to insulate the agency's Director from removal by the President. . . .

[Petitioner] asks us to deny the Government's petition to enforce the civil investigative demand and dismiss the case. The Government counters that the demand, though initially issued by a Director unconstitutionally insulated from removal, can still be enforced on remand because it has since been ratified by an Acting Director accountable to the President. The parties dispute whether this alleged ratification in fact occurred and whether, if so, it is legally sufficient to cure the constitutional defect in the original demand. That debate turns on case-specific factual and legal questions not addressed below and not briefed here. A remand for the lower Courts to consider those questions in the first instance is therefore the appropriate course — unless such a remand would be futile [because the removal position is not severable]. . . .

"Generally speaking, when confronting a constitutional flaw in a statute, we try to limit the solution to the problem, severing any problematic portions while leaving the remainder intact." Even in the absence of a severability clause, the "traditional" rule is that "the unconstitutional provision must be severed unless the statute created in its absence is legislation that Congress would not have enacted." When Congress has expressly provided a severability clause, our task is simplified. We will presume "that Congress did not intend the validity of the statute in question to depend on the validity of the constitutionally offensive provision . . . unless there is strong evidence that Congress intended otherwise."

The only constitutional defect we have identified in the CFPB's structure is the Director's insulation from removal. If the Director were removable at will by the President, the constitutional violation would disappear. . . . The provisions of the Dodd-Frank Act bearing on the CFPB's structure and duties remain fully operative without the offending tenure restriction. Those provisions are capable of functioning independently, and there is nothing in the text or history of the Dodd-Frank Act that demonstrates Congress would have preferred *no* CFPB to a CFPB supervised by the President. Quite the opposite. Unlike the Sarbanes-Oxley Act at issue in *Free Enterprise Fund*, the Dodd-Frank Act contains an express severability clause. There is no need to wonder what Congress would have wanted if "any provision of this Act" is "held to be unconstitutional" because it has told us: "the remainder of this Act" should "not be affected." . . .

Congress [may have] preferred an independent CFPB to a dependent one; but . . . the critical question [is] whether Congress would have preferred a dependent CFPB to *no agency at all.* That is the only question we have the authority to decide, and the answer seems clear. . . . Because we find the Director's removal protection severable from the other provisions of Dodd-Frank that establish the CFPB, we remand for the Court of Appeals to consider whether the civil investigative demand was validly ratified.

* * *

In our constitutional system, the executive power belongs to the President, and that power generally includes the ability to supervise and remove the agents who wield executive power in his stead. While we have previously upheld limits on the President's removal authority in certain contexts, we decline to do so when it comes to principal officers who, acting alone, wield significant executive power. The Constitution requires that such officials remain dependent on the President, who in turn is accountable to the people.

The judgment of the United States Court of Appeals for the Ninth Circuit is vacated, and the case is remanded for further proceedings consistent with this opinion.

It is so ordered.

Justice THOMAS, with whom Justice GORSUCH joins, concurring in part and dissenting in part.

[B]ecause the Court takes a step in the right direction by limiting *Humphrey's Executor* to "multimember expert agencies that *do not wield substantial executive power*," I join Parts I, II, and III of its opinion. I respectfully dissent from the Court's severability analysis, however, because I do not believe that we should address severability in this case.

The decision in *Humphrey's Executor* poses a direct threat to our constitutional structure and, as a result, the liberty of the American people. The Court concludes that it is not strictly necessary for us to overrule that decision. But with today's decision, the Court has repudiated almost every aspect of *Humphrey's Executor*. In a future case, I would repudiate what is left of this erroneous precedent. . . .

Despite the defined structural limitations of the Constitution and the clear vesting of executive power in the President, Congress has increasingly shifted executive power to a *de facto* fourth branch of Government — independent agencies. These agencies wield considerable executive power without Presidential oversight. They are led by officers who are insulated from the President by removal restrictions, "reduc[ing] the Chief Magistrate to [the role of] cajoler-in-chief." But "[t]he people do not vote for the Officers of the United States. They instead look to the President to guide the assistants or deputies subject to his superintendence." Because independent agencies wield substantial power with no accountability to either the President or the people, they "pose a significant threat to individual liberty and to the constitutional system of separation of powers and checks and balances." . . . Our tolerance of independent agencies in *Humphrey's Executor* is an unfortunate example of the Court's failure to apply the Constitution as written. That decision has paved the way for an ever-expanding encroachment on the power of the Executive, contrary to our constitutional design. . . .

Humphrey's Executor relies on one key premise: the notion that there is a category of "quasi-legislative" and "quasi-judicial" power that is not exercised by Congress or the Judiciary, but that is also not part of "the executive power vested by the Constitution in the President." . . . The problem is that the Court's premise was entirely wrong. The Constitution does not permit the creation of officers exercising "quasi-legislative" and "quasi-judicial powers" in "quasi-legislative" and "quasi-judicial agencies." No such powers or agencies exist. Congress lacks the authority to delegate its legislative power, *Whitman v. American Trucking Assns., Inc.*, 531 U.S. 457, 472 (2001), and it cannot authorize the use of judicial power by officers acting outside of the bounds of Article III, *Stern v. Marshall*, 564 U.S. 462, 484 (2011). Nor can Congress create agencies that straddle multiple branches of Government. The Constitution sets out three branches of Government and provides each with a different form of power—legislative, executive, and judicial. Free-floating agencies simply do not comport with this constitutional structure. "[A]gencies have been called quasi-legislative, quasi-executive or quasi-judicial, as the occasion required, in order to validate their functions within the separation-of-powers scheme of the Constitution." But "[t]he mere retreat to the qualifying 'quasi' is implicit with confession that all recognized classifications have broken down, and 'quasi' is a smooth cover which we draw over our confusion as we might use a counterpane to conceal a disordered bed."

That is exactly what happened in *Humphrey's Executor*. The Court upheld the FTC Act's removal restriction by using the "quasi" label to support its claim that the FTC "exercise[d] no part of the executive power vested by the Constitution in the President." But "it is hard to dispute that the powers of the FTC at the time of *Humphrey's Executor* would at the present time be considered 'executive,' at least to some degree." *Morrison*. . . .

Continued reliance on *Humphrey's Executor* to justify the existence of independent agencies creates a serious, ongoing threat to our Government's design. Leaving these unconstitutional agencies in place does not enhance this Court's legitimacy; it subverts political accountability and threatens individual liberty. . . . We simply cannot compromise when it comes to our Government's structure. Today, the Court does enough to resolve this case, but in the future, we should reconsider *Humphrey's Executor in toto*. And I hope that we will have the will to do so. . . .

While I think that the Court correctly resolves the merits of the constitutional question, I do not agree with its decision to sever the removal restriction. . . . I would simply deny the Consumer Financial Protection Bureau (CFPB) petition to enforce the civil investigative demand.

Article III of the Constitution vests "[t]he judicial Power of the United States" in the "supreme Court" and the lower federal courts established by Congress. § 1. "[T]he judicial power is, fundamentally, the power to render judgments in individual cases" or controversies that are properly before the court. . . . In the context of a constitutional challenge, "[i]t amounts to little more than the negative power to disregard an unconstitutional enactment." Thus, if a party argues that a statute and the Constitution conflict, "then courts must resolve that dispute and, . . . follow the higher law of the Constitution."

Consistent with this understanding, "[e]arly American courts did not have a severability doctrine." If a statute was unconstitutional, the court would just decline to enforce the statute in the case before it. That was the end of the matter. "[T]here was no 'next step' in which [a] cour[t]" severed portions of a statute.

Our modern severability precedents create tension with this historic practice. Instead of declining to enforce an unconstitutional statute in an individual case, this Court has stated that courts must "seve[r] and excis[e]" portions of a statute to "remedy" the constitutional problem. The Court's rhetoric when discussing severance implies that a court's decision to sever a provision "formally suspend[s] or erase[s it], when [the provision] actually remains on the books as a law." The Federal Judiciary does not have the power to excise, erase, alter, or otherwise strike down a statute. And the Court's reference to severability as a "remedy" is inaccurate. Traditional remedies—like injunctions, declarations, or damages—"'operate with respect to specific parties,' not 'on legal rules in the abstract.'"

Because the power of judicial review does not allow courts to revise statutes, the Court's severability doctrine must be rooted in statutory interpretation. But, even viewing severability as an interpretive question, I remain skeptical of our doctrine. As I have previously explained, "the severability doctrine often requires courts to weigh in on statutory provisions that no party has standing to challenge, bringing courts dangerously close to issuing advisory opinions." And the application of the doctrine "does not follow basic principles of statutory interpretation." Instead of determining the meaning of a statute's text, severability involves "nebulous inquir[ies] into hypothetical congressional intent." . . .

[T]he text of the severability clause cannot, in isolation, justify severance of the removal provision. In some instances, a constitutional injury arises as a result of two or more statutory provisions operating together. . . . That is precisely the situation we have in this case. . . . The constitutional violation results from, at a minimum, the combination of the removal provision, and the provision allowing the CFPB to seek enforcement of a civil investigative demand. When confronted with two provisions that operate together to violate the Constitution, the text of the severability clause provides no guidance as to *which* provision should be severed. Thus, we must choose, based on something other than the severability clause, which provision to sever. . . .

In short, when multiple provisions of law combine to cause a constitutional injury, the Court's current approach allows the Court to decide which provision to sever. The text of a severability clause does not guide that choice. Nor does the practice of early American courts. The Court is thus left to choose based on nothing more than speculation as to what the Legislature would have preferred. And the result of its choice can have a dramatic effect on the governing statutory scheme. This is not a simple matter of following the "plain language" of a statute. It is incumbent on us to take a close look at our precedents to make sure that we are not exceeding the scope of the judicial power.

Given my concerns about our modern severability doctrine and the fact that severability makes no difference to the dispute before us, I would resolve this case by simply denying the CFPB's petition to enforce the civil investigative demand.

Justice KAGAN, with whom Justice GINSBURG, Justice BREYER, and Justice SOTOMAYOR join, concurring in the judgment with respect to severability and dissenting in part.

Throughout the Nation's history, this Court has left most decisions about how to structure the Executive Branch to Congress and the President, acting through legislation they both agree to. In particular, the Court has commonly allowed those two branches to create zones of administrative independence by limiting the President's power to remove agency heads. The Federal Reserve Board. The Federal Trade Commission (FTC). The National Labor Relations Board. Statute after statute establishing such entities instructs the President that he may not discharge their directors except for cause — most often phrased as inefficiency, neglect of duty, or malfeasance in office. Those statutes, whose language the Court has repeatedly approved, provide the model for the removal restriction before us today. If precedent were any guide, that provision would have survived its encounter with this Court — and so would the intended independence of the Consumer Financial Protection Bureau (CFPB).

Our Constitution and history demand that result. The text of the Constitution allows these common for-cause removal limits. Nothing in it speaks of removal. And it grants Congress authority to organize all the institutions of American governance, provided only that those arrangements allow the President to perform his own constitutionally assigned duties. Still more, the Framers' choice to give the political branches wide discretion over administrative offices has played out through American history in ways that have settled the constitutional meaning. From the first, Congress debated and enacted measures to create spheres of administration — especially of financial affairs — detached from direct presidential control. As the years passed, and governance became ever more complicated, Congress continued to adopt and adapt such measures — confident it had latitude to do so under a Constitution meant to "endure for ages to come." *McCulloch v. Maryland*, 4 Wheat. 316, 415 (1819) (approving the Second Bank of the United States). Not every innovation in governance — not every experiment in administrative independence — has proved successful. And debates about the prudence of limiting the President's control over regulatory agencies, including through his removal power, have never abated.[1] But the Constitution — both as originally drafted and as practiced — mostly leaves disagreements about administrative structure to Congress and the President, who have the knowledge and experience needed to address them. Within broad bounds, it keeps the courts — who do not — out of the picture.

The Court today fails to respect its proper role. It recognizes that this Court has approved limits on the President's removal power over heads of agencies much like the CFPB. Agencies possessing similar powers, agencies charged with similar missions, agencies created for similar reasons. The majority's explanation is that the heads of those agencies fall within an "exception" — one for multimember bodies and another for inferior officers — to a "general rule" of unrestricted presidential removal power. And the majority says the CFPB Director does not. That account, though, is wrong in every respect. The majority's general rule does not exist. Its exceptions, likewise, are made up for the occasion — gerrymandered so the CFPB falls outside them. And the distinction doing most of the majority's work — between multimember bodies and single directors — does not respond to the constitutional values at stake. If a removal provision violates the separation of powers, it is because the measure so deprives the President of control over an official as to impede his own constitutional functions. But with or without a for-cause removal provision, the President has at least as much control over an individual as over a commission — and possibly more. That means the constitutional concern is, if anything, ameliorated when the agency has a single head. Unwittingly, the majority shows why courts should stay their hand in these matters. . . .

In second-guessing the political branches, the majority second-guesses as well the wisdom of the Framers and the judgment of history. It writes in rules to the Constitution that the drafters knew well enough not to put there. It repudiates the lessons of American experience, from the 18th century to the present day. And it commits the Nation to a static version of governance, incapable of responding to new conditions and challenges. Congress and the President established the CFPB to address financial practices that had brought on a devastating recession, and could do so again. Today's decision wipes out a feature of that agency its creators thought fundamental to its mission — a measure of independence from political pressure. I respectfully dissent.

I

The text of the Constitution, the history of the country, the precedents of this Court, and the need for sound and adaptable governance — all stand against the majority's opinion. They point not to the majority's "general rule" of "unrestricted removal power" with two grudgingly applied "exceptions." Rather, they bestow discretion on the legislature to structure administrative institutions as the times demand, so long as the President retains the ability to carry out his constitutional duties. And most relevant here, they give Congress wide leeway to limit the President's removal power in the interest of enhancing independence from politics in regulatory bodies like the CFPB.

What does the Constitution say about the separation of powers — and particularly about the President's removal authority? (Spoiler alert: about the latter, nothing at all.) . . .

[T]he separation of powers is, by design, neither rigid nor complete. Blackstone, whose work influenced the Framers on this subject as on others, observed that "every branch" of government "supports and is supported, regulates and is regulated, by the rest." 1 W. Blackstone, Commentaries on the Laws of England 151 (1765). So as James Madison stated, the creation of distinct branches "did not mean that these departments ought to have no partial agency in, or no controul over the acts of each other." The Federalist No. 47 (emphasis deleted). To the contrary, Madison explained, the drafters of the Constitution — like those of then-existing state constitutions — opted against keeping the branches of government "absolutely separate and distinct." Or as Justice Story reiterated a half-century later: "[W]hen we speak of a separation of the three great departments of government," it is "not meant to affirm, that they must be kept wholly and entirely separate." 2 J. Story, Commentaries on the Constitution of the United States § 524, p. 8 (1833). Instead, the branches have—as they must for the whole arrangement to work—"common link[s] of connexion [and] dependence."

One way the Constitution reflects that vision is by giving Congress broad authority to establish and organize the Executive Branch. Article II presumes the existence of "Officer[s]" in "executive Departments." § 2, cl. 1. But it does not, as you might think from reading the majority opinion, give the President authority to decide what kinds of officers—in what departments, with what responsibilities—the Executive Branch requires. Instead, Article I's Necessary and Proper Clause puts those decisions in the legislature's hands. Congress has the power "[t]o make all Laws which shall be necessary and proper for carrying into Execution" not just its own enumerated powers but also "all other Powers vested by this Constitution in the Government of the United States, or in any Department or Officer thereof." § 8, cl. 18. Similarly, the Appointments Clause reflects Congress's central role in structuring the Executive Branch. Yes, the President can appoint principal officers, but only as the legislature "shall . . . establish[ ] by Law" (and of course subject to the Senate's advice and consent). Art. II, § 2, cl. 2. And Congress has plenary power to decide not only what inferior officers will exist but also who (the President or a head of department) will appoint them. So as Madison told the first Congress, the legislature gets to "create[ ] the office, define[ ] the powers, [and] limit[ ] its duration." 1 Annals of Cong. 582 (1789). The President, as to the construction of his own branch of government, can only try to work his will through the legislative process.

Article II's Opinions Clause also demonstrates the possibility of limits on the President's control over the Executive Branch. Under that Clause, the President "may require the Opinion, in writing, of the principal Officer in each of the executive Departments, upon any Subject relating to the Duties of their respective Offices." § 2, cl. 1. For those in the majority's camp, that Clause presents a puzzle: If the President must always have the direct supervisory control they posit, including by threat of removal, why would he ever need a constitutional warrant to demand agency heads' opinions? The Clause becomes at least redundant—though really, inexplicable—under the majority's idea of executive power. [relocated footnote—eds.]

The majority relies for its contrary vision on Article II's Vesting Clause, but the provision can't carry all that weight. Or as Chief Justice Rehnquist wrote of a similar claim in *Morrison v. Olson*, 487 U.S. 654 (1988), "extrapolat[ing]" an unrestricted removal power from such "general constitutional language"—which says only that "[t]he executive Power shall be vested in a President"—is "more than the text will bear." Dean John Manning has well explained why, even were it not obvious from the Clause's "open-ended language." Separation of Powers as Ordinary Interpretation, 124 Harv. L. Rev. 1939, 1971 (2011). The Necessary and Proper Clause, he writes, makes it impossible to "establish a constitutional violation simply by showing that Congress has constrained the way '[t]he executive Power' is implemented"; that is exactly what the Clause gives Congress the power to do. Only "a *specific* historical understanding" can bar Congress from enacting a given constraint. And nothing of that sort broadly prevents Congress from limiting the President's removal power. I'll turn soon to the Decision of 1789 and other evidence of Post-Convention thought. For now, note two points about practice before the Constitution's drafting. First, in that era, Parliament often restricted the King's power to remove royal officers—and the President, needless to say, wasn't supposed to be a king. Second, many States at the time allowed limits on gubernatorial removal power even though their constitutions had similar vesting clauses. Historical understandings thus belie the majority's "general rule."

Nor can the Take Care Clause come to the majority's rescue. That Clause cannot properly serve as a "placeholder for broad judicial judgments" about presidential control. To begin with, the provision—"he shall take Care that the Laws be faithfully executed"—speaks of duty, not power. Art. II, § 3. New scholarship suggests the language came from English and colonial oaths taken by, and placing fiduciary obligations on, all manner and rank of executive officers. To be sure, the imposition of a duty may imply a grant of power sufficient to carry it out. But again, the majority's view of that power ill comports with founding-era practice, in which removal limits were common. See, *e.g.*, Corwin, Tenure of Office and the Removal Power Under the Constitution, 27 Colum. L. Rev. 353, 385 (1927) (noting that New York's Constitution of 1777 had nearly the same clause, though the State's executive had "very little voice" in removals). And yet more important, the text of the Take Care Clause requires only enough authority to make sure "the laws [are] faithfully executed"—meaning with fidelity to the law itself, not to every presidential policy preference. As this Court has held, a President can ensure " 'faithful execution' of the laws"—thereby satisfying his "take care" obligation—with a removal provision like the one here. *Morrison*. A for-cause standard gives him "ample authority to assure that [an official] is competently performing [his] statutory responsibilities in a manner that comports with the [relevant legislation's] provisions." *Ibid.*

Finally, recall the Constitution's telltale silence: Nowhere does the text say anything about the President's power to remove subordinate officials at will. The majority professes unconcern. After all, it says, "neither is there a 'separation of powers clause' or a 'federalism clause.'" But those concepts are carved into the Constitution's text—the former in its first three articles separating powers, the latter in its enumeration of federal powers and its reservation of all else to the States. And anyway, at-will removal is hardly such a "foundational doctrine[ ],": You won't find it on a civics class syllabus. That's because removal is a *tool*—one means among many, even if sometimes an important one, for a President to control executive officials. To find that authority hidden in the Constitution as a "general rule" is to discover what is nowhere there.

History no better serves the majority's cause. As Madison wrote, "a regular course of practice" can "liquidate & settle the meaning of" disputed or indeterminate constitutional provisions. The majority lays claim to that kind of record, asserting that its muscular view of "[t]he President's removal power has long been confirmed by history." But that is not so. The early history—including the fabled Decision of 1789—shows mostly debate and division about removal authority. And when a "settle[ment of] meaning" at last occurred, it was not on the majority's terms. Instead, it supports wide latitude for Congress to create spheres of administrative independence.

Begin with evidence from the Constitution's ratification. And note that this moment is indeed the beginning: Delegates to the Constitutional Convention never discussed whether or to what extent the President would have power to remove executive officials. As a result, the Framers advocating ratification had no single view of the matter. In Federalist No. 77, Hamilton presumed that under the new Constitution "[t]he consent of [the Senate] would be necessary to displace as well as to appoint" officers of the United States. He thought that scheme would promote "steady administration": "Where a man in any station had given satisfactory evidence of his fitness for it, a new president would be restrained" from substituting "a person more agreeable to him." By contrast, Madison thought the Constitution allowed Congress to decide how any executive official could be removed. He explained in Federalist No. 39: "The tenure of the ministerial offices generally will be a subject of legal regulation, conformably to the reason of the case, and the example of the State Constitutions." Neither view, of course, at all supports the majority's story. . . . The majority dismisses Federalist Nos. 77 and 39 as "reflect[ing] initial impressions later abandoned." . . . Assuming Hamilton gave up on the Senate's direct participation in removal (the evidence is sketchy but plausible), there is no evidence to show he accepted the majority's view. And while Madison opposed the first Congress's enactment of removal limits (as the majority highlights), he also maintained that the legislature had constitutional power to protect the Comptroller of the Treasury from at-will firing. In any event, such changing minds and inconstant opinions don't usually prove the existence of constitutional rules. [relocated footnote—eds.]

The second chapter is the Decision of 1789, when Congress addressed the removal power while considering the bill creating the Department of Foreign Affairs. Speaking through Chief Justice Taft—a judicial presidentialist if ever there was one—this Court in *Myers v. United States*, 272 U.S. 52 (1926), read that debate as expressing Congress's judgment that the Constitution gave the President illimitable power to remove executive officials. The majority rests its own historical claim on that analysis (though somehow also finding room for its two exceptions). But Taft's historical research has held up even worse than *Myers'* holding (which was mostly reversed). As Dean Manning has concluded after reviewing decades' worth of scholarship on the issue, "the implications of the debate, properly understood, [are] highly ambiguous and prone to overreading."

The best view is that the First Congress was "deeply divided" on the President's removal power, and "never squarely addressed" the central issue here. The congressional debates revealed three main positions. Some shared Hamilton's Federalist No. 77 view: The Constitution required Senate consent for removal. At the opposite extreme, others claimed that the Constitution gave absolute removal power to the President. And a third faction maintained that the Constitution placed Congress in the driver's seat: The legislature could regulate, if it so chose, the President's authority to remove. In the end, Congress passed a bill saying nothing about removal, leaving the President free to fire the Secretary of Foreign Affairs at will. But the only one of the three views definitively rejected was Hamilton's theory of necessary Senate consent. As even strong proponents of executive power have shown, Congress never "endorse[d] the view that [it] lacked authority to modify" the President's removal authority when it wished to. The summer of 1789 thus ended without resolution of the critical question: Was the removal power "beyond the reach of congressional regulation?"

At the same time, the First Congress gave officials handling financial affairs — as compared to diplomatic and military ones — some independence from the President. . . . Congress left the organization of the Departments of Foreign Affairs and War skeletal, enabling the President to decide how he wanted to staff them. By contrast, Congress listed each of the offices within the Treasury Department, along with their functions. Of the three initial Secretaries, only the Treasury's had an obligation to report to Congress when requested. And perhaps most notable, Congress soon deemed the Comptroller of the Treasury's settlements of public accounts "final and conclusive." That decision, preventing presidential overrides, marked the Comptroller as exercising independent judgment. True enough, no statute shielded the Comptroller from discharge. But even James Madison, who at this point opposed most removal limits, told Congress that "there may be strong reasons why an officer of this kind should not hold his office at the pleasure" of the Secretary or President. At the least, as Professor Prakash writes, "Madison maintained that Congress had the [constitutional] authority to modify [the Comptroller's] tenure."

Contrary to the majority's view, then, the founding era closed without any agreement that Congress lacked the power to curb the President's removal authority. And as it kept that question open, Congress took the first steps — which would launch a tradition — of distinguishing financial regulators from diplomatic and military officers. The latter mainly helped the President carry out his own constitutional duties in foreign relations and war. The former chiefly carried out statutory duties, fulfilling functions Congress had assigned to their offices. In addressing the new Nation's finances, Congress had begun to use its powers under the Necessary and Proper Clause to design effective administrative institutions. And that included taking steps to insulate certain officers from political influence. . . .

As the decades and centuries passed, those efforts picked up steam. Confronting new economic, technological, and social conditions, Congress — and often the President — saw new needs for pockets of independence within the federal bureaucracy. And that was especially so, again, when it came to financial regulation. . . . Enacted under the Necessary and Proper Clause, those measures — creating some of the Nation's most enduring institutions — themselves helped settle the extent of Congress's power. "[A] regular course of practice," to use Madison's phrase, has "liquidate[d]" constitutional meaning about the permissibility of independent agencies.

Take first Congress's decision in 1816 to create the Second Bank of the United States — "the first truly independent agency in the republic's history." Of the twenty-five directors who led the Bank, the President could appoint and remove only five. Yet the Bank had a greater impact on the Nation than any but a few institutions, regulating the Nation's money supply in ways anticipating what the Federal Reserve does today. . . . [B]y the early 19th century, Congress established a body wielding enormous financial power mostly outside the President's dominion. . . .

In response to wartime economic pressures, President Lincoln (not known for his modest view of executive power) asked Congress to establish an office called the Comptroller of the Currency. The statute he signed made the Comptroller removable only with the Senate's consent — a version of the old Hamiltonian idea, though this time required not by the Constitution itself but by Congress. A year later, Congress amended the statute to permit removal by the President alone, but only upon "reasons to be communicated by him to the Senate." The majority dismisses the original version of the statute as an "aberration." But in the wake of the independence given first to the Comptroller of the Treasury and then to the national Bank, it's hard to conceive of this newest Comptroller position as so great a departure. And even the second iteration of the statute preserved a constraint on the removal power, requiring a President in a firing mood to explain himself to Congress — a demand likely to make him sleep on the subject. In both versions of the law, Congress responded to new financial challenges with new regulatory institutions, alert to the perils in this area of political interference.

And then, nearly a century and a half ago, the floodgates opened. In 1887, the growing power of the railroads over the American economy led Congress to create the Interstate Commerce Commission. Under that legislation, the President could remove the five Commissioners only "for inefficiency, neglect of duty, or malfeasance in office" — the same standard Congress applied to the CFPB Director. More — many more — for-cause removal provisions followed. In 1913, Congress gave the Governors of the Federal Reserve Board for-cause protection to ensure the agency would resist political pressure and promote economic stability. The next year, Congress provided similar protection to the FTC in the interest of ensuring "a continuous policy" "free from the effect" of "changing [White House] incumbency." The Federal Deposit Insurance Corporation (FDIC), the Securities and Exchange Commission (SEC), the Commodity Futures Trading Commission. In the financial realm, "independent agencies have remained the bedrock of the institutional framework governing U.S. markets." By one count, across all subject matter areas, 48 agencies have heads (and below them hundreds more inferior officials) removable only for cause. So year by year by year, the broad sweep of history has spoken to the constitutional question before us: Independent agencies are everywhere.

What is more, the Court's precedents before today have accepted the role of independent agencies in our governmental system. To be sure, the line of our decisions has not run altogether straight. But we have repeatedly upheld provisions that prevent the President from firing regulatory officials except for such matters as neglect or malfeasance. In those decisions, we sounded a caution, insisting that Congress could not impede through removal restrictions the President's performance of his own constitutional duties. (So, to take the clearest example, Congress could not curb the President's power to remove his close military or diplomatic advisers.) But within that broad limit, this Court held, Congress could protect from at-will removal the officials it deemed to need some independence from political pressures. Nowhere do those precedents suggest what the majority announces today: that the President has an "unrestricted removal power" subject to two bounded exceptions.

The majority grounds its new approach in *Myers*, ignoring the way this Court has cabined that decision. *Myers*, the majority tells us, found an unrestrained removal power "essential to the [President's] execution of the laws." What the majority does not say is that within a decade the Court abandoned that view (much as later scholars rejected Taft's one-sided history). In *Humphrey's Executor* v. *United States*, 295 U.S. 602 (1935), the Court unceremoniously — and unanimously — confined *Myers* to its facts. "[T]he narrow point actually decided" there, *Humphrey's* stated, was that the President could "remove a postmaster of the first class, without the advice and consent of the Senate." Nothing else in Chief Justice Taft's prolix opinion "c[a]me within the rule of *stare decisis.*" (Indeed, the Court went on, everything in *Myers* "out of harmony" with *Humphrey's* was expressly "disapproved.") Half a century later, the Court was more generous. Two decisions read *Myers* as standing for the principle that Congress's own "participation in the removal of executive officers is unconstitutional." *Bowsher* v. *Synar*, 478 U.S. 714, 725 (1986); see *Morrison.* *Bowsher* made clear that *Myers* had nothing to say about Congress's power to enact a provision merely "limit[ing] the President's powers of removal" through a for-cause provision. That issue, the Court stated, was "not presented" in "the *Myers* case." Instead, the relevant cite was *Humphrey's.*

And *Humphrey's* found constitutional a statute identical to the one here, providing that the President could remove FTC Commissioners for "inefficiency, neglect of duty, or malfeasance in office." The *Humphrey's* Court, as the majority notes, relied in substantial part on what kind of work the Commissioners performed. (By contrast, nothing in the decision turned — as the majority suggests — on any of the agency's organizational features.) According to *Humphrey's*, the Commissioners' primary work was to "carry into effect legislative policies" — "filling in and administering the details embodied by [a statute's] general standard." In addition, the Court noted, the Commissioners recommended dispositions in court cases, much as a special master does. Given those "quasi-legislative" and "quasi-judicial" — as opposed to "purely executive" — functions, Congress could limit the President's removal authority. Or said another way, Congress could give the FTC some "independen[ce from] executive control."

The majority is quite right that today we view *all* the activities of administrative agencies as exercises of "the 'executive Power.'" But we well understand, just as the *Humphrey's* Court did, that those activities may "take 'legislative' and 'judicial' forms." The classic examples are agency rulemakings and adjudications, endemic in agencies like the FTC and CFPB. In any event, the Court would soon make clear that Congress can also constrain the President's removal authority over officials performing even the most "executive" of functions. [relocated footnote — eds.]

About two decades later, an again-unanimous Court in *Wiener v. United States*, 357 U.S. 349 (1958), reaffirmed *Humphrey's*. The question in *Wiener* was whether the President could dismiss without cause members of the War Claims Commission, an entity charged with compensating injuries arising from World War II. Disdaining *Myers* and relying on *Humphrey's*, the Court said he could not. The Court described as "short-lived" *Myers'* view that the President had "inherent constitutional power to remove officials, no matter what the relation of the executive to the discharge of their duties." Here, the Commissioners were not close agents of the President, who needed to be responsive to his preferences. Rather, they exercised adjudicatory responsibilities over legal claims. Congress, the Court found, had wanted the Commissioners to do so "free from [political] control or coercive influence." And that choice, as *Humphrey's* had held, was within Congress's power. The Constitution enabled Congress to take down "the Damocles' sword of removal" hanging over the Commissioners' heads.

Another three decades on, *Morrison* both extended *Humphrey's* domain and clarified the standard for addressing removal issues. The *Morrison* Court, over a one-Justice dissent, upheld for-cause protections afforded to an independent counsel with power to investigate and prosecute crimes committed by high-ranking officials. The Court well understood that those law enforcement functions differed from the rulemaking and adjudicatory duties highlighted in *Humphrey's* and *Wiener*. But that difference did not resolve the issue. An official's functions, *Morrison* held, were relevant to but not dispositive of a removal limit's constitutionality. The key question in all the cases, *Morrison* saw, was whether such a restriction would "impede the President's ability to perform his constitutional duty." Only if it did so would it fall outside Congress's power. And the protection for the independent counsel, the Court found, did not. Even though the counsel's functions were "purely executive," the President's "need to control the exercise of [her] discretion" was not "so central to the functioning of the Executive Branch as to require" unrestricted removal authority. True enough, the Court acknowledged, that the for-cause standard prevented the President from firing the counsel for discretionary decisions or judgment calls. But it preserved "ample authority" in the President "to assure that the counsel is competently performing" her "responsibilities in a manner that comports with" all legal requirements. That meant the President could meet his own constitutional obligation "to ensure 'the faithful execution' of the laws."

. . . In [the majority's] view, a test asking whether a for-cause provision impedes the President's ability to carry out his constitutional functions has "no real limiting principle." If the provision leaves the President with constitutionally sufficient control over some subordinates (like the independent counsel), the majority asks, why not over even his close military or diplomatic advisers? But the Constitution itself supplies the answer. If the only presidential duty at issue is the one to ensure faithful execution of the laws, a for-cause provision does not stand in the way: As *Morrison* recognized, it preserves authority in the President to ensure (just as the Take Care Clause requires) that an official is abiding by law. But now suppose an additional constitutional duty is implicated — relating, say, to the conduct of foreign affairs or war. To carry out those duties, the President needs advisers who will (beyond complying with law) help him devise and implement policy. And that means he needs the capacity to fire such advisers for disagreeing with his policy calls. [relocated footnote — eds.] . . .

Even *Free Enterprise Fund*, in which the Court recently held a removal provision invalid, operated within the framework of this precedent — and in so doing, left in place a removal provision just like the one here. . . . Members of an accounting board were protected from removal by SEC Commissioners, who in turn were protected from removal by the President. The Court found that the two-layer structure deprived the President of "adequate control" over the Board members. . . . The Court observed that it did not "take issue with for-cause limitations in general" — which *do* enable the President to determine whether good cause for discharge exists (because, say, an official has violated the law). And the Court's solution to the constitutional problem it saw was merely to strike one level of insulation, making the Board removable by the SEC at will. That remedy left the SEC's own for-cause protection in place. The President could thus remove Commissioners for malfeasance or neglect, but not for policy disagreements.

[F]or almost a century, this Court has made clear that Congress has broad discretion to enact for-cause protections in pursuit of good governance. . . . The deferential approach this Court has taken gives Congress the flexibility it needs to craft administrative agencies. Diverse problems of government demand diverse solutions. They call for varied measures and mixtures of democratic accountability and technical expertise, energy and efficiency. Sometimes, the arguments push toward tight presidential control of agencies. The President's engagement, some people say, can disrupt bureaucratic stagnation, counter industry capture, and make agencies more responsive to public interests. See, well, Kagan, Presidential Administration, 114 Harv. L. Rev. 2245, 2331-2346 (2001). At other times, the arguments favor greater independence from presidential involvement. Insulation from political pressure helps ensure impartial adjudications. It places technical issues in the hands of those most capable of addressing them. It promotes continuity, and prevents short-term electoral interests from distorting policy. (Consider, for example, how the Federal Reserve's independence stops a President trying to win a second term from manipulating interest rates.) Of course, the right balance between presidential control and independence is often uncertain, contested, and value-laden. No mathematical formula governs institutional design; trade-offs are endemic to the enterprise. But that is precisely why the issue is one for the political branches to debate — and then debate again as times change. And it's why courts should stay (mostly) out of the way. Rather than impose rigid rules like the majority's, they should let Congress and the

President figure out what blend of independence and political control will best enable an agency to perform its intended functions.

Judicial intrusion into this field usually reveals only how little courts know about governance. Even everything I just said is an over-simplification. It suggests that agencies can easily be arranged on a spectrum, from the most to the least presidentially controlled. But that is not so. A given agency's independence (or lack of it) depends on a wealth of features, relating not just to removal standards, but also to appointments practices, procedural rules, internal organization, oversight regimes, historical traditions, cultural norms, and (inevitably) personal relationships. It is hard to pinpoint how those factors work individually, much less in concert, to influence the distance between an agency and a President. In that light, even the judicial opinions' perennial focus on removal standards is a bit of a puzzle. Removal is only the most obvious, not necessarily the most potent, means of control. That is because informal restraints can prevent Presidents from firing at-will officers — and because other devices can keep officers with for-cause protection under control. Of course no court, as *Free Enterprise Fund* noted, can accurately assess the "bureaucratic minutiae" affecting a President's influence over an agency. But that is yet more reason for courts to defer to the branches charged with fashioning administrative structures, and to hesitate before ruling out agency design specs like for-cause removal standards. . . .

II

As the majority explains, the CFPB emerged out of disaster. The collapse of the subprime mortgage market "precipitat[ed] a financial crisis that wiped out over $10 trillion in American household wealth and cost millions of Americans their jobs, their retirements, and their homes." In that moment of economic ruin, the President proposed and Congress enacted legislation to address the causes of the collapse and prevent a recurrence. An important part of that statute created an agency to protect consumers from exploitative financial practices. The agency would take over enforcement of almost 20 existing federal laws. And it would administer a new prohibition on "unfair, deceptive, or abusive act[s] or practice[s]" in the consumer-finance sector.

No one had a doubt that the new agency should be independent. As explained already, Congress has historically given — with this Court's permission — a measure of independence to financial regulators like the Federal Reserve Board and the FTC. And agencies of that kind had administered most of the legislation whose enforcement the new statute transferred to the CFPB. The law thus included an ordinary for-cause provision — once again, that the President could fire the CFPB's Director only for "inefficiency, neglect of duty, or malfeasance in office." That standard would allow the President to discharge the Director for a failure to "faithfully execute[ ]" the law, as well as for basic incompetence. But it would not permit removal for policy differences. . . .

The CFPB Director exercises the same powers, and receives the same removal protections, as the heads of other, constitutionally permissible independent agencies [such as the FTC, the SEC, and the Federal Reserve Board]. How could it be that this opinion is a dissent?

The majority briefly mentions, but understandably does not rely on, two . . . features of Congress's scheme. First, the majority notes that the CFPB receives its funding outside the normal appropriations process. But so too do other financial regulators, including the Federal Reserve Board and the FDIC. And budgetary independence comes mostly at the expense of Congress's control over the agency, not the President's. (Because that is so, it actually works to the President's advantage.) Second, the majority complains that the Director's five-year term may prevent a President from "shap[ing the agency's] leadership" through appointments. But again that is true, to one degree or another, of quite a few longstanding independent agencies, including the Federal Reserve, the FTC, the Merit Systems Protection Board, and the Postal Service Board of Governors. If you think the last is unimportant, just ask the current President whether he agrees. [relocated footnote—eds.]

The majority focuses on one (it says sufficient) reason: The CFPB Director is singular, not plural. "Instead of placing the agency under the leadership of a board with multiple members," the majority protests, "Congress provided that the CFPB would be led by a single Director." And a solo CFPB Director does not fit within either of the majority's supposed exceptions. He is not an inferior officer, so (the majority says) *Morrison* does not apply; and he is not a multimember board, so (the majority says) neither does *Humphrey's*. Further, the majority argues, "[a]n agency with a [unitary] structure like that of the CFPB" is "novel"—or, if not quite that, "almost wholly unprecedented." Finally, the CFPB's organizational form violates the "constitutional structure" because it vests power in a "single individual" who is "insulated from Presidential control."

I'm tempted at this point just to say: No. All I've explained about constitutional text, history, and precedent invalidates the majority's thesis. But I'll set out here some more targeted points, taking step by step the majority's reasoning.

First, as I'm afraid you've heard before, the majority's "exceptions" (like its general rule) are made up. To begin with, our precedents reject the very idea of such exceptions. "The analysis contained in our removal cases," *Morrison* stated, shuns any attempt "to define rigid categories" of officials who may (or may not) have job protection. Still more, the contours of the majority's exceptions don't connect to our decisions' reasoning. The analysis in *Morrison* . . . extended far beyond inferior officers. And of course that analysis had to apply to *individual* officers: The independent counsel was very much a person, not a committee. So the idea that *Morrison* is in a separate box from this case doesn't hold up.

The majority . . . asserts that the independent counsel's "duties" were more "limited" than the CFPB Director's. That's true in a sense: All (all?) the special counsel had to do was decide whether the President and his top advisers had broken the law. But I doubt (and I suspect Presidents would too) whether the need to control those duties was any less "central to the functioning of the Executive Branch" than the need to control the CFPB's. And in any event, as I've shown, *Morrison* did much more than approve a specific removal provision; it created a standard to govern all removal cases that is at complete odds with the majority's reasoning. [relocated footnote — eds.]

Similarly, *Humphrey's* and later precedents give no support to the majority's view that the number of people at the apex of an agency matters to the constitutional issue. Those opinions mention the "groupness" of the agency head only in their background sections. The majority picks out that until-now-irrelevant fact to distinguish the CFPB, and constructs around it an until-now-unheard-of exception. So if the majority really wants to see something "novel," it need only look to its opinion.

By contrast, the CFPB's single-director structure has a fair bit of precedent behind it. The Comptroller of the Currency. The Office of the Special Counsel (OSC). The Social Security Administration (SSA). The Federal Housing Finance Agency (FHFA). Maybe four prior agencies is in the eye of the beholder, but it's hardly nothing. I've already explained why the earliest of those agencies — the Civil-War-era Comptroller — is not the blip the majority describes. The office is one in a long line, starting with the founding-era Comptroller of the Treasury (also one person), of financial regulators designed to do their jobs with some independence. As for the other three, the majority objects: too powerless and too contested. I think not. On power, the SSA runs the Nation's largest government program — among other things, deciding all claims brought by its 64 million beneficiaries; the FHFA plays a crucial role in overseeing the mortgage market, on which millions of Americans annually rely; and the OSC prosecutes misconduct in the two-million-person federal workforce. All different from the CFPB, no doubt; but the majority can't think those matters beneath a President's notice. (Consider: Would the President lose more votes from a malfunctioning SSA or CFPB?) And controversial? Well, yes, they are. Almost *all* independent agencies are controversial, no matter how many directors they have. Or at least controversial among Presidents and their lawyers. That's because whatever might be said in their favor, those agencies divest the President of some removal power. If signing statements and veto threats made independent agencies unconstitutional, quite a few wouldn't pass muster. Maybe that's what the majority really wants (I wouldn't know) — but it can't pretend the disputes surrounding these agencies had anything to do with whether their heads are singular or plural.

Still more important, novelty is not the test of constitutionality when it comes to structuring agencies. See *Mistretta v. United States*, 488 U.S. 361, 385 (1989) ("[M]ere anomaly or innovation" does not violate the separation of powers). Congress regulates in that sphere under the Necessary and Proper Clause, not (as the majority seems to think) a Rinse and Repeat Clause. The Framers understood that new times would often require new measures, and exigencies often demand innovation. See *McCulloch*. In line with that belief, the history of the administrative sphere — its rules, its practices, its institutions — is replete with experiment and change. Indeed, each of the agencies the majority says now fits within its "exceptions" was once new; there is, as the saying goes, "a first time for everything." So even if the CFPB differs from its forebears in having a single director, that departure is not itself "telling" of a "constitutional problem." In deciding what *this* moment demanded, Congress had no obligation to make a carbon copy of a design from a bygone era.

And Congress's choice to put a single director, rather than a multimember commission, at the CFPB's head violates no principle of separation of powers. The purported constitutional problem here is that an official has "slip[ped] from the Executive's control" and "supervision"—that he has become unaccountable to the President. So to make sense on the majority's own terms, the distinction between singular and plural agency heads must rest on a theory about why the former more easily "slip" from the President's grasp. But the majority has nothing to offer. In fact, the opposite is more likely to be true: To the extent that such matters are measurable, individuals are easier than groups to supervise. . . .

Presidential control, as noted earlier, can operate through many means—removal to be sure, but also appointments, oversight devices (*e.g.,* centralized review of rulemaking or litigating positions), budgetary processes, personal outreach, and more. The effectiveness of each of those control mechanisms, when present, can then depend on a multitude of agency-specific practices, norms, rules, and organizational features. In that complex stew, the difference between a singular and plural agency head will often make not a whit of difference. Or to make the point more concrete, a multimember commission may be harder to control than an individual director for a host of reasons unrelated to its plural character. That may be so when the two are subject to the same removal standard, or even when the individual director has greater formal job protection. Indeed, the very category of multimember commissions breaks apart under inspection, spoiling the majority's essential dichotomy. Some of those commissions have chairs appointed by the President; others do not. Some of those chairs are quite powerful; others are not. Partisan balance requirements, term length, voting rules, and more—all vary widely, in ways that make a significant difference to the ease of presidential control. Why, then, would anyone distinguish along a simple commission/single-director axis when deciding whether the Constitution requires at-will removal?

[T]he majority's distinction cuts the opposite way: More powerful control mechanisms are needed (if anything) for commissions. Holding everything else equal, those are the agencies more likely to "slip from the Executive's control." Just consider your everyday experience: It's easier to get one person to do what you want than a gaggle. So too, you know exactly whom to blame when an individual—but not when a group—does a job badly. The same is true in bureaucracies. A multimember structure reduces accountability to the President because it's harder for him to oversee, to influence—or to remove, if necessary—a group of five or more commissioners than a single director. Indeed, that is *why* Congress so often resorts to hydra-headed agencies. "[M]ultiple membership," an influential Senate Report concluded, is "a buffer against Presidential control" (especially when combined, as it often is, with partisan-balance requirements). Senate Committee on Governmental Affairs, Study on Federal Regulation, S. Doc. No. 95-91, vol. 5, p. 75 (1977). So, for example, Congress constructed the Federal Reserve as it did because it is "easier to protect a board from political control than to protect a single appointed official." R. Cushman, The Independent Regulatory Commissions 153 (1941). It is hard to know why Congress did not take the same tack when creating the CFPB. But its choice brought the agency only closer to the President — more exposed to his view, more subject to his sway. In short, the majority gets the matter backward: Where presidential control is the object, better to have one than many.

Because it has no answer on that score, the majority slides to a different question: Assuming presidential control of any independent agency is vanishingly slim, is a single-head or a multi-head agency more capable of exercising power, and so of endangering liberty? The majority says a single head is the greater threat because he may wield power *"unilaterally"* and "[w]ith no colleagues to persuade." So the CFPB falls victim to what the majority sees as a constitutional anti-power-concentration principle (with an exception for the President).

If you've never heard of a statute being struck down on that ground, you're not alone. It is bad enough to "extrapolat[e]" from the "general constitutional language" of Article II's Vesting Clause an unrestricted removal power constraining Congress's ability to legislate under the Necessary and Proper Clause. It is still worse to extrapolate from the Constitution's general structure (division of powers) and implicit values (liberty) a limit on Congress's express power to create administrative bodies. And more: to extrapolate from such sources a distinction as prosaic as that between the SEC and the CFPB — *i.e.,* between a multi-headed and single-headed agency. That is, to adapt a phrase (or two) from our precedent, "more than" the emanations of "the text will bear." By using abstract separation-of-powers arguments for such purposes, the Court "appropriate[s]" the "power delegated to Congress by the Necessary and Proper Clause" to compose the government. In deciding for itself what is "proper," the Court goes beyond its own proper bounds.

And in doing so, the majority again reveals its lack of interest in how agencies work. First, the premise of the majority's argument — that the CFPB head is a mini-dictator, not subject to meaningful presidential control — is wrong. As this Court has seen in the past, independent agencies are not fully independent. A for-cause removal provision, as noted earlier, leaves "ample" control over agency heads in the hands of the President. He can discharge them for failing to perform their duties competently or in accordance with law, and so ensure that the laws are "faithfully executed." U.S. Const., Art. II, § 3. And he can use the many other tools attached to the Office of the Presidency — including in the CFPB's case, rulemaking review — to exert influence over discretionary policy calls. Second, the majority has nothing but intuition to back up its essentially functionalist claim that the CFPB would be less capable of exercising power if it had more than one Director (even supposing that were a suitable issue for a court to address). Maybe the CFPB would be. Or maybe not. Although a multi-member format tends to frustrate the President's control over an agency, it may not lessen the agency's own ability to act with decision and dispatch. (Consider, for a recent example, the Federal Reserve Board.) That effect presumably would depend on the agency's internal organization, voting rules, and similar matters.

At the least: If the Court is going to invalidate statutes based on empirical assertions like this one, it should offer some empirical support. It should not pretend that its assessment that the CFPB wields more power more dangerously than the SEC comes from someplace in the Constitution. But today the majority fails to accord even that minimal respect to Congress.

III

Recall again how this dispute got started. In the midst of the Great Recession, Congress and the President came together to create an agency with an important mission. It would protect consumers from the reckless financial practices that had caused the then-ongoing economic collapse. Not only Congress but also the President thought that the new agency, to fulfill its mandate, needed a measure of independence. So the two political branches, acting together, gave the CFPB Director the same job protection that innumerable other agency heads possess. All in all, those branches must have thought, they had done a good day's work. Relying on their experience and knowledge of administration, they had built an agency in the way best suited to carry out its functions. They had protected the public from financial chicanery and crisis. They had governed.

And now consider how the dispute ends — with five unelected judges rejecting the result of that democratic process. The outcome today will not shut down the CFPB: A different majority of this Court, including all those who join this opinion, believes that *if* the agency's removal provision is unconstitutional, it should be severed. But the majority on constitutionality jettisons a measure Congress and the President viewed as integral to the way the agency should operate. The majority does so even though the Constitution grants to Congress, acting with the President's approval, the authority to create and shape administrative bodies. And even though those branches, as compared to courts, have far greater understanding of political control mechanisms and agency design.

Nothing in the Constitution requires that outcome; to the contrary. "While the Constitution diffuses power the better to secure liberty, it also contemplates that practice will integrate the dispersed powers into a workable government." *Youngstown Sheet & Tube Co. v. Sawyer*, 343 U.S. 579, 635 (1952) (Jackson, J., concurring). The Framers took pains to craft a document that would allow the structures of governance to change, as times and needs change. The Constitution says only a few words about administration. As Chief Justice Marshall wrote: Rather than prescribing "immutable rules," it enables Congress to choose "the means by which government should, in all future time, execute its powers." *McCulloch*. It authorizes Congress to meet new exigencies with new devices. So Article II does not generally prohibit independent agencies. Nor do any supposed structural principles. Nor do any odors wafting from the document. Save for when those agencies impede the President's performance of his own constitutional duties, the matter is left up to Congress. . . .

The Constitution does not distinguish between single-director and multi-member independent agencies. It instructs Congress, not this Court, to decide on agency design. Because this Court ignores that sensible — indeed, that obvious — division of tasks, I respectfully dissent.

Discussion

1. Seila Law *and the "unitary executive."* Behind the debate between Chief Justice Roberts, Justice Thomas, and Justice Kagan is a longer debate over the theory of the "unitary executive." The theory of a "unitary executive" emerged in the conservative movement during the 1970s, and was further articulated in the decades that followed. Stephen Skowronek, The Conservative Insurgency and Presidential Power: A Developmental Perspective on the Unitary Executive, 122 Harv. L. Rev. 2070 (2009). The theory was originally developed in the context of the Nixon, Ford, and Reagan Administrations, when a Republican President faced a liberal Democratic Congress and a bureaucracy and civil service developed during the New Deal/Civil Rights regime.

The unitary executive theory made sense given the goals of the conservative movement. The point was to make the conservative insurgency more effective by allowing the President to get control of the bureaucracy, and to resist congressional interference with the President's exercise of powers, both in domestic and foreign affairs.

Of course, if the tables were turned, and Congress were controlled by Republicans and the White House by Democrats, the unitary executive might sometimes assist liberal causes. But conservative insurgents realized that their real opponent was government bureaucracies and the growing activist state. Because bureaucracies tend over time to increase regulation, it is better to get control over them. Analogous considerations applied to foreign policy: Presidents of both parties like to exercise their foreign policy powers without congressional interference, so it is better to give them a freer hand. Thus, for a political movement that sought to dismantle regulation and promote a muscular approach to foreign policy, empowering the presidency at the expense of the bureaucracy and Congress seemed like a good bet.

Conservative lawyers in the Reagan Justice Department, many of whom became distinguished lawyers and scholars, grounded the theory of the unitary executive in the initial grant in Article II, section 1, that "The executive power shall be vested in a President of the United States of America." They argued that this vesting clause demanded a unitary executive. As Chief Justice Roberts, who served as a young lawyer in the Reagan Justice Department, puts it in *Seila Law*, "The entire 'executive Power' belongs to the President alone," and "lesser officers must remain accountable to the President, whose authority they wield."

The idea that the executive is "unitary" is sometimes associated with three ideas, two of which are closely connected, and the third of which is quite different:

The first idea is that because the executive is unitary, the President must have complete and exclusive power over the choice of people who work under him and who exercise any part of "the executive power of the United States." Under the text of the Constitution, the President does not have complete power to *hire*. See Art. II, § 2 (noting Senate's role in advice and consent, and Congress's role in the appointment of inferior officers). So the unitary executive theory has focused instead on the power to *fire* officials. But this idea has never been fully realized in practice: Congress has provided tenure protection for civil servants, for-cause protections for inferior officers, and similar protections for members of multi-member "independent" federal agencies. The issue in *Seila Law* was whether to extend these practices to a regulatory agency with a single head.

The second, closely related idea is the President's complete power to *direct* executive officials. Taken literally, this would mean that the President has complete power to direct executive officials in all of their functions, including those that Congress has assigned to those officials — and perhaps even that the President could countermand those decisions or perform them himself.

This, too, has never been the way the federal bureaucracy has been run, especially given the vast growth of the federal bureaucracy in the twentieth century. In fact, the idea was rejected early on. Attorney General William Wirt explained in the first of a series of opinions that where Congress has clearly indicated that an officer's decision is to be final and conclusive within the Executive branch, the President may not review the "correctness" of the officer's judgment, let alone execute the authority himself. The President and Accounting Offices, 1 Op. Att'y Gen. 624, 625-629 (1823). The idea has also not been realized in "independent" federal agencies, versions of which have existed since the First Bank of the United States.

A third idea, which is sometimes confusingly associated with the "unitary executive," but is logically distinct, is that the President has broad inherent powers that Congress may not interfere with. This idea of inherent executive power became especially important during the George W. Bush Administration, when Administration lawyers argued that, because the President was "Commander in Chief of the Army and Navy of the United States," he had the unilateral power to use military force overseas; he could engage in foreign surveillance practices without congressional authorization; and, in general, he was subject only to very limited congressional oversight in foreign affairs. If Congress wanted to check the Executive, the proper way to do it was to threaten to withhold funding, using the spending powers granted to Congress under Article I, section 8.

A broad theory of inherent executive power has also never been fully realized in practice. Congress can shape the structure of federal offices and the duties of federal officers; under *Youngstown* it has concurrent authority with the President to regulate in a wide range of situations, including in foreign policy. Outside of a small number of areas in which the Constitution gives complete authority to the President, see, e.g., *Zivitofsky* (presidential power to recognize foreign governments), Congress may limit or direct the exercise of executive authority.

Although it may not seem obvious at first, the idea that Congress may not interfere with executive branch functions is actually in some tension with the first two ideas, which concern presidential control over the federal bureaucracy. As the federal government grew larger and larger, more and more of the people who actually governed were part of the executive branch and the President grew more and more powerful. If the President had complete control over all of these people, *and* could avoid substantial congressional control and oversight, the president would become increasingly like a dictator. This would be inconsistent with the constitutional idea that branches were separated but with checks and balances, so that no branch could be a law unto itself.

Put another way, the founders thought that Congress, and not the President, would be the most dangerous branch. They probably did not expect that the President would eventually become the most powerful actor in the constitutional system and have at his command an enormous federal bureaucracy and huge military forces that could be stationed or dispatched around the globe. But the rise of the administrative state and America's status as world superpower undermined those assumptions. The greater the President's powers grew in the twentieth century, the more he needed checking by the other branches. Justice Thomas' concurrence argues that checks on the President's power undermine individual liberty. But it is at least as plausible to argue that an unconstrained president is a threat to liberty.

We see this tension in Chief Justice Roberts' account. He notes that the framers wanted to separate and check power and avoid the concentration of power in any part of the government. But he treats the presidency as an exception: "Aside from the sole exception of the Presidency, that structure scrupulously avoids concentrating power in the hands of any single individual." Later he says that " 'The Framers recognized that, in the long term, structural protections against abuse of power were critical to preserving liberty.' . . . Their solution to governmental power and its perils was simple: divide it. . . . The Executive Branch is a stark departure from all this division."

2. *Independent agencies: normal, exceptional, or unconstitutional?* Faced with a history of independent agencies and a large federal bureaucracy that the President cannot dismiss at will, Roberts attempts to describe these practices as exceptional, preserving the ones that currently exist but not extending them.

He explains that the basic principle of the unitary executive does not apply to inferior officers "with limited duties and no policymaking or administrative authority." They may have tenure or for-cause protections. This is how he explains the independent counsel statute upheld in *Morrison v. Olson.*

Second, Roberts argues that there is an exception for "a multimember body of experts, balanced along partisan lines, that performed legislative and judicial functions and was said not to exercise any executive power." (citing *Humphrey's Executor v. United States*, 295 U.S. 602 (1935).) Of course, as Roberts concedes, the idea that independent federal agencies do not actually exercise executive power makes little sense today. Taken literally, this exception would not be much of an exception at all, because most of today's independent agencies wouldn't fit within it. (Justice Thomas emphasizes this point.)

Roberts notes the problem but does not really resolve it. He says only that there is an exception for "multimember expert agencies that do not wield substantial executive power." He then argues that deviations from any of the current exceptions are presumptively unconstitutional. New innovations are suspect. (The question Roberts leaves hanging is whether *existing* independent agencies, which may wield "substantial executive power," are also unconstitutional, as Justice Thomas contends.)

Justice Kagan, by contrast, sees for-cause protections and independent federal agencies as perfectly normal, rather than exceptional. Citing *McCulloch v. Maryland*, she argues that the Constitution was designed to allow Congress to experiment with different ways of solving problems of governance, and that the President does not have immunity from these experiments. Of course, this principle, taken too far, would swallow up the presidency. So, she argues that there are limits where legislation would "impede . . . the President's performance of his own constitutional duties," so that, "to take the clearest example, Congress could not curb the President's power to remove his close military or diplomatic advisers."

Justice Thomas, who is far more of a revolutionary than the Chief Justice, wants to take the unitary executive theory to its logical conclusion. What Justice Kagan calls normal, and Chief Justice Roberts calls exceptional, is simply unconstitutional. Thomas speaks of the continued presence of independent agencies as "a serious, ongoing threat to our Government's design. Leaving these unconstitutional agencies in place does not enhance this Court's legitimacy; it subverts political accountability and threatens individual liberty. . . . We simply cannot compromise when it comes to our Government's structure." It is not a surprise, then, that Thomas believes the courts have no power to sever the for-cause provision and that the entire CFPB should be eliminated.

Because of Roberts' deliberate ambiguity, as noted above, Thomas's position on independent agencies has not yet been definitively ruled out. The question is whether there are five votes for it.

3. *What's at stake? Political accountability versus non-partisan expertise.* Why the Justices care so much about the structure of the CFPB may be mystifying at first. It is not immediately clear what values are at stake. Chief Justice Roberts sums up the issue this way: "the expansion of [the federal] bureaucracy into new territories the Framers could scarcely have imagined only sharpens our duty to ensure that the Executive Branch is overseen by a President accountable to the people." The idea is that the people who exercise governance — who make decisions that affect our lives — should be accountable through elections. Since members of the bureaucracy are not elected, they need to be controlled by an official who is elected. So, if members of the bureaucracy perform badly or prove to be corrupt, the public can pressure the President, who can fire them or order them to shape up.

This model of political accountability faces two difficulties. First, it may not be a very realistic account of how the public actually holds bureaucrats accountable. A second term president faces very few electoral pressures. A first term president is unlikely to be thrown out of office because of a particular policy decision by the head of an agency. Most decisions by the bureaucracy pass unnoticed by the public, although they matter greatly to particular businesses. In many contexts, the accountability argument seems fairly weak.

A better argument for political accountability would be the old political saw that "personnel is politics." Elect a conservative Republican to the presidency, and you can more or less be assured that conservative Republicans will be carrying out the government's agenda. Conversely, if officials stray from the party's agenda, the President will be more likely to get rid of them.

That explanation makes more sense from the perspective of the conservative movement that pushed for the theory of the unitary executive in the first place. Presidential ability to hire and fire helps guarantee that officials subject to dismissal will be ideologically consistent with the White House. It does not, however, guarantee that they will be competent or not be corrupt. And this kind of accountability seems orthogonal to the question of "liberty" emphasized by Justice Thomas. The President's ability to control subordinates to effectuate the President's ideological program may increase or decrease liberty, depending on one's perspective. And the ability of the public to hold presidents accountable for the actions of their subordinates may increase liberty, or it may have precisely the opposite effect. Presidents Trump and Obama, for example, both were responsive to the public (or at least, the part of the public that voted for them) but both had very different accounts of the kinds of liberty they wanted executive branch officials to protect and how best to protect them.

The second problem is that not all governing problems respond well to this kind of political accountability. Some kinds of government decisions are best insulated from everyday electoral politics, and certainly from the executive's desire to settle scores. Justice Kagan gives the example of the Federal Reserve: "the Federal Reserve's independence stops a President trying to win a second term from manipulating interest rates." Throughout the nineteenth century, monetary policy was a hot political question shaped by partisan politics. This encouraged short-term political thinking that sometimes led to panics and economic disasters. The creation of a central bank in 1913 was designed to put the control of the money supply—and interest rates—in the hands of experts relatively isolated from day-to-day political pressure.

Once you see the problem, it becomes ubiquitous. We don't want the President to use the FBI and the Justice Department to protect the President's friends and punish the President's enemies. We want the prosecutorial power to reflect the larger policy concerns of an Administration, but not fine-grained political determinations and score settling. (This has been a recurrent problem in the Trump Administration: the President has cast aside post-Watergate norms that restrain the political and self-dealing use of prosecutorial power.)[7] We want the military

---

7. See, e.g., Katie Benner, Charlie Savage, Sharon LaFraniere and Ben Protess, After Stone Case, Prosecutors Say They Fear Pressure From Trump, N.Y. Times, February 12, 2020, https://www .nytimes.com/2020/02/12/us/politics/justice-department-roger-stone-sentencing.html ("numerous legal scholars say that Mr. Trump has shredded norms that kept presidents in check for decades, undermining public trust in federal law enforcement and creating at least the perception that criminal cases are now subject to political influence from the White House.").

to serve the foreign policy aims of successive presidents, and not become the ideological arm of the party in power. We want the Post Office just to deliver the mail, and so on.

Political accountability and non-partisan expertise must be balanced, and the right balance might be different in different contexts and subject matters. Chief Justice Roberts argues that multiple-member independent agencies give presidents of different parties a chance to shape the direction of these agencies without dominating them, so it strikes a good balance. By contrast, "[b]ecause the CFPB is headed by a single Director with a five-year term, some Presidents may not have any opportunity to shape its leadership and thereby influence its activities." Does Roberts' logic allow for fully non-partisan commissions, as employed in some states?

4. *Five heads are better than one?* Even if we grant Justice Kagan's argument that for-cause provisions and independent federal agencies are perfectly consistent with the separation of powers, it does not follow that Congress made the right choice in designing the CFPB. Why might Congress have chosen an agency with a single head rather than multiple heads? What are the problems both for political accountability and for non-partisan expertise with a single head? Suppose that a multi-member body would have been a better design choice on both counts. Justice Kagan's argument is that the choice is Congress's call, and not the Supreme Court's.

Does this follow from *McCulloch*, or does the argument prove too much? Why shouldn't the Court subject Congress's design choices to some measure of scrutiny, requiring that Congress justify its reasons, rather than simply defer (Kagan) or ask whether the design is exactly the same as previous designs (Roberts)? Can you think of a third approach that would allow Congress some leeway for innovation without offering complete deference?

5. *Two's company, but one's a crowd?* Justice Thomas would argue that a multi-member agency is no more constitutional than a single-member agency. Justice Kagan would turn this logic around and argue that a single-member agency is no more unconstitutional than a multi-member agency. If one director is unconstitutional, how many extra directors does it take to make the CFPB constitutional? Would two be enough? Would three? If so, why? Chief Justice Roberts avoids the issue by getting rid of the for-cause provision. How would you resolve the question he avoided?

6. *The unitary executive in the states.* It is worth noting that most state constitutions have nothing like a unitary executive. For example, fewer than 10% of the fifty states allow their governors to appoint the state attorney general. Most elect the attorney general (along with several other state officials) — which solves the political accountability problem in a different way. (In fact, the attorney general and the governor can, in theory, be from different political parties.) On the other hand, the Tennessee Supreme Court picks the state's Attorney General for an eight year term, which tends to insulate that official from direct political control. Many states also have bipartisan or nonpartisan commissions for different purposes, including legislative

redistricting. Should the federal system adopt innovations in design from the states? Which ones?

Add the following at the end of p. 1012, immediately before Note: Presidential Selection:

Note: The Emoluments Clauses

President Donald Trump is unique among modern American presidents for the vast financial holdings he had accumulated at the time he assumed office. In contrast to other modern chief executives such as Barack Obama, most of his wealth has not been in the form of holdings of securities and mutual funds, which could, in theory, be converted into holdings placed in a blind trust. Instead, much of President Trump's wealth comes from his leadership of a family business and its various real estate holdings and licensing deals around the globe.

Traditionally, incoming presidents have worked with ethics counsels to place their assets in a blind trust or to otherwise minimize conflicts of interest during the period they are in office. Shortly after the 2016 election, Trump brushed aside concerns about conflicts of interest, stating that "the law is totally on my side, meaning, the president can't have a conflict of interest."[8] Nevertheless, on January 11, 2017, President Trump promised to distance himself from his businesses, and to hand over operations to his two sons (although he would retain ownership); he also promised that the Trump Organization would not engage in any new deals in foreign countries while he was in office. Even so, his business affairs continue to be carried on by members of his immediate family who are in constant contact with the President,[9] the no-new-foreign-deals pledge has turned out to be an empty promise,[10] and far from being unaware of his holdings and how they are doing, the President regularly visits many of his properties.[11] Perhaps unsurprisingly, a number of foreign states and officials have switched their business to Trump-owned or -branded properties.

The U.S. Constitution contains two clauses that are designed to prevent financial conflicts of interest and both the appearance and the reality of financial

---

8. The Editors, Donald Trump's New York Times Interview: Full Transcript, N.Y. Times, November 23, 2016, https://www.nytimes.com/2016/11/23/us/politics/trump-new-york-times-interview-transcript.html.

9. For a summary as of July 2017, see Kate Brannen, Trump Family's Endless Conflicts of Interest: Chapter and Verse, Newsweek, July 3, 2017, at http://www.newsweek.com/trump-familys-endless-conflicts-interest-chapter-and-verse-631216.

10. See Jeremy Venook, Donald Trump's Conflicts of Interest: A Crib Sheet, The Atlantic, June 28, 2017, at https://www.theatlantic.com/business/archive/2017/06/donald-trump-conflicts-of-interests/508382/.

11. Sam Petulla, Tracking President Trump's Visits to Trump Properties, NBC News, July 3, 2017, at http://www.nbcnews.com/politics/donald-trump/how-much-time-trump-spending-trump-properties-n753366.

corruption. These are the Foreign and Domestic Emoluments Clauses of Article I, section 9, clause 8, and Article 2, section 1, clause 7.

The Foreign Emoluments Clause, Article I, section 9, clause 8, provides that "no Person holding any Office of Profit or Trust under [the United States], shall, without the Consent of the Congress, accept of any present, Emolument, Office, or Title, of any kind whatever, from any King, Prince, or foreign State."

During the Philadelphia Convention, on August 23, 1787, Charles Pinckney "urged the necessity of preserving foreign Ministers & other officers of the U.S. independent of external influence," and he moved to insert a provision which ultimately became Article I, section 9, clause 8.[12] This language was similar to that in Article VI of the Articles of Confederation, except that the new version applied only to federal officers, and allowed Congress to authorize exceptions.[13] The proposed language was adopted without objection.

At the Virginia ratifying convention, Governor Randolph explained that "[t]his restriction was provided to prevent corruption. . . . An accident, which actually happened, operated in producing the restriction. A box was presented to our ambassador by the king of our allies. It was thought proper, in order to exclude corruption and foreign influence, to prohibit any one in office from receiving or holding any emoluments from foreign states."[14] Randolph was apparently referring to the gift of a very expensive diamond encrusted snuffbox, with a portrait of King Louis XVI, that had been given by the King to then-Ambassador Benjamin Franklin.[15]

The reason for prohibiting all such gifts in advance (at least without congressional "Consent"), Randolph explained, was that one could not rely on individual ministers to turn down such gifts when they were bestowed: "I believe, that if at that moment, when we were in harmony with the King of France, we had supposed that he was corrupting our ambassador, it might have disturbed that confidence, and diminished that mutual friendship, which contributed to carry us through the war."

In his commentaries on the Constitution, St. George Tucker, a Jeffersonian, pointed to the example of Charles II, who was said to be under the pay of Louis XIV: "In the reign of Charles the second of England, that prince, and almost all his officers of state were either actual pensioners of the court of France, or supposed to be under its influence, directly, or indirectly, from that cause. The reign of that monarch has been, accordingly, proverbially disgraceful to his memory." 1 St. George Tucker, Blackstone's Commentaries 295-96 & n.* (1803; reprint

---

12. 2 The Records of the Federal Convention of 1787 389 (Max Farrand ed., 1911).

13. Article VI provided: "[N]or shall any person holding any office of profit or trust under the United States, or any of them, accept any present, emolument, office or title of any kind whatever from any King, Prince or foreign State."

14. 2 The Debates of the Several State Conventions on the Adoption of the Federal Constitution 344 (Jonathan Elliot ed., 1937); 3 Farrand 327.

15. Franklin requested and received permission to keep it, even though it is unclear from the text of the Articles of Confederation that Congress could give consent.

1996). Tucker explained that "[t]he economy which ought to prevail in republican governments, with respects to salaries and other emoluments of office, might encourage the offer of presents from abroad, if the constitution and laws did not reprobate their acceptance."

The requirement of congressional consent serves two functions. First, it gives federal officials an excuse to turn down or donate gifts without offending foreign governments. Second, requiring Congress to consider the matter draws public attention to attempts to influence federal officials. Publicity gives federal officials incentives to avoid the appearance of impropriety. Moreover, even when Congress permits officials to accept foreign gifts or emoluments, the transparency that comes with congressional deliberation and approval makes it more likely that federal officials will not be influenced by a foreign state's generosity in their official conduct.

As of July 2019, Congress had not passed any resolutions with respect to Trump's holdings or income derived from them.

The Domestic Emoluments Clause of Article 2, section 1, clause 7, states that "The President shall, at stated Times, receive for his Services, a Compensation, which shall neither be increased nor diminished during the Period for which he shall have been elected, and he shall not receive within that Period any other Emolument from the United States, or any of them."

Unlike the Foreign Emoluments Clause, the Domestic Emoluments Clause applies only to the President, and Congress cannot make exceptions by giving its consent. In *The Federalist* 73, Alexander Hamilton explained that the requirement of fixed compensation was designed to prevent corruption of the President either by threats or temptations: Congress and the states "will have no power to alter it, either by increase or diminution, till a new period of service by a new election commences. They can neither weaken his fortitude by operating on his necessities, nor corrupt his integrity by appealing to his avarice. Neither the Union, nor any of its members, will be at liberty to give, nor will he be at liberty to receive, any other emolument than that which may have been determined by the first act."

Several lawsuits have been filed charging President Trump with violations of the Foreign and/or Domestic Emoluments Clause. One suit, CREW v. Trump, 276 F.Supp.3d 174 (S.D.N.Y. 2017), was brought by Citizens for Responsibility and Ethics in Washington (CREW), a progressive government-watchdog organization. They have been joined by an association of restaurants and restaurant workers and by a person who books events at various hotels that compete with Trump-branded properties for business from foreign guests and state officials staying in Washington, D.C. They allege that Trump's violations of the Foreign and Domestic Emoluments Clauses harm their economic interests. The district court dismissed the Domestic Emoluments Clause claims for lack of standing, and the Foreign Emoluments Clause claims because they were both a nonjusticiable political question and, in the alternative, not ripe for judicial resolution. As of the summer of 2019, the case was on appeal before the Second Circuit.

A second suit, District of Columbia v. Trump, 291 F.Supp.3d 725 (D. Maryland 2018), was brought by the Attorney Generals of the District of Columbia and Maryland, respectively. They argue that the President's Trump International Hotel in Washington, near the White House, draws business from taxpayer-financed convention centers and facilities in D.C. and Maryland. The hotel gives the President income both from foreign countries and officials, and from state and local government officials, who might be eager to please him.

D.C. and Maryland also argue that Trump's business practices generate pressure and competition among state and local governments to provide the Trump Organization with concessions and exemptions in taxation, environmental protection, land use, and zoning. This undermines their budgets, tax revenues, and regulatory authority. They argue that "the Domestic Emoluments Clause aims to prevent 'the United States, or any of them,' from feeling compelled (or being compelled) to confer private financial benefits on the President in order to compete for influence and favor."

In this case, the district court held that plaintiffs had standing to raise claims under the "Foreign and Domestic Emoluments Clauses of the Constitution by reason of [the President's] involvement with and receipt of benefits from the Trump International Hotel and its appurtenances in Washington, D.C. as well as the operations of the Trump Organization with respect to the same." At the same time, it held that "Plaintiffs lack standing to challenge possible constitutional violations by the President involving operations of the Trump Organization outside the District of Columbia from which the President may receive personal benefits." Finally, the court held that the surviving claims were not barred by the political question doctrine. On appeal, a panel of the Fourth Circuit initially dismissed the plaintiffs' claims for lack of standing, but the Court of Appeals en banc kept the litigation alive for now. See In re Trump, 958 F.3d 274 (4th Cir. 2020) (en banc).

A third suit, Blumenthal v. Trump, No. 1:17-cv-01154 (D.D.C. 2017), was brought by the Constitutional Accountability Center (CAC), a liberal public-interest organization devoted to constitutional issues. The plaintiffs in the suit include approximately 160 Congressmen and 30 senators, led by Connecticut Senator Richard Blumenthal and Michigan Congressman John Conyers. All are Democrats. The plaintiffs seek to enforce the Foreign Emoluments Clause. They argue that President Trump is receiving many different kinds of profits for his businesses from foreign governments and officials—many of whom wish to curry favor with him—but that the President has made no effort to seek Congress's permission or to provide Congress with the information necessary to judge whether he is in compliance with the Constitution. Their complaint argues that "[b]ecause Defendant has failed to come to Congress and seek consent before accepting foreign emoluments that have been confirmed through public reporting, it is impossible to know whether Defendant is accepting other foreign emoluments that have not yet been made public. Indeed, through his personal attorney, Defendant has indicated that he does not believe the Constitution requires him to seek or obtain Congress's consent before accepting benefits arising out of exchanges between foreign states and his businesses." The District

Court subsequently held that the controversy was justiciable, and that the plaintiffs had standing. Blumenthal v. Trump, 335 F.Supp.3d 45, 72 (D.D.C. 2018), but the D.C. Circuit disagreed. Blumenthal v. Trump, 949 F.3d 14 (D.C. Cir. 2020).

Discussion

1. *Standing.* All three suits raise important standing questions. Under the Supreme Court's modern doctrine, standing to bring suit under Article III of the Constitution requires that the plaintiff show three things: First, the plaintiff must have suffered an "injury in fact" — an invasion of a legally-protected interest which is (a) concrete and particularized, and (b) actual or imminent, not conjectural or hypothetical. Second, there must be a causal connection between the injury and the conduct complained of; the injury has to be fairly traceable to the challenged action of the defendant, and not the result of the independent action of some third party not before the court. Third, it must be likely, as opposed to merely speculative, that the injury will be redressed by a favorable decision. Lujan v. Defenders of Wildlife, 504 U.S. 555, 560-61 (1992). These three requirements are usually referred to for short as the requirements of (1) injury-in-fact, (2) causation and (3) redressability.

Do the *CREW* and *D.C.* plaintiffs have standing to challenge violations of the Foreign and Domestic Emoluments Clauses?

One might assume that the answer is yes, because the Emoluments Clauses are designed to benefit *all* Americans by ensuring that their elected officials are not unduly influenced by considerations that might conflict with the best interests of the nation as a whole. On this view, we are all injured if those officials are beholden to foreign powers or otherwise diverted from serving the public interest. The Supreme Court, however, has in recent decades repeatedly held that a "generalized grievance" in *seeing that officials obey the law*, suffered in common by all Americans, or by all taxpayers, is insufficient to establish Article III standing for any one of those aggrieved Americans. In such cases, the Court has reasoned, "the political process, rather than the judicial process, may provide the more appropriate remedy for a widely shared grievance."

Accordingly, the plaintiffs in the emoluments litigation would only have standing to challenge those violations that in some way affect them *personally.* So, for example, if the Philippines agrees to make it easier for the Trump Organization to build a new hotel in Manila that might produce lots of income, or Chinese officials decide to play on Trump golf courses in Scotland or New Jersey, it is not immediately apparent how such conduct would harm the plaintiffs personally and distinctly, even if President Trump's receipt of the income does violate the Foreign Emoluments Clause.

It is plausible to think that Trump's hotel in D.C. might hurt local businesses because it draws away business from foreign and state officials eager to ingratiate themselves with the Trump Administration. But is the economic loss caused by Trump's acceptance of the extra profits? If a court required the Trump Organization to disgorge any profits from foreign and state officials, isn't it possible that at least some of these foreign and state officials would keep patronizing Trump's establishments anyway, just to please him? If so, then plaintiffs may not have shown causation and redressability. What is the plaintiffs' best response? (Hint: Consider changing the kind of remedy that plaintiffs seek.)[16] What do you make of D.C. and Maryland's other argument under the Domestic Emoluments Clause—that they are harmed by having to compete with other jurisdictions in offering tax breaks and regulatory concessions?[17] See Citizens for Responsibility and Ethics in Washington v. Trump, 939 F.3d 131 (2d Cir. 2019) (holding that the plaintiffs had standing because they plausibly alleged a competitive injury).

  Blumenthal v. Trump presents a different set of standing issues. Here the question is whether a group of individual members of Congress—not Congress as a whole or even one House—have standing to enforce the Foreign Emoluments Clause. In Raines v. Byrd, 521 U.S. 811 (1997), the Supreme Court held that six individual Members of Congress lacked standing to challenge the Line Item Veto Act. It "attach[ed] some importance to the fact that [the Raines plaintiffs had] not been authorized to represent their respective Houses of Congress." Id., at 829. "[I]ndeed," the Court observed, "both houses actively oppose[d] their suit." Id. Thus, the plaintiffs were asserting the institutional interests of Congress as a whole even though Congress did not want to assert those interests or did not believe that they were injured. By contrast, in Arizona Legislature v. Arizona Redistricting Commission, 135 S.Ct. 2652 (2015), the Supreme Court distinguished *Raines* and upheld the standing of the *entire* Arizona Legislature to protect its authority under the Elections Clause, Art. I, § 4, cl. 1, to establish redistricting maps for federal House seats.[18] The Arizona legislature, the Court explained, "is an institutional plaintiff asserting an institutional injury, and it commenced this action after authorizing votes in both of its chambers." Is *Blumenthal v. Trump* closer to *Raines* or *Arizona Legislature*? Does the currently Republican-controlled Congress want to oversee Trump? If not, then does this mean that that the *Blumenthal* plaintiffs will have to wait until Trump's political opponents control both Houses of Congress?

  On appeal, the D.C. Circuit applied *Raines* and held that *Blumenthal* plaintiffs lacked standing. Blumenthal v. Trump, 949 F.3d 14 (D.C. Cir. 2020). See also Virginia House Of Delegates v. Bethune-Hill, 139 S.Ct. 1945 (2019) (holding

---

  16. See Leah Littman, On Standing in *CREW v. Trump* Part I: Defining The Injury, Take Care, April 27, 2017, https://takecareblog.com/blog/on-standing-in-crew-v-trump-part-i-defining-the-injury.

  17. There are additional theories of standing based on Maryland's sovereign and quasi-sovereign interests. For a discussion, see Laurence H. Tribe and Joshua Matz, Maryland and DC Have Standing to Sue Trump for Emoluments Violations, Take Care, June 12, 2017, https://takecareblog.com/blog/maryland-and-dc-have-standing-to-sue-trump-for-emoluments-violations.

  18. See Art. I, § 4, cl. 1 ("The Times, Places and Manner of holding Elections for Senators and Representatives, shall be prescribed in each State by the Legislature thereof"). The legislature argued that an Amendment to the Arizona Constitution by a statewide popular initiative, which had transferred the redistricting function to an expert commission, violated the Elections Clause.

that a single house of the Virginia legislature lacked standing to contest a state redistricting plan).

2. *Political Question Doctrine.* The Supreme Court's 1962 decision in Baker v. Carr, 369 U.S. 186, 217 (1962) described six circumstances in which a legal issue might be nonjusticiable because it is a political question: (1) where the Constitution makes a textually demonstrable constitutional commitment of the issue to another branch of government; (2) where there is a lack of judicially discoverable and manageable standards for resolving it; (3) where the court would have to make a policy determination of a kind clearly for nonjudicial discretion; (4) where a decision would be disrespectful to coordinate branches of government; (5) where there is an unusual need to treat a political branch's decision as final; and (6) where it is necessary for the federal government to speak with one voice on an issue. In Zivotofsky v. Clinton, 132 S. Ct. 1421, 1427-28 (*Zivotofsky I*) (2012), the Court maintained that the first two of these six factors are virtually determinative, and emphasized that the political question doctrine is "a narrow exception to [the] rule" that "the Judiciary has a responsibility to decide cases properly before it, even those it 'would gladly avoid.'"

Whether a President has violated the Foreign Emoluments Clause may turn on whether Congress gives its consent. Therefore, one might argue that the Constitution has assigned *to Congress* the exclusive power to decide whether something is an "emolument" and whether the President may accept it. Application of the Clause often implicates delicate foreign relations, which are inappropriate for courts to handle.

On the other hand, Congress's ability to bless what would otherwise be a violation of the Emoluments Clause doesn't mean that Congress is the sole check on Presidential corruption. Moreover, Congress has by statute permitted a range of transactions for various federal officials, and cases construing these statutes are almost certainly justiciable.

In any case, this argument would not affect claims under the Domestic Emoluments Clause, under which congressional consent is immaterial. (Would it make sense if courts could adjudicate Domestic Emoluments Clause cases, but not those involving foreign enticements?)

A second and related argument for treating the clauses as non-justiciable is that, unless Congress specifically passes a statute governing gifts to Presidents, the sole remedy for violations of both clauses is impeachment and removal.

The problem with this theory is that it would give bad incentives to unscrupulous Presidents.[19] If courts can rule on emoluments claims, presidents would have an incentive to get permission from both houses of Congress before accepting gifts from foreign governments. If the President does not wait, he or she will be subject to a lawsuit (assuming, of course, that someone has standing

---

19. Richard Primus, Two thoughts on the Government's Motion to Dismiss in the CREW emoluments case, Balkinization, June 9, 2017, https://balkin.blogspot.com/2017/06/two-thoughts-on-governments-motion-to.html.

to sue). If the question is not justiciable, however, the incentives would work in the opposite direction. Presidents could accept gifts and dare Congress to impeach and remove (or they could just keep the income and gifts secret). It is politically very hard to impeach a president, and even harder to remove one. To be sure, Congress might try to pass a statute that limits the President's conduct and requires disclosure of income from foreign governments. But because the President can veto any such law, Congress would have to obtain a two-thirds majority in both houses—a even larger majority in the House than is required for impeachment. In short, although the Clause contemplates that Presidents will not accept foreign gifts or emoluments unless both houses of Congress give permission, holding that the Clause is nonjusticiable would render this requirement effectively irrelevant.

3. *Does the Foreign Emoluments Clause apply to the President?* The text of the Domestic Emoluments Clause clearly applies to the President. It has long been assumed by Congress and the Executive Branch that the President holds an "Office of Profit or Trust under" the United States and therefore the Foreign Emoluments Clause applies to the President as well. Moreover, this reading is consistent with the central purpose of the Clause—to prevent foreign influence and corruption.

Nevertheless, Seth Barrett Tillman has recently argued that the Clause does not actually apply to the President, because although he is an "Officer," he does not hold an "Office of Profit or Trust under" the United States.[20] Tillman's view is that the latter group includes only appointed officials, not elected officials such as the President, Vice President, and members of Congress. Tillman points out that President George Washington received the key to the French Bastille and a portrait of Louis XVI from French officials without asking Congress's permission—apparently without anyone raising a constitutional objection. It is of course possible that Congress found it imprudent to object to Washington's probity; nevertheless these examples offer an argument from early practice that might gloss the text.

One difficulty with the argument is that it might prove too much.[21] If the President does not hold an "Office of Profit or Trust" under the United States, then the rest of the clause doesn't apply either. This means that foreign governments could hire the President as an employee and give him or her foreign titles of nobility as well. The idea that the President could accept a foreign title from the King of England (for example) would have been unthinkable to the Framers. (Incidentally, the Titles of Nobility Clause, which immediately precedes the Foreign Emoluments Clause in Article I, section 9, clause 8, says only that "No

---

20. Seth Barrett Tillman, The Original Public Meaning of The Foreign Emoluments Clause: A Reply to Professor Zephyr Teachout, 107 Nw. L. Rev. Colloquy 180 (2013).

21. See Marty Lederman, How the DOJ Brief in *CREW v. Trump* Reveals that Donald Trump Is Violating the Foreign Emoluments Clause, Take Care, June 12, 2017, https://takecareblog .com/blog/how-the-doj-brief-in-crew-v-trump-reveals-that-donald-trump-is-violating-the-foreign-emoluments-clause.

Title of Nobility shall be granted by the *United States*." The ban on accepting foreign titles is in the Emoluments Clause.)

For this reason, the Justice Department has long taken the position that the President is bound by both the Foreign and the Domestic Emoluments Clauses. As a result, when President Barack Obama won the Nobel Prize in 2009 (along with an award of approximately 1.4 million dollars), it raised a Foreign Emoluments Clause question. The OLC issued an opinion explaining that he could keep the prize because the Nobel Committee that awards the Peace Prize was not a "King, Prince, or Foreign State" under the meaning of the Clause. Obama nevertheless donated the proceeds to charity.[22]

4. *What is an Emolument?* The final question is whether President Trump accepts an "emolument" when he benefits from profits flowing to Trump-owned and licensed businesses, or from concessions, benefits, and tax breaks to Trump-owned and licensed businesses.

John Mikhail has argued that the predominant meaning of the term "emolument" at the time of the founding was "anything of value," and that this is how the term was frequently used by Blackstone and by various Framers.[23] Under this definition, if the President receives anything of value from a foreign or state government, this violates the Foreign and Domestic Emoluments Clauses, respectively.[24]

If one accepts this definition, however, it is still necessary to adopt some sort of limiting construction. Otherwise, the clauses would produce any number of implausible results. It would follow, for example, that federal officials could not, without congressional consent, own index or other mutual funds that included any companies that do business globally. A President could not own federal or state bonds because interest from the bonds would violate the Domestic Emoluments Clause. And officials could not receive royalties for books — even from books written and published before they took office — because some foreign or state government's library might have purchased the book. A simple

22. See Applicability of the Emoluments Clause and the Foreign Gifts and Decorations Act to the President's Receipt of the Nobel Peace Prize 33 Op. O.L.C. 1 (2009); Alister Bull & Mohammad Zargham, Obama gives $1.4 million Nobel prize to 10 charities, Reuters, Mar 11th, 2010, http://www.reuters.com/article/us-obama-donation-idUSTRE62A5EN20100311.

23. John Mikhail, A Note on the Original Meaning of "Emolument," Balkinization, January 18, 2017, https://balkin.blogspot.com/2017/01/a-note-on-original-meaning-of-emolument.html; John Mikhail, Other uses of "emolument" in The Federalist (and the fallacy of affirming the consequent), Balkinization, January 25, 2017, https://balkin.blogspot.com/2017/01/other-uses-of-emolument-in-federalist.html; John Mikhail, "Emolument" in Blackstone's Commentaries, May 28, 2017, https://balkin.blogspot.com/2017/05/emolument-in-blackstones-commentaries.html.

24. See District of Columbia v. Trump, 315 F.Supp.3d 875, 900 (D. Maryland 2018) ("An 'emolument' within the meaning of the Emoluments Clauses was intended to reach be-yond simple payment for services rendered by a federal official in his official capacity, which in effect would merely restate a prohibition against bribery. The term was in-tended to embrace and ban anything more than de minimis profit, gain, or advantage offered to a public official in his private capacity as well, wholly apart from his official salary."). Accord, Blumenthal v. Trump, 373 F.Supp.3d 191, 207 (D.D.C. 2019) (" 'Emolument' is broadly defined as any profit, gain, or advantage.").

reading of "emolument" as "anything of value" is too broad. Hence, the key substantive issue in *CREW* and other cases is what kind of limiting construction courts should adopt.

The employment theory. A relatively narrow construction would be that "emolument" refers only to compensation for services rendered in an employment or consulting relationship. Hence, the President violates the Foreign Emoluments Clause when he or she receives compensation for services arising out of an employment or consulting relationship with a foreign government. See Andy Grewal, The Foreign Emoluments Clause and the Chief Executive, SSRN, January 19, 2017, at https://papers.ssrn.com/sol3/papers.cfm?abstract_id=2902391. These situations, in which the President is directly in the pay of a foreign power, are likely to be very rare.

The nexus theory. In the *CREW* litigation, the Department of Justice has taken the view that an emolument need not require an employment or consulting relationship with a foreign government. It can also cover "benefits arising from services the President provides to [a] foreign state . . . as President (e.g., making executive decisions favorable to the paying foreign power)." "Neither the text nor the history of the Clauses," the DOJ explains, "shows that they were intended to reach benefits arising from a President's private business pursuits having nothing to do with his office or personal service to a foreign power." That is because "the evils sought to be prevented by the Clause are inducements in the forms of pecuniary compensation and other benefits for the President's services *as President*, as such benefits would pose the greatest danger of undermining the President's independence." Therefore, the DOJ argues, there must be a *nexus* between the payments or benefits that flow to the President and his or her office as President. Relying heavily on *one* definition in a handful of Founding-era dictionaries, the DOJ argues that an "emolument" includes any profit "*arising from* an office or employ" or the "receipt of value for services rendered or for a position held."

Under the DOJ's account, the fact that Trump obtains income from foreign officials staying at his hotels is not an emolument; nor is China's decision to authorize trademarks for Trump Organization businesses. The money does not flow to the President in his official capacity or because of any actions he has taken in his official capacity as President.

On the other hand, the CREW plaintiffs allege that foreign governments are shifting their business to Trump properties and that China has granted trademarks *in order to curry favor with the President*—that is, in the hope that he will use his official powers in ways that will benefit them (or not harm them). According to the CREW plaintiffs, then, the profits *do* "arise from" Trump's office, and thus satisfy even the DOJ's definition, because the President receives these benefits as a result of his office, not in spite of it.[25]

To avoid this conclusion, the DOJ argues that plaintiffs must also show that the money flowed to Trump as compensation for *actions* he takes as President. It may

---

25. See Lederman, *supra*, note 21.

be very difficult to prove that the President actually changed his decision-making because of the money flowing to his businesses from foreign governments. If the DOJ's nexus test requires this, it would make the Foreign Emoluments Clause largely unenforceable, absent proof of a deliberate quid pro quo.

The functional theory. A different view of the two clauses would be functional: an emolument is any income, gift or present that might have the potential of influencing or corrupting the integrity of the recipient, whether or not the income arises out of their actions as an officer.[26] This is the view that the Office of Legal Counsel (OLC) took in a 1981 opinion about the Domestic Emoluments Clause.[27] It argued that President Reagan could receive California state retirement benefits arising from his service as governor of California because the income was already vested before he became President, and could not be withdrawn by the state. Therefore, there was no danger that it could influence his decisionmaking.[28]

In 1993, the OLC held that the Foreign Emoluments Clause prevented members of the Administrative Conference (who are government officers operating in a federal agency) from drawing shares of their law firms' profits because those firms had clients who were foreign governments and money from client services went into the partnership pool.[29] The prohibition applied even though the officials "did not personally represent a foreign government, . . . had no personal contact with that client of the firm, [and] could not be said to be subject to the foreign government's 'control' in his or her activities on behalf of the partnership." Rather, the OLC argued, "[m]ore important . . . is the fact that the Conference member would draw a proportionate share of the partnership's pooled profits, which would include any profits the firm earned from representing its foreign governmental client. Because the amount the Conference member would receive from the partnership's profits would be a function of the amount paid to the firm by the foreign government, the partnership would in effect be a conduit for that government. Thus, some portion of the member's income could fairly be attributed to a foreign government." Presumably, the practical concern was that if a foreign government were unhappy with the Conference's work, it

---

26. See Jane Chong, Reading the Office of Legal Counsel on Emoluments: Do Super-Rich Presidents Get a Pass?, Lawfare, July 1, 2017, https://lawfareblog.com/reading-office-legal-counsel- emoluments-do-super-rich-presidents-get-pass.

27. President Reagan's Ability to Receive Retirement Benefits from the State of California, 5 Op. O.L.C. 187 (1981).

28. See District of Columbia v. Trump, 315 F.Supp. at 904 ("Based on precedent from the OLC and Comptroller General, there would be an exception, at least under the Domestic Emoluments Clause, where the thing of value received by the federal office holder, after the fashion of the Reagan-California pension precedent, was fully vested and indefeasi-ble before the federal official became a federal official, the rationale being that the ben-efit would lack any potential to influence the federal office-holder in his decision-making.")

29. Applicability of the Emoluments Clause to Non-Government Members of ACUS, 17 Op. O.L.C. 114, 119 (1993).

could switch law firms, affecting the partnership pool, and creating indirect pressure on the official from the partnership.

Which of these accounts best serves the purposes of the two Clauses? Which is likely to produce the most coherent and administrable doctrine?

Add the following at the end of p. 1014:

CHIAFALO v. WASHINGTON
2020 WL 3633779

Justice KAGAN delivered the opinion of the Court.

Every four years, millions of Americans cast a ballot for a presidential candidate. Their votes, though, actually go toward selecting members of the Electoral College, whom each State appoints based on the popular returns. Those few "electors" then choose the President.

The States have devised mechanisms to ensure that the electors they appoint vote for the presidential candidate their citizens have preferred. With two partial exceptions, every State appoints a slate of electors selected by the political party whose candidate has won the State's popular vote. Most States also compel electors to pledge in advance to support the nominee of that party. This Court upheld such a pledge requirement decades ago, rejecting the argument that the Constitution "demands absolute freedom for the elector to vote his own choice." *Ray v. Blair*, 343 U.S. 214, 228 (1952).

Today, we consider whether a State may also penalize an elector for breaking his pledge and voting for someone other than the presidential candidate who won his State's popular vote. We hold that a State may do so.

I

Our Constitution's method of picking Presidents emerged from an eleventh-hour compromise. . . . Th[e original version of the electoral college] failed to anticipate the rise of political parties, and soon proved unworkable. . . . The result was the Twelfth Amendment, [ratified in 1804] whose main part provided that electors would vote separately for President and Vice President. . . . The Amendment thus brought the Electoral College's voting procedures into line with the Nation's new party system.

Within a few decades, the party system also became the means of translating popular preferences within each State into Electoral College ballots. In the Nation's earliest elections, state legislatures mostly picked the electors, with the majority party sending a delegation of its choice to the Electoral College. By 1832, though, all States but one had introduced popular presidential elections. At first, citizens voted for a slate of electors put forward by a political party . . . By the early 20th century, citizens in most States voted for the presidential candidate himself; ballots increasingly did not even list the electors. . . .

In the 20th century, many States enacted statutes meant to guarantee that out-come — that is, to prohibit so-called faithless voting. Rather than just assume that party-picked electors would vote for their party's winning nominee, those States insist that they do so. As of now, 32 States and the District of Columbia have such statutes on their books. They are typically called pledge laws because most demand that electors take a formal oath or pledge to cast their ballot for their party's presidential (and vice presidential) candidate. Others merely impose that duty by law. Either way, the statutes work to ensure that the electors vote for the candidate who got the most statewide votes in the presidential election.

Most relevant here, States began about 60 years ago to back up their pledge laws with some kind of sanction. By now, 15 States have such a system. Almost all of them immediately remove a faithless elector from his position, substituting an alternate hose vote the State reports instead. A few States impose a monetary fine on any elector who flouts his pledge. . . .

This case involves three Washington electors [nominated by the Washington State Democratic Party] who violated their pledges [to vote for Hillary Clinton] in the 2016 presidential election. . . . [T]he State fined the Electors $1,000 apiece for breaking their pledges to support the same candidate its vot-ers had. . . .

Our decision in *Ray* held that "Neither the language of Art. II, § 1, nor that of the Twelfth Amendment," we explained, prohibits a State from appointing only electors committed to vote for a party's presidential candidate. . . . *Ray*, how-ever, reserved a question not implicated in the case: Could a State enforce those pledges through legal sanctions? . . . Today, we take up that question. We uphold Washington's penalty-backed pledge law for reasons much like those given in *Ray*. The Constitution's text and the Nation's history both support allowing a State to enforce an elector's pledge to support his party's nominee — and the state voters' choice — for President.

Article II, § 1 's appointments power gives the States far-reaching authority over presidential electors, absent some other constitutional constraint.[4] [E]ach State may appoint electors "in such Manner as the Legislature thereof may direct." Art. II, § 1, cl. 2; see *supra*, at 2. This Court has described that clause as "conveying the broadest power of determination" over who becomes an elec-tor. *McPherson v. Blacker*, 146 U.S. 1, 27 (1892). And the power to appoint an elector (in any manner) includes power to condition his appointment — that is, to say what the elector must do for the appointment to take effect. A State can require, for example, that an elector live in the State or qualify as a regular voter during the relevant time period. Or more substantively, a State can insist (as *Ray* allowed) that the elector pledge to cast his Electoral College ballot for his party's presidential nominee, thus tracking the State's popular vote. Or — so long as nothing else in the Constitution poses an obstacle — a State can add, as Washington did, an associated condition of appointment: It can demand that the elector actually live up to his pledge, on pain of penalty. Which is to say that the State's appointment power, barring some outside constraint, enables the enforce-ment of a pledge like Washington's.

Checks on a State's power to appoint electors, or to impose conditions on an appointment, can theoretically come from anywhere in the Constitution. A State, for example, cannot select its electors in a way that violates the Equal Protection Clause. And if a State adopts a condition on its appointments that effectively imposes new requirements on presidential candidates, the condition may conflict with the Presidential Qualifications Clause, see Art. II, § 1, cl. 5. [relocated footnote — eds.]

[N]othing in the Constitution expressly prohibits States from taking away presidential electors' voting discretion as Washington does. The Constitution is barebones about electors. Article II includes only the instruction to each State to appoint, in whatever way it likes, as many electors as it has Senators and Representatives (except that the State may not appoint members of the Federal Government). The Twelfth Amendment then tells electors to meet in their States, to vote for President and Vice President separately, and to transmit lists of all their votes to the President of the United States Senate for counting. Appointments and procedures and . . . that is all. . . .

The Electors [make a textual argument.] Article II, § 1 . . . names the members of the Electoral College: "electors." The Twelfth Amendment . . . says that electors shall "vote" and that they shall do so by "ballot." The "plain meaning" of those terms, the Electors say, requires electors to have "freedom of choice." . . . But those words need not always connote independent choice. Suppose a person always votes in the way his spouse, or pastor, or union tells him to. We might question his judgment, but we would have no problem saying that he "votes" or fills in a "ballot." In those cases, the choice is in someone else's hands, but the words still apply because they can signify a mechanical act. Or similarly, suppose in a system allowing proxy voting (a common practice in the founding era), the proxy acts on clear instructions from the principal, with no freedom of choice. Still, we might well say that he cast a "ballot" or "voted," though the preference registered was not his own. For that matter, some elections give the voter no real choice because there is only one name on a ballot (consider an old Soviet election, or even a down-ballot race in this country). Yet if the person in the voting booth goes through the motions, we consider him to have voted. . . . [A]lthough voting and discretion are usually combined, voting is still voting when discretion departs. Maybe most telling, switch from hypotheticals to the members of the Electoral College. For centuries now, as we'll later show, almost all have considered themselves bound to vote for their party's (and the state voters') preference. Yet there is no better description for what they do in the Electoral College than "vote" by "ballot." And all these years later, everyone still calls them "electors" — and not wrongly, because even though they vote without discretion, they do indeed elect a President.

The Electors and their *amici* object that the Framers using those words expected the Electors' votes to reflect their own judgments. Hamilton praised the Constitution for entrusting the Presidency to "men most capable of analyzing the qualities" needed for the office, who would make their choices "under circumstances favorable to deliberation." The Federalist No. 68. So too, John Jay predicted that the Electoral College would "be composed of the most enlightened and respectable citizens," whose choices would reflect "discretion and discernment." *Id.*, No. 64.

But even assuming other Framers shared that outlook, it would not be enough. Whether by choice or accident, the Framers did not reduce their thoughts about electors' discretion to the printed page. All that they put down about the electors was what we have said: that the States would appoint them, and that they would meet and cast ballots to send to the Capitol. Those sparse instructions took no position on how independent from—or how faithful to—party and popular preferences the electors' votes should be. On that score, the Constitution left much to the future. And the future did not take long in coming. Almost immediately, presidential electors became trusty transmitters of other people's decisions.

"Long settled and established practice" may have "great weight in a proper interpretation of constitutional provisions." *The Pocket Veto Case*, 279 U.S. 655, 689 (1929). As James Madison wrote, "a regular course of practice" can "liquidate & settle the meaning of" disputed or indeterminate "terms & phrases." Letter to S. Roane (Sept. 2, 1819), in 8 Writings of James Madison 450 (G. Hunt ed. 1908); see The Federalist No. 37, at 225. The Electors make an appeal to that kind of practice. . . . But "our whole experience as a Nation" points in the opposite direction. *NLRB v. Noel Canning*, 573 U.S. 513, 557 (2014). Electors have only rarely exercised discretion in casting their ballots for President. From the first, States sent them to the Electoral College—as today Washington does—to vote for pre-selected candidates, rather than to use their own judgment. And electors (or at any rate, almost all of them) rapidly settled into that non-discretionary role.

Begin at the beginning—with the Nation's first contested election in 1796. Would-be electors declared themselves for one or the other party's presidential candidate. . . . The Twelfth Amendment embraced this new reality—both acknowledging and facilitating the Electoral College's emergence as a mechanism not for deliberation but for party-line voting. . . . [T]he Twelfth Amendment made party-line voting [for both President and Vice-President] safe. The Amendment thus advanced, rather than resisted, the practice that had arisen in the Nation's first elections. . . . [A]s the Court wrote in *Ray*, the new procedure allowed an elector to "vote the regular party ticket" and thereby "carry out the desires of the people" who had sent him to the Electoral College. No independent electors need apply.

Courts and commentators throughout the 19th century recognized the electors as merely acting on other people's preferences. . . . State election laws evolved to reinforce that development, ensuring that a State's electors would vote the same way as its citizens. . . . Washington's law, penalizing a pledge's breach, is only another in the same vein. It reflects a tradition more than two centuries old. In that practice, electors are not free agents; they are to vote for the candidate whom the State's voters have chosen.

The history going the opposite way is one of anomalies only. The Electors stress that since the founding, electors have cast some 180 faithless votes for either President or Vice President. But that is 180 out of over 23,000. And more than a third of the faithless votes come from 1872, when the Democratic Party's nominee (Horace Greeley) died just after Election Day. Putting those aside, faithless votes represent just one-half of one percent of the total. Still, the Electors counter, Congress has counted all those votes. But because faithless votes have never come close to affecting an outcome, only one has ever been challenged. True enough, that one was counted. But the Electors cannot rest a claim of historical tradition on one counted vote in over 200 years. And anyway, the State appointing that elector had no law requiring a pledge or otherwise barring his use of discretion. Congress's deference to a state decision to tolerate a faithless vote is no ground for rejecting a state decision to penalize one.

The Electors contend that elector discretion is needed to deal with the possibility that a future presidential candidate will die between Election Day and the Electoral College vote. We do not dismiss how much turmoil such an event could cause. In recognition of that fact, some States have drafted their pledge laws to give electors voting discretion when their candidate has died. And we suspect that in such a case, States without a specific provision would also release electors from their pledge. Still, we note that because the situation is not before us, nothing in this opinion should be taken to permit the States to bind electors to a deceased candidate. [footnote relocated—eds.]

The judgment of the Supreme Court of Washington is

Affirmed.

Justice THOMAS, with whom Justice GORSUCH joins as to Part II, concurring in the judgment.

The Court correctly determines that States have the power to require Presidential electors to vote for the candidate chosen by the people of the State. I disagree, however, with its attempt to base that power on Article II. In my view, the Constitution is silent on States' authority to bind electors in voting. I would resolve this case by simply recognizing that "[a]ll powers that the Constitution neither delegates to the Federal Government nor prohibits to the States are controlled by the people of each State." *U.S. Term Limits, Inc. v. Thornton*, 514 U.S. 779, 848 (1995) (Thomas, J., dissenting).

I

The Constitution does not address—expressly or by necessary implication—whether States have the power to require that Presidential electors vote for the candidates chosen by the people. Article II, § 1, and the Twelfth Amendment provide for the election of the President through a body of electors. But neither speaks directly to a State's power over elector voting. . . .

Clause 2 of Article II, § 1 . . . provides, in relevant part, that "[e]ach State shall appoint, in such Manner as the Legislature thereof may direct, a Number of Electors." As I have previously explained, this language "imposes an affirmative obligation on the States" to establish the manner for appointing electors. . . . This obligation to provide the manner of appointing electors does not expressly delegate power to States; it simply imposes an affirmative duty. . . .

The Court appears to misinterpret Article II, § 1, by overreading its language as authorizing the broad power to impose and enforce substantive conditions on appointment. The Court then misconstrues the State of Washington's law as enforcing a condition of appointment. . . . Article II, § 1, provides that States shall appoint electors "in such Manner as the Legislature thereof may direct." . . . At the time of the founding, the term "manner" referred to a "[f]orm" or "method." 1 S. Johnson, A Dictionary of the English Language (6th ed. 1785); see also 1 J. Ash, The New and Complete Dictionary of the English Language (2d ed. 1795). These definitions suggest that Article II requires state legislatures merely to set the approach for selecting Presidential electors, not to impose substantive limitations on whom may become an elector. And determining the "Manner" of appointment certainly does not include the power to impose requirements as to how the electors vote *after they are appointed*, which is what the Washington law addresses. . . .

[T]he Court's interpretation gives the same term—"Manner"—different meanings in two parallel provisions of the Constitution. Article I, § 4, states that "[t]he Times, Places and Manner of holding Elections for Senators and Representatives, shall be prescribed in each State by the Legislature thereof." In *U.S. Term Limits*, the Court concluded that the term "Manner" in Article I includes only "a grant of authority to issue procedural regulations," not "the broad power to set qualifications." 514 U.S., at 832-833 (majority opinion); see also *id.,* at 861-864 (Thomas, J., dissenting). Yet, today, the Court appears to take the exact opposite view. The Court interprets the term "Manner" in Article II, § 1, to include the power to impose conditions or qualifications on the appointment of electors. . . .

Washington's law . . . did not involve the enforcement of a pledge or relate to the appointment process at all. It simply regulated electors' votes, unconnected to the appointment process. . . . Some States expressly require electors to pledge to vote for a party nominee as a condition of appointment and then impose a penalty if electors violate that pledge. . . . But not all States attempt to bind electors' votes through the appointment process. Some States simply impose a legal duty that has no connection to elector appointment. . . . The Court does not, and cannot, claim that the text of Article II provides States power over anything other than the *appointment* of electors.

Here, the challenged Washington law did not enforce any appointment condition. It provided that "[a]ny elector who votes for a person or persons not nominated by the party of which he or she is an elector is subject to a civil penalty of up to one thousand dollars." . . . Thus, even accepting the Court's strained reading of Article II, § 1's text, I cannot agree with the Court's effort to reconcile Washington's law with its desired theory.

In short, the Constitution does not speak to States' power to require Presidential electors to vote for the candidates chosen by the people. . . . Rather than contort the language of both Article II and the state statute, I would acknowledge that the Constitution simply says nothing about the States' power in this regard.

II

When the Constitution is silent, authority resides with the States or the people. This allocation of power is both embodied in the structure of our Constitution and expressly required by the Tenth Amendment. The application of this fundamental principle should guide our decision here. . . .

This fundamental allocation of power applies in the context of the electoral college. Article II, § 1, and the Twelfth Amendment address the election of the President through a body of electors. These sections of the Constitution provide the Federal Government with limited powers concerning the election, set various requirements for the electors, and impose an affirmative obligation on States to appoint electors. Art. II, § 1; Amdt. 12. Each of these directives is consistent with the general structure of the Constitution and the principle of reserved powers. Put simply, nothing in the text or structure of Article II and the Twelfth Amendment contradicts the fundamental distribution of power preserved by the Tenth Amendment. . . .

As the Court recognizes, nothing in the Constitution prevents States from requiring Presidential electors to vote for the candidate chosen by the people. . . . Petitioners ask us to infer a constitutional right to elector independence by interpreting the terms "appoint," "Electors," "vote," and "by Ballot" to align with the Framers' *expectations* of discretion in elector voting. But the Framers' expectations aid our interpretive inquiry only to the extent that they provide evidence of the original public meaning of the Constitution. They cannot be used to change that meaning. As the Court explains, the plain meaning of the terms relied on by petitioners do not appear to "connote independent choice." Thus, "the original expectation[s]" of the Framers as to elector discretion provide "no reason for holding that the power confided to the States by the Constitution has ceased to exist." *McPherson.*

Discussion

1. Do the textual arguments of the Justices prove too much? Both Justice Kagan and Justice Thomas argue that nothing in the meaning of the word "vote" prevents a State from using fines to get electors to vote in a certain way. But the word "vote" appears in many places in the Constitution, for example, in the guarantees of the Fifteenth and Nineteenth Amendments. There the term "vote" clearly refers to a free choice. Presumably it would not be constitutional for a state to require that all voters vote for a preselected group of candidates, as long as the same obligation applied to all voters regardless of race and sex.

2. This example shows a general principle in constitutional interpretation: Behind arguments from text are usually other kinds of arguments that make the textual arguments plausible: for example, arguments of purpose, structure,

and consequences. What structural reasons can you give for allowing states to determine the votes of electors? How does the result further the way that the electoral system is supposed to function? How would the contrary result damage, if at all, the proper functioning of the system for choosing presidents?

3. What arguments from the purpose of the Electoral College could you offer to support the result in *Chiafalo*? Note that these are not arguments about the *original* purpose, since at the founding it was assumed that electors would vote their consciences. This is clear in Hamilton's arguments in Federalist 68, where he argues that the Electoral College will prevent people unfit from office from gaining power. Rather, these are arguments about the purpose that the Electoral College came to have in the early years of the Republic — to translate voters' political preferences into a system for electing presidents. (In the alternative, one might argue that these new purposes were implicit in the adoption of the Twelfth Amendment, which acquiesced in the new system of party politics.)

4. What bad consequences for democratic government might flow from states' inability to fine faithless electors? Are these dangers real, since, as the Court points out, few electors have been faithless? If the Court announced that states could not fine electors for being faithless, would this mean that there would be many more faithless electors? Or would it mean, instead, that state parties would be even more careful about whom they made electors, and that state *parties*, and not state governments, would offer threats and penalties to keep electors in line? Put another way, is the result in *Chiafalo* necessary to avoid chaos, or does it simply reflect the Justices' view that they should not tempt fate?

5. The Court also makes arguments from tradition, or more correctly, from a long course of conduct of states and state-appointed electors over the Nation's history. Can there still be a tradition of practice if it has not always been honored and some electors have been faithless? What is the reason for following past practices or traditions in these situations, as opposed to following past practices in the areas of race and sex discrimination?

6. Justice Kagan drops a footnote explaining that: "if a State adopts a condition on its appointments that effectively imposes new requirements on presidential candidates, the condition may conflict with the Presidential Qualifications Clause, see Art. II, § 1, cl. 5." Does this mean that Washington could not require that electors may not vote for any candidate who has not disclosed the last ten years of their tax returns?

Replace Note on Presidential Impeachment on p. 1015 with the following:

Note: Presidential Impeachment

Article II, section 4 states that "The President, Vice President and all civil officers of the United States, shall be removed from Office on Impeachment for, and Conviction of, Treason, Bribery, or other high Crimes and Misdemeanors." Article I prescribes that the House of Representatives is entrusted with the power to impeach, the Senate with the power to try impeachments, and the Chief Justice of the Supreme Court acts as the presiding officer at Presidential impeachments.

Three presidents, Andrew Johnson, Bill Clinton, and Donald Trump, have been impeached by the House. No President has ever been convicted and removed by the Senate. Richard Nixon resigned to avoid impeachment.

This Note discusses the history of the three most recent impeachment controversies, the structural issues involved in impeachment, and finally, the meaning of "high Crimes and Misdemeanors" as the potential grounds for impeachment.[30]

1. Three modern impeachments. The three modern impeachment controversies involved Richard Nixon, Bill Clinton, and Donald Trump.

a. Nixon's resignation. The House Judiciary Committee voted to recommend the first of three articles of impeachment of President Richard Nixon to the full House on July 27, 1974. The primary accusation was that Nixon had attempted to cover up and impede the investigation of the burglary at the Watergate Hotel in July 1972, when five men broke into the Democratic National Committee headquarters at the Watergate office complex in Washington. Nixon attempted to cover up his Administration's involvement in the burglary.

The Watergate scandal ultimately led to the discovery of multiple abuses of power by the Nixon Administration, including secret wiretapping of political activists, and the use of the FBI, the CIA, and the IRS to investigate and/or harass political opponents. Ultimately, 69 people were indicted, leading to 48 convictions, including Attorney General John Mitchell, the President's chief of staff, H.R. Haldeman, the President's chief domestic policy advisor, John Ehrlichman, and many other high Administration officials.

Upon the revelation that Nixon had taped many of his conversations in the Oval Office, a protracted legal and political struggle began to get access to the Watergate tapes. Nixon resisted until the Supreme Court ordered him to hand over the tapes in United States v Nixon on July 24, 1974. The White House finally complied on August 5, 1974. The tapes revealed, among other things, that Nixon had ordered the CIA to get the FBI to stop investigating the Watergate burglary on grounds of national security; and that Nixon had ordered his aides to engage in a cover up. At this point Nixon's faced almost certain impeachment in the House and conviction in the Senate. Political leaders in his own party now urged him to give up the fight. He resigned on August 8, 1974. This avoided impeachment by the full House. His former Vice-President, President Gerard

---

30. For two recent studies of the law of impeachment, see Cass R. Sunstein, Impeachment: A Citizen's Guide (2017); Laurence Tribe & Joshua Matz, To End a Presidency: The Power of Impeachment (2018). A classic account from 1974 is Charles L. Black, Jr. Impeachment: A Handbook, Philip Bobbitt ed. (2d ed. 2018). See also the discussion of the Clinton impeachment in Akhil Reed Amar, The Constitution Today: Timeless Lessons for the Issues of Our Era 273-326 (2016).

Ford, pardoned him a month later, on September 8, 1974. As a result, Nixon never faced criminal prosecution.

b. Clinton's impeachment and acquittal. In 1998, the House impeached Bill Clinton for perjury and obstruction of justice arising out of his affair with a White House intern, Monica Lewinsky. In a deposition arising out of a sexual harassment lawsuit brought by Paula Jones, Clinton had denied having "sexual relations" with Lewinsky. That lawsuit was later settled out of court. However, Independent Counsel Kenneth Starr, who had been investigating the Whitewater land deal, learned that Clinton and Lewinsky had an affair. He convened a grand jury, threatened Lewinsky with prosecution for false testimony in the Jones lawsuit, and reached an immunity deal in return for her grand jury testimony. Lewinsky testified that she had engaged in various forms of intimate physical relations with the President. Before the grand jury, Clinton testified that his statements during the Jones deposition were technically accurate (because of the convoluted definition of "sexual relations" and related terms that the attorneys had agreed to in that case). However, he admitted to "inappropriate contact" with Lewinsky. Starr issued a report to Congress on September 9, 1998, detailing his findings and grounds for impeachment of Clinton.

The House began impeachment hearings on October 8, 1998, which were marked by acrimony between Democrats and Republicans. In the November 1998 mid-term elections, the Republicans lost five seats in the House. Opposition parties in the sixth term of a presidency usually gain twenty or more seats, so this was regarded as an unusually poor showing. Many commentators blamed the rebuff on the national party's decision to make Clinton and the Lewinsky affair an issue in selected House races; and public opinion polls suggested that the public was wearying of months of media coverage of the scandal and that a substantial majority opposed impeachment.

Apparently, although the public had a low opinion of Clinton's ethics, his approval ratings as President remained high. Nevertheless, the House hearings continued after the election under the leadership of the lame duck Congress, and in December 1998, a bitterly divided Congress passed two of four proposed articles of impeachment, essentially along party lines, with almost all Republicans supporting impeachment and almost all Democrats opposing it. The two articles accused Clinton of perjuring himself before the grand jury and of obstructing justice. On February 12, 1999, the Senate voted to acquit Clinton of both charges. The vote was 55 for acquittal and 45 for conviction on the perjury count, and 50-50 on the obstruction of justice count. Once again the votes were strongly partisan: all 45 Democrats voted for acquittal on both counts and most Republicans voted for conviction.

c. Trump's impeachment and acquittal. The most recent impeachment, of Donald Trump, arose out of the Ukraine Scandal. In August 2019, a whistle-blower complaint charged that Trump had attempted to coerce the government of Ukraine to benefit him politically in the upcoming 2020 elections. First, Trump wanted the government of Ukraine to announce a corruption investigation into Joe Biden, Trump's most likely Democratic opponent in the 2020 elections, as well as Biden's son Hunter. (There was no evidence that either Biden had done anything illegal or corrupt in Ukraine.) Second, Trump sought to get the government of Ukraine to support a theory, discredited by American intelligence agencies, that it was Ukraine, and not Russia, that interfered in the 2016 presidential election; and, moreover, that the interference was not to benefit Trump, but rather Trump's opponent, Hillary Clinton.

The scandal led to an investigation by the House of Representatives, which produced testimony by Trump Administration officials and others that Trump had used his personal lawyer, Rudy Giuliani, and members of his Administration to pressure Ukraine for announcements about Biden and about Ukrainian interference in the 2016 election to benefit Hillary Clinton. In order to provide further pressure, Trump also initially blocked payment of a congressional appropriation of 400 million dollars of military aid to Ukraine. After the scandal broke and members of Congress demanded that the payments be made, Trump released the funds. In January 2020, just before the Senate impeachment trial began, the Government Accountability Office issued a report finding that Trump had illegally withheld the money.

Trump denied any wrongdoing, arguing that he had a perfect right to ask foreign governments to investigate corruption by his political opponents. On October 3rd, 2019, while the House of Representatives was conducting its investigations of Trump, Trump told members of the press on the South Lawn of the White House that he hoped Ukraine would investigate the Bidens, and he also called on China to start an investigation. Trump declared the House investigation into his conduct illegitimate. He refused to hand over any documents to the House or to allow any government officials to testify. Testimony came primarily from civil servants who defied his wishes.

On December 3, the House Judiciary Committee voted to send a report to the full House calling for impeachment. The report stated that Trump had used his personal attorney and members of his Administration to solicit the government Ukraine to interfere in the upcoming presidential election to benefit him personally. It found that in order to pressure Ukraine, Trump had withheld a White House meeting sought by Ukraine's new president, Volodymyr Zelensky, as well as much-needed military aid to fight Russian interference in eastern Ukraine. (Russia had seized Crimea from Ukraine in 2014 and Russian and Russian-allied troops were fighting Ukraine in the eastern part of the country).

On December 13, the House Judiciary committee voted on two articles of impeachment. The first article charged Trump with abuse of power. The second charged him with obstruction of Congress for refusing to cooperate with the House investigations. The vote was 23-17, with all Democrats voting for and all Republicans voting against. An accompanying report explained that the first abuse of power count included violations of multiple federal crimes, including wire fraud and bribery (that is, that Trump had sought to bribe the President of Ukraine with withheld military aid and a White House meeting in return for announcements about the Bidens and about Ukrainian interference in the 2016 election).

On December 18th, the House of Representatives voted on the two articles of impeachment. The vote on abuse of power was 230-197-1. The vote on obstruction of Congress was 229-198-1. All House Republicans voted against the two articles. Justin Amash, a former Republican who became an independent in July 2019, voted for both.

Preparations began for a trial in the Senate, where the Republicans held a 53-47 majority. Republicans were strongly opposed to impeachment and wanted to end the trial quickly. Senate Majority Leader Mitch McConnell explained that "I'm not an impartial juror." "This is a political process. There is not anything judicial about it. Impeachment is a political decision."[31] In an interview with Fox News he explained that he would work closely with the Trump Administration: "Everything I do during this I'm coordinating with the White House counsel. There will be no difference between the president's position and our position as to how to handle this."[32] Similarly, Senate Judiciary Committee Chair Lindsey Graham explained that "I am trying to give a pretty clear signal I have made up my mind. I'm not trying to pretend to be a fair juror here. . . . I will do everything I can to make [the impeachment trial] die quickly."[33]

Democrats delayed sending the articles of impeachment to the Senate, hoping to get assurances that the Senate would hear witnesses, but McConnell rebuffed them. The articles were finally delivered on January 15th, 2020. Opening arguments began on January 22nd. Trump's defense began on the 25th. Trump's defenders argued that there was no evidence of wrongdoing, and that the Democrats were attempting to undermine the result of the 2016 election and steal the upcoming 2020 election.

One of Trump's counsels, Harvard Professor Alan Dershowitz, argued that Trump could not be removed from office without proof of a criminal act or "criminal-like behavior."[34] Neither abuse of power nor Trump's refusal to cooperate with Congress's impeachment investigations were federal crimes. Offering a quid pro quo to Ukraine could not be a federal crime because what Trump asked for was not illegal and there was no corrupt motive. It was legal to ask a foreign government for an investigation of corruption. Even if Trump had mixed motives in making the request, politicians often make decisions with a view to increasing their chances for election. Performing an otherwise lawful act out of a desire to be re-elected, Dershowitz argued, did not constitute a corrupt motive.

31. Ted Barrett & Ali Zaslav, Mitch McConnell: "I'm not an impartial juror" ahead of Senate impeachment trial, CNN, December 17, 2019, https://www.cnn.com/2019/12/17/politics/mcconnell-impartial-juror-impeachment/index.html.

32. Jordain Carney, McConnell says he'll be in "total coordination" with White House on impeachment trial strategy, The Hill, December 12, 2019, https://thehill.com/homenews/senate/474399-mcconnell-says-hell-be-in-total-coordination-with-white-house-on-impeachment.

33. Veronica Stracqualursi, "I'm not trying to pretend to be a fair juror here": Graham predicts Trump impeachment will "die quickly" in Senate, CNN.com, December 14, 2019, https://www.cnn.com/2019/12/14/politics/lindsey-graham-trump-impeachment-trial/index.html.

34. Alan M. Dershowitz, Democrats Are Lying About My Argument, Wall St. J., February 3, 2020, https://www.wsj.com/articles/democrats-are-lying-about-my-argument-11580773517.

On January 31, the Senate voted 51-49 against hearing any witnesses. Two Republican senators, Mitt Romney and Susan Collins, voted for witnesses. On February 5, 2020, the Senate acquitted Trump on both counts. The vote on the first count was 52-48, with one Republican Senator, Mitt Romney, voting to convict. The vote on the second count was 53-47, with all Republican Senators voting to acquit.

Trump's approval ratings went up slightly during the impeachment trial, reaching a new high of 49 percent in early February 2020. The months-long intensely bitter fight over impeachment was quickly forgotten as the country focused on a global pandemic.

In the Johnson and Clinton impeachments, no Senator of the President's own party (the Democrats) voted to convict. Thus, Senator Romney's vote on the first count of abuse of power is the only example of a Senator from the President's own party voting to convict in an impeachment trial. On the other hand, President Nixon predicted that he would lose votes from his own party, and he resigned before either an impeachment vote or an impeachment trial could be held.

2. *The House's Role.* How should responsible members of the House of Representatives think about their vote?

Here it is important to distinguish between impeachments of presidents and impeachments of judges. In fact, there have been many more impeachments of judges than of presidents—some fifteen in all—and many more judges have been investigated without impeachment.[35]

One might think that judicial independence requires that judges should not be removed for political reasons. (This is one of the lessons of the Chase impeachment in the early Republic, see Casebook, p. 116). By contrast, the impeachment of a president sits between a legal and a political judgment and has aspects of both. Moreover, although impeachment is akin to a judicial proceeding, it is not part of the Article III process for judging disputes. It takes place in an Article I institution—part of the representative and political branches.

Under Article I, the House can impeach the President by a simple majority. Note that conviction by the Senate requires a two-thirds vote. Does this suggest that the standard of proof for the House is different than for the Senate?

If one adopts a judicial model, one might argue that the House is equivalent to a grand jury considering an indictment. Under this analogy, it needs only probable cause to believe that the President (or other officer) has committed an impeachable offense. On the other hand, there are significant differences between the House and a grand jury. There is no prosecutor to guide the House; thus House members must play both the role of prosecutor and grand jury. (Query: Why couldn't an Independent Counsel like Kenneth Starr play that

---

35. See Impeachments of Federal Judges, Federal Judicial Center, https://www.fjc.gov/history/judges/impeachments-federal-judges (listing impeachments); Warren S. Grimes, Hundred-Ton-Gun Control: Preserving Impeachment as the Exclusive Removal Mechanism for Federal Judges, 38 U.C.L.A. L. Rev. 1209, 1216 (1991) (compiling numbers of federal judges investigated for impeachment up to 1989).

role? Think about the separation of powers discussions following Morrison and Edmond in Chapter Six, pp. 892-98, 901).

Because the House must play two roles, its considerations are arguably different from those of a grand jury. Moreover, the House is an elected body whose members take an oath to uphold the Constitution and also owe responsibilities to their constituents. See Neil S. Siegel, After the Trump Era: A Constitutional Role Morality for Presidents and Members of Congress, 107 Geo. L.J. 109 (2018). Are there tensions in these duties?

There is also the question of hijacking the nation's attention and agenda. Here again, we should distinguish between impeaching judges and impeaching presidents. A president has been elected by the people and removal from office through impeachment short-circuits the democratic process, and so may be deeply divisive. The House must decide whether it is worth it to put the country through a presidential impeachment. Obviously, impeachments of both presidents and judges cost the Senate valuable time, but presidential impeachments in particular are likely to consume the lion's share of the Senate's time and attention.

Should a conscientious House member vote against impeachment if he or she believes that the Senate will not convict? Or should the member vote for impeachment on the grounds that there is an independent constitutional duty to say what the appropriate legal standard is?

Consider the possibility that House members in Clinton's case might have voted for impeachment on the ground that (1) they knew the Senate would not convict, or (2) that they wanted to show their disapproval of Clinton akin to a motion for censure. Is either or both of these reasons constitutionally appropriate?

By the time the House impeached Trump, it was clear that he had the unwavering loyalty of most Republican politicians, and that there was no chance that he would be convicted in the Senate. (Republican politicians said as much before the trial.) Was the vote to impeach therefore inappropriate?

Is it appropriate for the House to begin impeachment proceedings to get access to information from the President when the President refuses to cooperate with oversight investigations? In *United States v. Nixon*, the Court held that executive privilege must yield to the need for information in an ongoing criminal investigation. Does the same logic apply to an impeachment investigation, which, as noted above, is akin to a judicial proceeding?

3. Impeachment as a Political Act. To what extent should impeachment and conviction depend on the President's popularity? On the public's view whether the President should not be impeached and/or convicted? Compare Charles L. Black, Jr., Impeachment: A Handbook 20 (1974) ("taking, at intervals, of public opinion polls on guilt or innocence, should be looked on as an unspeakable indecency.") with Michael J. Klarman, Constitutional Fetishism and the Clinton Impeachment Debate, 85 Va. L. Rev. 631 (1999) ("If popular majorities get to elect a President, it is hard to see why they should be ignored on the question of whether he remains fit to hold office.")

In this light, consider Senate Majority Leader Mitch McConnell's remarks that he regarded the entire process as political through and through and would cooperate with the White House counsel. What, if anything, is wrong with these remarks? During the impeachment proceedings, President Clinton's approval ratings were quite high, particularly for a President in his sixth year in office. They got even higher as a response to the House's impeachment resolutions. President Trump's approval ratings also moved up slightly. By contrast, President Nixon was deeply unpopular by the time he resigned in August 1974, and politicians of both parties were calling for his resignation.

Consider the following arguments and counterarguments:

(a) *Constitutional obligations.* Impeachment and conviction are constitutional obligations of the House and the Senate, respectively. They cannot be shirked no matter how popular a president is or what his poll numbers might be. A House member must vote for impeachment if there are reasonable grounds for impeachment, and a Senator must convict if he or she believes that the President has committed a high crime or misdemeanor judged by the appropriate standard of proof.

(b) *Prosecutorial Discretion and Jury Deliberation.* Impeachment is a prosecutorial act. Prosecutors engage in prosecutorial discretion all the time, and they should do so in the interests of the public. (See the discussion of the *Cox* and *Nixon* cases in Chapter Six for a list of justifications for prosecutorial discretion). Hence the House must consider whether proceeding with impeachment is for the good of the country. One important consideration is whether House members are going against the will of the people who elected the President to office.

Textually, note that Article I, Section 3 gives the House "the sole Power of Impeachment" but says nothing about any duty to impeach. Intratextually, note that the Framers knew how to use the word "duty"—indeed they used it twice in Article II. On this view, House impeachment is about power, not duty—about choices, not obligations. A related point: The House's inherent power of mercy is all the more vital given that the ordinary locus of pretrial mercy in our constitutional system—the President's pardon power—is inapplicable. As we have seen, under Article II, Section 2, a president may ordinarily pardon at any time and for any reason (recall Gerald Ford's pretrial pardon of Nixon and George Bush's pretrial pardon of Caspar Weinberger), but not "in cases of impeachment." Thus, in impeachment prosecutions, the Framers took the power of executive clemency away from the President and gave it to the House.

Similarly, Senators must consider whether conviction and removal would be in the best interests of the country. If House members are roughly in the role of prosecutors, Senators are roughly in the role of jurors. Like any ordinary criminal juror, each Senator is free to be merciful for a wide variety of reasons—because she thinks the defendant has suffered enough, or because the punishment doesn't fit the crime, or because punishing the defendant would impose unacceptable costs on innocent third parties. Moreover unlike ordinary jurors, Senators are elected, and thus they are also free to consult their constituents. Sometimes, deferring to "the masses" might be irresponsible—for example, if the citizenry were ignorant of the facts or incapable of thinking through the complicated legal question at hand. But Senators should not ignore their constituents where these circumstances do not apply.

If Senators are like jurors, was it appropriate for Senate Judiciary Committee Chairman Lindsey Graham (who had been one of the floor managers in the Clinton impeachment) to announce that he had made up his mind even before the trial even began? Was it permissible for him to have his mind made up but not say so in public?

(c) *The "Coup' D'Etat" Argument.* Because presidential impeachment is a fundamentally political decision to remove an elected president from office, it should not be undertaken without solid popular support. Although solid popular support may not be sufficient to justify impeachment, it is necessary because impeachment overturns the results of a national election; at the very least it involves a transfer of the most important office in the country without direct popular approval.[36] The country was fairly evenly divided on President Trump's impeachment. His base of Republican voters was very loyal to him, and there was little chance that they would abandon him. Does this mean that the House of Representatives should not have forged ahead under these conditions, even if members were convinced that he was corrupt?

Consider the following response: Because of the twelfth and twenty-fifth amendments, the successor to the President will most likely be a member of his own party. (Note that if the President and Vice President are both impeached, the presidency would fall to the Speaker of the House. But see the discussion of presidential succession in Chapter Six).

Compare the impeachments of Bill Clinton, Donald Trump, and Andrew Johnson. In Clinton's case, Al Gore, a Democrat would have become president. In Trump's case, Mike Pence, a Republican, would have become president. In Johnson's case, there was no vice-president, because the twenty-fifty amendment had not yet been ratified. Johnson was a War Democrat who disagreed with Republicans on many issues. His successor would have been Ben Wade, the Speaker of the House and a Radical Republican who would, most likely, have let the Congress accelerate the process of Reconstruction. (Would Wade's ascension to the Presidency have been a good thing or a bad thing from the standpoint of American democracy?) Note that Andrew Johnson himself had never been elected President by the American people.

Even if a Vice President of the same party succeeds the President, one can still argue that impeachment is a counter-majoritarian assertion that should not proceed without broad popular support. The opposition party may have good reasons to prefer the Vice-President in office, even if he is thereby strengthened for a subsequent run at the presidency. A successful conviction may weaken the presidency and confirm the power of the opposition party. (Consider whether successful conviction of Andrew Johnson in 1868 or Bill Clinton in 1999 would have confirmed the dominance of the Republican Party in either era. Note also that in 1868, putting Ben Wade in White House would have created an obstacle

---

36. Jack M. Balkin, "An Implosion of Democracy," *Boston Globe*, January 17, 1999, at C07.

to the election of the Republicans' favored candidate in the 1868 elections, Ulysses S. Grant.)

(d) *The Asymmetrical Importance of Popular Will.* Consider the argument that popular will is most important in cases where it speaks against impeachment and removal of a President:

> If in her heart a Congressperson or Senator thinks the President is innocent in fact (he actually didn't do it) or in law (even if he did it, it is not a "high crime or misdemeanor"), then she must vote not guilty—even if she thereby offends her constituents, who want the man's head. She has taken a solemn oath to do justice, and she would violate that oath if she voted to convict a man she believed innocent. [Moreover, in the Senate] impeachment rules are not symmetric between conviction and acquittal. It takes 67 votes to convict, but only 34 to acquit. On this view, although no Senator may vote to convict a man she deems innocent, any Senator may vote to acquit a man she deems guilty.[37]

(e) *The Political context in which impeachment occurs.* Consider the fact that the Johnson impeachment occurred in the wake of the Civil War, the Nixon resignation during the height of the Cold War, and the Clinton impeachment after the Cold War. The Trump impeachment took place when the country was involved in decades-long military engagements in the Middle East. Note also the "dog that didn't bark"—the Iran Contra scandal of 1986-87, which did not lead to impeachment proceedings against Ronald Reagan, and which also occurred during the Cold War. To what extent do foreign policy and global military obligations of the United States affect the willingness of Congress to proceed against a sitting President? The Johnson impeachment seems to have been largely about the Republican Congress's desire to have its way on Reconstruction against a President bent on undermining that Reconstruction. (See the discussion of the procedural history of the Fourteenth Amendment in Chapter Four, *supra*). Is the failure of the Iran-Contra scandal to result in impeachment in part explained on the grounds that Democrats lacked the political will to attack a popular president during the height of the Cold War unless there was clear proof of the very gravest offenses? If so, what explains the proceedings against Nixon, which also occurred during the Cold War?

Trump's impeachment probably reflects a special set of political circumstances—both the Russian interference in the 2016 election and Trump's abundant personal flaws. Democrats (and even some Republicans) believed that Trump was a deeply corrupt individual who was unfit for office and should never have become president in the first place. His Administration was full of scandals, and he repeatedly sought to profit from his office shamelessly. Many Democrats probably hoped that Special Counsel Robert Mueller's investigation into Russian interference in the 2016 election would be his undoing. For multiple reasons, these hopes proved unavailing, and Trump adeptly used repeated accusations of a "witch hunt" against him to solidify his base of support.

---

37. Akhil Reed Amar, The People's Court, Legal Times, February 1, 1999.

Ironically, Trump's phone call to the President of Ukraine in July 2019 that precipitated the Ukraine Scandal occurred immediately after it became clear that the Mueller Report on Russian interference would *not* lead to his impeachment. Trump may have taken the conclusion of the Russia investigation as evidence that he was essentially beyond accountability for his actions. In a sense, Trump was proven right by the subsequent Senate trial. But this did not stop Democrats from impeaching him.

(f) *The effects of political polarization.* One of the most important element of the political context is the degree of partisan polarization in the country. Nixon was president during a relatively depolarized politics, and that made it possible for members of his party to threaten to abandon him. But Johnson, Clinton, and Trump held office when politics was polarized, and in Trump's case, hyper-polarized. Most Republican Senators who abandoned Trump would face serious political retribution, both in their home states and, equally important, from political donors. Senator Romney, who was the 2012 GOP nominee for President, was one of the few senators who could risk crossing the President.

When politics is strongly polarized, as it is today, there is almost no chance that a president can be removed through impeachment, as long as his or her party has more than one third of the votes in the Senate. If removal is not possible in a highly polarized politics, what purpose does impeachment serve?

4. *The Senate Trial.* Article I, section 3 states that "The Senate shall have the sole Power to try all Impeachments." Does the power to try include a duty to try? Suppose that the President's party has a majority in the Senate and the Senate leadership concludes that there is no chance that the President will be convicted. If the House impeaches, must the Senate hold a trial at all? Can the Senate hold a perfunctory trial leading to a quick vote of acquittal without hearing evidence? In this respect, is there anything wrong with Senate Majority Leader McConnell's decision to accelerate the trial, or the vote of Trump's fellow Republicans not to hear any witnesses?

When a president is not being tried, the Constitution specifies in Article I, section 3 that the presiding officer is the Vice President of the United States (who also serves as the president of the Senate.) In presidential impeachments, however, the Chief Justice of the United States, who plays no role in any other impeachment, must "preside" over the Senate trial. There are good structural reasons for this: the Framers excluded the Vice-President from a trial that could end with his winning the defendant's job. This mandatory recusal rule made even more sense at the Founding, when presidents did not handpick their vice presidents, who were more likely to be rivals than partners.

The Constitution specifies that the Chief Justice "shall" preside. Can the Chief Justice refuse, if he or she thinks that the trial is unfair and improper? Could the trial properly proceed without the presence of its constitutionally-prescribed presiding officer? Note that another reason for the chief's presence is also structural: It reminds the Senators that this inherently political trial must be scrupulously fair to the President in both reality and appearance. Not only the

American people, but other countries around the world will be watching this test of American democracy.

The role of the Chief Justice has profound implications for the proper ethical relations between senators and the President. Suppose a sudden illness were to require the chief to resign. Although the senior associate justice might presumably fill in temporarily,[38] at some point a new chief would need to be installed. According to Article II, section 2, the President would appoint, with the advice and consent of the Senate, a new chief. In other words, even in the middle of a trial, the judges and the judged might need to confer and collaborate to pick the permanent presiding officer!

This points up a unique feature of Presidential impeachments: the need for coordination between the two branches even as they are at loggerheads. The Senate and the President must work together to do the people's business. Vacant appointments must be filled, treaties considered, laws enacted, budgets approved, foreign policy—even war—conducted. (Note that as the House was considering impeachment of the President, President Clinton was launching airstrikes against terrorist camps halfway around the globe.) Even as senators sit as detached judges and jurors over a presidential defendant every afternoon (bound by an oath of impartiality as prescribed under Article I, section 3), they must as legislators work closely with the President every morning. This also suggests an important difference from impeachments of federal district judges. In these low-level impeachments, senators are more likely to shun all contact with the defendant, analogizing such meetings to "jury tampering."

5. Indictment and Conviction before Impeachment. Presidential and non-presidential impeachments also tend to differ because the latter class of officials can be and often are indicted and convicted before impeachments begin.[39] Presidential impeachments are different. First of all, as discussed below, it is doubtful that an indictable offense is required for impeachment and conviction of the President. Given his unique and awesome constitutional powers, the President can often inflict great harm on the nation without violating any specific

---

38. What, precisely, is the basis for this presumption? Pure pragmatism? A structural inference of sorts? The traditions of the Supreme Court, or the history of predecessor courts in England?

39. Indeed, in two of the three district judge impeachments during the 1980s, Senate trials occurred after the judges had been tried and convicted of statutory crimes in ordinary courts. Although the Constitution does not require this sequence, the Framers expected that it would often make sense for geographic reasons. District judges in the late eighteenth century would be scattered across the continent, as would the evidence of and witnesses to their wrongdoing. Congress, by contrast, would sit in the capital, weeks away from the most remote hinterlands. Given this geography, the Founders anticipated that the easiest venue to gather all the evidence and witnesses would often be in a trial held in the judge's home district. See Maria Simon, Note, Bribery and Other Not So "Good Behavior": Criminal Prosecution as a Supplement to Impeachment of Federal Judges, 94 Colum. L. Rev. 1617 (1999). After such a trial, the Senate's job in impeachment would be much easier—senators could simply take as given the facts duly found beyond reasonable doubt in an ordinary court following strict evidentiary rules and affording procedural rights and other safeguards to the defendant.

criminal statute. As a result, presidential impeachments are less likely to simply track ordinary prosecutions and may more often charge the chief executive with abuses of power beyond the criminal code.

Second, many commentators (and the Justice Department) hold that a sitting president may not be forced to stand trial in an ordinary criminal court. (See also the discussion following *Clinton v. Jones*, Chapter Six, pp. 1009-1012). In two Federalist Papers (Numbers 69 and 77), Hamilton suggested that an incumbent president must first be tried in the Senate; only after his removal (via conviction or resignation or the natural expiration of his term) would ordinary courts have a opportunity to prosecute him.[40] As noted in the discussion of *Clinton v. Jones*, there is a structural argument for the rule: A president represents the nation and may need to pursue sound national policies that will render him unpopular in certain localities—consider Lincoln's popularity in South Carolina in early

40. See The Federalist No. 69 ("The President . . . would be liable to be impeached, tried, and upon conviction . . . would afterwards be liable to prosecution and punishment in the ordinary course of law.") (emphasis added); Id. No. 77 (discussing presidential impeachment and "subsequent prosecution in the common course of law") (emphasis added). Note that Hamilton here was trying to reassure his readers that the President would not be overly powerful; if he in fact believed that a sitting President could be forced to stand trial in an ordinary criminal prosecution, he had a strong incentive to say so, but in fact he said the opposite. This impeachment-first rule has a strong bipartisan pedigree—affirmed two centuries ago by Senator (and later Chief Justice) Oliver Ellsworth, Vice President John Adams, and President Thomas Jefferson. See The Diary of William Maclay and Other Notes on Senate Debates 168 (Kenneth R. Bowling & Helen E. Veit eds., 1988) (reporting that Adams and Ellsworth argued that a sitting President could be impeached, but "no other process [w]hatever lay against him. . . . When he is no longer President, [y]ou can indict him."); 10 Works of Thomas Jefferson 404 (Paul L. Ford ed., 1905) (Letter to George Hay, June 20, 1807) ("The leading principle of our Constitution is the independence of the Legislature, executive, and judiciary of each other, and none are more jealous of this than the judiciary. But would the executive be independent of the judiciary, if he were subject to the commands of the latter, [and] to imprisonment for disobedience; if the several courts could bandy him from pillar to post, keep him constantly trudging from north to south [and] east to west.").

The point was reiterated during the Nixon impeachment crisis by then-Solicitor General Robert Bork on the right and Professor Charles Black on the left. See John Hart Ely, On Constitutional Ground 140-41 (1996) (detailing Robert Bork's argument that the President could not be indicted prior to being impeached.); Charles L. Black, Jr., Impeachment: A Handbook 40 (1974) ("[A]n incumbent president cannot be put on trial in the ordinary courts for ordinary crime, and if the crime he is charged with is not an impeachable offense, the simple and obvious solution would either be to indict him and delay trial until after his term has expired, or to delay indictment until after his term, with the statute of limitations tolled . . . until the president's term is over."). See also Alexander M. Bickel, the Constitutional Tangle, New Republic, October 6, 1973 (the "presidency cannot be conducted from jail, nor can it be effectively carried on while an incumbent is defending himself in a criminal trial"); Terry Eastland, The Power to Control Prosecution, 2 Nexus 43, 49 (1997) ("the President may be prosecuted, but . . . only to the extent he allows himself to be"); Stephen G. Calabresi, Caesarism, Departmentalism, and Professor Paulsen, 83 Minn. L. Rev. 1421 (1999) ("the President cannot be prosecuted until he has first been impeached and removed"). But see Ronald D. Rotunda, Can a President Plumbing the Constitutional Depths of *Clinton v. Jones* be Imprisoned?, Legal Times, July 21, 1997 ("*Clinton v. Jones* thus establishes that a sitting president may be [criminally] indicted and tried"). Compare the discussion in Chapter Six, *supra*, pointing out some ways in which Jones seems distinguishable.

1861. While in office, the President should not be obstructed by a grand or petit jury from any one locality, whether Charleston or Little Rock or the District of Columbia. The House and the Senate represent the entire nation, and therefore are the only grand and petit juries that a sitting president must answer to.

However, if the President is not subject to trial before impeachment, a Senate trial will (and did in Clinton's case) pose enormous complications concerning issues of evidentiary procedure and proof. The Senate will not be able to simply point to an earlier judicial proceeding that clearly established the relevant facts beyond reasonable doubt. Instead, the Senate is obliged to find the facts for itself. In Clinton's trial, the Senate elected not to hear live witnesses, but instead relied on the record compiled by the House (which drew heavily on the Independent Counsel's report) and videotapes and transcripts of depositions of three witnesses conducted by the House Managers in charge of the President's prosecution. In the Trump impeachment, the Senate did without witnesses entirely.

The Senate is not (unless it chooses to be) bound by federal rules of evidence, including the hearsay rules, which express (with many exceptions) a preference for live testimony subject to cross-examination. Why do you think the Senate did not choose to call witnesses in Clinton's case (and in particular live testimony of Monica Lewinsky, which would, presumably, involve discussions of her affair with President Clinton on national television)? Why do you think the Senate chose not to hear witnesses in the Trump impeachment? Does this confirm the inherently political nature of presidential impeachments?

By contrast, in the 1980's impeachments of judges the Senate delegated fact-gathering to a committee. Could the Senate do so constitutionally in the case of presidential impeachments? Would it be politically possible to do so even if it were constitutional? Consider whether the committee could meet outside of the presence of the Chief Justice, or whether, on the other hand, the Chief Justice could preside over such a "rump" Senate?

Acting as the jury in an impeachment trial, the Senate also exercises discretion. Even if it considers the President's crimes technically impeachable, it need not vote to convict unless it also thinks that the punishment—mandatory removal from office, under Article II, section 4—fits the crime. (Analogously, every criminal trial jury has the inherent power to acquit against the evidence if it deems punishment unjust.).

6. *Remedies upon Conviction by the Senate.* As you read Article II, can the Senate convict the President without removing him from office? Can the Senate pass a censure motion in lieu of conviction? Some Senators and Congressmen argued that because the Constitution says nothing about censure, a censure motion was unconstitutional. Why doesn't the fact that the Constitution says nothing about censure mean that nothing prohibits censure? (Note that Andrew Jackson was censured in 1834 by a Whig-controlled Senate for his opposition to the Second Bank, but when the Democrats came to power they removed the censure.).

7. *What are "High Crimes and Misdemeanors"?* The Constitution's language raises two complementary questions. First, are all violations of the criminal code committed by a President High Crimes and Misdemeanors under the meaning of

Article II, section 4? One of the central questions in the Clinton impeachment trial was whether perjury about his sexual affair with Monica Lewinsky was a "high Crime and Misdemeanor" under the meaning of Article II, section 4. One argument that it was not was that the President's perjury, although a crime, was not related to his official duties.[41]

Second, and conversely, must the President's conduct be a crime in order to be a High Crime and Misdemeanor under the meaning of the Constitution? In the Clinton impeachment, for example, the question would have been whether Clinton's behavior — concealing the affair, lying about it to the American people for months, and engaging in evasive maneuvers before Congress and a grand jury constituted impeachable offenses even if they do not technically constitute criminal offenses.

One of the key issues in the Trump impeachment was whether Trump's solicitation of Ukraine to announce an investigation of his likely opponent in the 2020 elections in return for military support and a White House meeting was an impeachable offense even if it was not criminal. (On the other hand, House Democrats regarded Trump's action as an attempted bribe, which is covered by the text of the Impeachment Clause. Their report also argued that the abuse of power count involved multiple federal criminal offenses, including wire fraud. And the G.A.O. report found that Trump's withholding of funding to Ukraine was unlawful.)

There are several ways of approaching these questions, corresponding to familiar modalities of constitutional argument.

a. Historical Arguments. The original understandings of the impeachment power are provocative but inconclusive. Several proposals at the Constitutional Convention attempted to limit the grounds for impeachment to neglect of duty or abuse of official power. One proposal argued for limiting the power to "treason or bribery." George Mason opposed this formula and proposed adding "maladministration" to the grounds for impeachment and removal. Madison in turn opposed Mason's amendment, arguing that "[so] vague a term will be equivalent to a tenure during the pleasure of the Senate."

Mason then withdrew his motion and moved to substitute the words "treason, bribery and other high crimes or misdemeanors against the State," which was accepted by the convention. This wording was later changed to "against the United States." Finally, the Committee of Style and Arrangement eliminated the words "against the United States" apparently on the grounds that these words were redundant.

What relevance, if any, should this history have in interpreting Article II, section 4?

---

41. A separate question is whether one should distinguish between perjury before a deposition in a civil matter and perjury before a grand jury convened by the Independent Counsel.

Consider the following arguments:

(a) Impeachable offenses must be offenses against the State similar to treason and bribery. Perjury, especially about matters unrelated to the President's duties is much less damaging to the State and hence is not impeachable. What about obstruction of justice?

(b) Impeachable offenses must be offenses against the State, and not merely crimes. Bribery is impeachable only because the President might trade secrets with the enemy or compromise the national interest for private gain. Crimes that are unrelated to the President's duties are not a crimes against the State and is therefore not impeachable.

How do we tell what is unrelated to the President's duties? Suppose the President commits a crime in order to be elected? For example, suppose that the President arranges for hush money payments to a former mistress to prevent embarrassing information coming out before the election, and the secret payments violate campaign finance law?

What if the President obstructs investigations into his or his employees' misconduct? Suppose that the President asks his associates to lie before Congress about whether the President was pursuing a real estate deal in Moscow during the presidential campaign? If a cover-up might allow a foreign power leverage over the President, should this be impeachable?

(c) The President is the chief law enforcement officer of the United States and therefore either perjury in official proceedings or obstruction of justice are offenses against the State because they fundamentally undermine confidence in his office and in the government of the United States. (If a President commits any crime to further his political objectives, to hinder his political enemies, or to avoid political embarrassment, should it be regarded as a high crime or misdemeanor?)

(d) Given the language of Article II, section 4, impeachable offenses need not be crimes, much less crimes against the State. A President who abuses his power, or who fundamentally disgraces his office — for example, by raping a person — can be impeached and removed. The question whether the matter is a "public" abuse of power or part of his "private" life is irrelevant.

(e) The question of what a "high Crime and Misdemeanor" consists in is fundamentally political. It is up to the American people, through their elected representatives, to determine when a President has so lost the confidence of the People that he can no longer remain in office.

b. Textual Arguments. The argument that not every crime is impeachable would seem to be bolstered by the following textual argument: Ordinary citizens can be tried and convicted for any crime, but the President may be impeached and removed only for "high" crime. This word must have limiting significance: In two other places in the Constitution (Article I, Section 6 and Article IV, Section 2), the Framers speak about treason and other crimes without using the word "high." This suggests that the adjective was added to the impeachment clause of Article II, Section 4 to make clear that not all crime is impeachable. This argument, however, does not mean that only crimes are impeachable: The word "misdemeanor" is easily read to mean misbehavior or misconduct generally, though it, too, must be "high" misconduct to warrant impeachment.

c. Precedental Arguments. Another approach to the question is to look for precedents in past practice. As noted earlier, in 1998, Bill Clinton was impeached on two counts: perjury and obstruction of justice.

In 1974, the House impeached Richard Nixon on three counts. The first count was obstruction of justice in the covering up and impeding the investigation of the Watergate burglary. The second count was abuse of power: that Nixon had "repeatedly engaged in conduct violating the constitutional rights of citizens, impairing the due and proper administration of justice and the conduct of lawful inquiries, or contravening the laws governing agencies of the executive branch and the purposes of these agencies." The third count was contempt of Congress, stating that Nixon "failed without lawful cause or excuse to produce papers and things as directed by duly authorized subpoenas issued by the Committee on the Judiciary of the House of Representatives on April 11, 1974, May 15, 1974, May 30, 1974, and June 24, 1974, and willfully disobeyed such subpoenas."

d. Precedental and Structural Arguments: Comparing presidents to other kinds of officers. Because there are so few precedents of presidential impeachments, one might look to precedents concerning the impeachments of other officers, including federal judges. However, because these offices have different functions, the precedents may not apply to presidential impeachments. As a result, precedental arguments about the meaning of "high Crimes and Misdemeanors" cannot be easily extricated from structural arguments. (And, as we shall see, each also relies on a series of textual arguments). Hence we consider them together.

Here is an example: During the impeachment proceedings against Richard Nixon, the House Impeachment Committee considered and rejected an article that accused Nixon of backdating his tax returns in order to take advantage of more favorable tax laws. That might suggest that perjury for private gain is not an impeachable offense. On the other hand, during the 1980's two federal judges, Walter Nixon (no relation to Richard) and Alcee Hastings, were impeached and removed for perjury.

One can make a textual argument that high crimes and misdemeanors for presidents and judges should be the same: Article II, section 4 states that "[t]he President, Vice President and all civil officers of the United States, shall be removed from Office on Impeachment for, and Conviction of, Treason, Bribery, or other high Crimes and Misdemeanors." Because Article II, section 4 lumps together presidential impeachments with all others (vice presidents, judges, justices, Cabinet officers, inferior officers) and uses the same linguistic standard (high crimes), the test is the same.

But one can argue in the opposite direction, too: According to Article II, section 2, "by and with the Advice and Consent of the Senate, [the President] shall appoint Ambassadors, other public Ministers and Consuls, Judges of the Supreme Court, and . . . other Officers of the United States." Senators usually

give Presidents much more leeway in executive and ambassadorial appointments than judicial appointments, even though the text of the appointments
clause is the same for both. If the Senate's Advise and Consent power is different
depending on the nature of the office, why not the meaning of High Crimes and
Misdemeanors?[42]

Akhil Amar argues that, quite apart from text, there are good structural
grounds for treating presidents and judges differently: "When senators remove
one of 1,000 federal judges (or even one of nine justices), they are not transform-
ing an entire branch of government. . . . Presidential impeachments involve high
statecraft and international affairs—the entire world is watching—in a manner
wholly unlike other impeachments. Most important, when senators oust a judge,
they undo their own prior vote (via advice and consent to judicial nominees).
When they remove a duly elected president, they undo the votes of millions of
ordinary Americans on Election Day. This is not something that senators should
do lightly, lest we slide toward a kind of parliamentary government that our
entire structure of government was designed to repudiate."[43]

For a similar effort to ponder post-Founding presidential precedents, see Cass
R. Sunstein, Impeaching the President, 147 U. Pa. L. Rev. 279 (1998). Sunstein
concludes that "historical practice suggests a broader congressional power to
impeach judges than presidents, and indeed, it suggests a special congressional
reluctance to proceed against the President."[44]

42. Consider Laurence Tribe's response to this textual argument:

[A]lthough the Appointments Clause calls in the same words for the Senate's advice and consent regardless of the office involved, that clause says nothing about what standard the Senate
is to employ in giving or withholding its consent in any particular category of appointments,
and might best be read as agnostic on the question whether that standard is the dependent
on the office to which an appointment has been made or is instead to be office-independent.
The Impeachment Clause, in contrast, purports to specify the standard for impeachment and
removal and seemingly does so in the same terms—"high Crimes and Misdemeanors"—for
judges and presidents alike.

1 Laurence H. Tribe, American Constitutional Law 165-69 & n.57 (3rd ed. 1999).
43. Amar, Trial and Tribulation, The New Republic, January 18, 1999. See also Tribe, *supra*:

[Even though Article II section 4 defines impeachable offenses for all federal officers], the
Constitution nowhere mandates that the *definition* of a high crime be independent of the
nature of the office from which it is proposed that someone be removed—independent for
example, . . . of the mode of the office's selection (whether by the people in a national election, for example, or by the President with the concurrence of the Senate). . . . [A judge may
well be] removable for conduct that would not warrant removal of a president, particularly
since Senate removal of a judge entails reversing the Senate's own action in confirming the
judge whereas Senate removal of a president entails reversing an action of the entire national
electorate.

44. With Amar and Sunstein, compare John O. McGinnis, Impeachment: The Structural
Understanding, 67 Geo. Wash. L. Rev. 650, 660 (1999) (pointing to certain antipopulist features
of the original Constitution, and rejecting the argument that the "legal standard for impeaching a

8. Must the Senate remove a President who has committed a High Crime and Misdemeanor? Finally, assume that two-thirds of the Senators (or more) are convinced that the President has committed a high crime and misdemeanor. Must the Senate remove him from office, or does the Senate's decision also depend on larger political considerations? Consider the following structural argument:

[S]enators must . . . decide whether a given perjury warrants removal as a matter of sound judgment and statesmanship. In making this decision, they must be sensitive to the ways in which the presidency is a very different office from a federal district judgeship. Where extremely "high crimes" are implicated—treason or tyranny—senators should probably be quicker to pull the trigger on a bad president, whose office enables him unilaterally to do many dangerous things. (A single bad judge, by contrast, is hemmed in by colleagues and higher courts.) But where borderline or low "high crimes" are involved, the Senate would be wise to spare the people's president—especially if his crimes reflect character flaws that the people duly considered before voting for him, or if the people continue to support him even after the facts come to light.

[Consider] Andrew Jackson, who killed a man in a duel before he was elected president. Technically, this was a crime, although it was rarely prosecuted in Jackson's day. Should Congress have impeached and removed Jackson even if the people who elected him knew about his crime and voted for him anyway? The duel Jackson fought concerned his wife's honor and chastity. Suppose Jackson had lied under oath to protect his wife's honor. Again, suppose the people knew all this when they voted for him. Should Congress have undone the people's votes on a theory that all crime is high crime, and that all perjury is the same?

Now consider the next presidential Andrew—Johnson, that is. Given our structural analysis, it seems relevant that Johnson was never elected president in his own right and that he was in fact working to undo the policies of the man the people did elect, Abraham Lincoln. If ever our structural argument cautioning restraint in ousting an elected president were weak, it was here, since Johnson lacked a genuine electoral mandate. And his policies toward unrepentant rebels could have been viewed as akin to treason, giving aid and comfort to men who were—not to mince words—traitors. And yet even here—an unelected president cozying up to actual traitors—the Senate acquitted.

Finally, consider President Nixon, whose extremely "high crimes" and gross abuses of official power posed a threat to our basic constitutional system. Although Nixon was elected by the people, his own unprecedented use of political espionage and sabotage tainted his mandate, in the same way that bribing electors would have. When all the facts were brought to light and the tapes came out, the people did indeed turn against him, prompting leaders of both parties to conclude that the time had come for him to go.[45]

President should be higher than the legal standard for impeaching a judge because the President has been elected by the people whereas a judge has been appointed. . . . Indeed, important considerations of constitutional structure might well suggest the opposite conclusion, that we should be more loathe to retain a President in office who has breached the public trust than any other official, including a judge.").

45. Amar, *supra.*

How should this analysis apply to President Trump? Trump's lying, immorality, and unethical business practices were well known before he was elected. Trump lost the popular vote, and has been one of the more unpopular presidents in modern history. However, he has a devoted base of supporters, and his party has a majority in the Senate. Is his situation most like Jackson's, Johnson's, Nixon's, or none of the above?

Chapter 7

Race and the Equal Protection Clause

Insert at the end of p. 1247:

TRUMP v. HAWAII
138 S.Ct. 2392 (2018)

[During the 2016 Presidential campaign, Donald Trump ran on a platform of restricting illegal immigration, deporting undocumented aliens, and preventing the United States from being invaded by radical Islamists. He strongly opposed receiving refugees from Syria fleeing that country's civil war. On December 7, 2015, following a mass shooting in San Bernadino, California, candidate Trump gave a speech in which he called for "a total and complete shutdown of Muslims entering the United States until our country's representatives can figure out what is going on." The proposal for what became known as a "Muslim ban" was posted on Trump's campaign website until March 2017. During the 2016 campaign Trump and his surrogates alternatively described the proposal as a ban on people coming from countries known to produce terrorism, along with a call for "extreme vetting" of people entering the United States.

Shortly after taking office, President Trump signed Executive Order No. 13769, Protecting the Nation From Foreign Terrorist Entry Into the United States. 82 Fed. Reg. 8977 (2017) (EO-1). EO-1 directed the Secretary of Homeland Security to conduct a review to examine the adequacy of information provided by foreign governments about their nationals seeking to enter the United States. Pending that review, the order suspended for 90 days the entry of foreign nationals from seven countries — Iran, Iraq, Libya, Somalia, Sudan, Syria, and Yemen — that had been previously identified by Congress or prior administrations as posing heightened terrorism risks. EO-1 also modified refugee policy. It suspended the United States Refugee Admissions Program (USRAP) for 120 days and reduced the number of refugees eligible to be admitted to the United States during fiscal year 2017 from 110,000 to 50,000. The refugee provisions were not at issue in the litigation before the Supreme Court.

EO-1 created enormous confusion at airports around the United States, in part because it was not immediately clear — even to federal officials — whether the order applied to permanent residents of the United States (green card holders) who were also nationals of the seven countries. On January 28, protests against the order began around the country and at various airports. A week after EO-1 was issued, a Federal District Court in Washington state entered a nationwide temporary restraining order enjoining enforcement of several of its key provisions. Six days later, the Ninth Circuit denied the Government's emergency motion to stay the order pending appeal. Washington v. Trump, 847 F.3d 1151 (2017) (*per curiam*).

In response, the President revoked EO-1, replacing it with Executive Order No. 13780 (EO-2), which again directed a worldwide review. EO-2 also temporarily restricted the entry (with case-by-case waivers) of foreign nationals from six of the countries covered by EO-1: Iran, Libya, Somalia, Sudan, Syria, and Yemen, eliminating Iraq. The order explained that those countries had been selected because each "is a state sponsor of terrorism, has been significantly compromised by terrorist organizations, or contains active conflict zones." The entry restriction was to stay in effect for 90 days, pending completion of the worldwide review.

EO-2 was immediately challenged in court, and district courts in Maryland and Hawaii issued nationwide preliminary injunctions barring enforcement of the entry suspension; the Fourth and Ninth circuits affirmed. The Supreme Court granted certiorari, staying the injunctions — allowing the entry suspension to go into effect — with respect to foreign nationals who lacked a "credible claim of a bona fide relationship" with a person or entity in the United States. However, the temporary restrictions in EO-2 expired before a decision on the merits, and so the Supreme Court vacated the lower court decisions as moot.

Shortly thereafter, President Trump issued a third executive order, Proclamation No. 9645, Enhancing Vetting Capabilities and Processes for Detecting Attempted Entry Into the United States by Terrorists or Other Public–Safety Threats, which was immediately challenged in court.

Plaintiffs — the State of Hawaii, three individuals with foreign relatives affected by the entry suspension, and the Muslim Association of Hawaii — argued that the Proclamation violated the Immigration and Nationality Act (INA) and the Establishment Clause.]

CHIEF JUSTICE ROBERTS delivered the opinion of the Court.

I

The Proclamation (as its title indicates) sought to improve vetting procedures [for foreign nationals traveling to the United States] by identifying ongoing deficiencies in the information needed to assess whether nationals of particular countries present "public safety threats." § 1(a). To further that purpose, the Proclamation placed entry restrictions on the nationals of eight foreign states whose systems for managing and sharing information about their nationals the President deemed inadequate.

The Proclamation described how foreign states were selected for inclusion based on the review undertaken pursuant to EO-2. [T]he Department of Homeland Security (DHS), in consultation with the State Department and several intelligence agencies, developed [an informational and risk assessment] "baseline" for . . . foreign governments. . . . DHS collected and evaluated data regarding all foreign governments [identifying] countries [that had or risked] having deficient information-sharing practices and [that] present[ed] national security concerns. The State Department then undertook diplomatic efforts over a 50-day period to encourage all foreign governments to improve their practices.

Following the 50-day period, the Acting Secretary of Homeland Security concluded that eight countries—Chad, Iran, Iraq, Libya, North Korea, Syria, Venezuela, and Yemen—remained deficient in terms of their risk profile and willingness to provide requested information. The Acting Secretary recommended that the President impose entry restrictions on certain nationals from all of those countries except Iraq [because the United States was working with Iraq to combat ISIS]. She also [recommended including] Somalia [because it had a] "significant terrorist presence."

After consulting with multiple Cabinet members and other officials, the President adopted the Acting Secretary's recommendations and issued the Proclamation. Invoking his authority under 8 U.S.C. §§ 1182(f) and 1185(a), the President determined that certain entry restrictions were necessary to "prevent the entry of those foreign nationals about whom the United States Government lacks sufficient information"; "elicit improved identity management and information-sharing protocols and practices from foreign governments"; and otherwise "advance [the] foreign policy, national security, and counterterrorism objectives" of the United States. . . .

The Proclamation imposed a range of restrictions that vary based on the "distinct circumstances" in each of the eight countries. . . . [It] exempts lawful permanent residents and foreign nationals who have been granted asylum. It also provides for case-by-case waivers when a foreign national demonstrates undue hardship, and that his entry is in the national interest and would not pose a threat to public safety. § 3(c)(i); see also § 3(c)(iv) (listing examples of when a waiver might be appropriate, such as if the foreign national seeks to reside with a close family member, obtain urgent medical care, or pursue significant business obligations). The Proclamation further directs DHS to assess on a continuing basis whether entry restrictions should be modified or continued, and to report to the President every 180 days. Upon completion of the first such review period, the President, on the recommendation of the Secretary of Homeland Security, determined that Chad had sufficiently improved its practices, and he accordingly lifted restrictions on its nationals. . . .

III

. . . Congress has . . . delegated to the President authority to suspend or restrict the entry of aliens in certain circumstances. The principal source of that authority, . . . § 1182(f), states: "Whenever the President finds that the entry of any aliens or of any class of aliens into the United States would be detrimental to the interests of the United States, he may by proclamation, and for such period as he shall deem necessary, suspend the entry of all aliens or any class of aliens as immigrants or nonimmigrants, or impose on the entry of aliens any restrictions he may deem to be appropriate."

By its terms, § 1182(f) exudes deference to the President in every clause. It entrusts to the President the decisions whether and when to suspend entry . . . ; whose entry to suspend . . . ; for how long . . . ; and on what conditions. . . . The Proclamation falls well within this comprehensive delegation. The sole prerequisite set forth in § 1182(f) is that the President "find[]" that the entry of the covered aliens "would be detrimental to the interests of the United States." The President has undoubtedly fulfilled that requirement here. He first ordered DHS and other agencies to conduct a comprehensive evaluation of every single country's compliance with the information and risk assessment baseline. The President then issued a Proclamation setting forth extensive findings describing how deficiencies in the practices of select foreign governments — several of which are state sponsors of terrorism — deprive the Government of "sufficient information to assess the risks [those countries' nationals] pose to the United States." Based on that review, the President found that it was in the national interest to restrict entry of aliens who could not be vetted with adequate information — both to protect national security and public safety, and to induce improvement by their home countries. . . .

Plaintiffs . . . argue . . . that the Proclamation fails to provide a persuasive rationale for why nationality alone renders the covered foreign nationals a security risk. And they further discount the President's stated concern about deficient vetting because the Proclamation allows many aliens from the designated countries to enter on nonimmigrant visas.

Such arguments [assume] that § 1182(f) not only requires the President to *make* a finding that entry "would be detrimental to the interests of the United States," but also to explain that finding with sufficient detail to enable judicial review. That premise is questionable. But even assuming that some form of review is appropriate, plaintiffs' attacks on the sufficiency of the President's findings cannot be sustained. The 12-page Proclamation — which thoroughly describes the process, agency evaluations, and recommendations underlying the President's chosen restrictions — is more detailed than any prior order a President has issued under § 1182(f). Moreover, plaintiffs' request for a searching inquiry into the persuasiveness of the President's justifications is inconsistent with the broad statutory text and the deference traditionally accorded the President in this sphere. "Whether the President's chosen method" of addressing perceived risks is justified from a policy perspective is "irrelevant to the scope of his [§ 1182(f)] authority." *Sale v. Haitian Centers Council, Inc.,* 509 U.S. 155, 187-188 (1993). And when the President adopts "a preventive measure . . . in the context of international affairs and national security," he is "not required to conclusively link all of the pieces in the puzzle before [courts] grant weight to [his] empirical conclusions." *Holder v. Humanitarian Law Project,* 561 U.S. 1, 35 (2010).

The Proclamation also comports with the remaining textual limits in § 1182(f). We agree with plaintiffs that the word "suspend" often connotes a "defer[ral] till later." But that does not mean that the President is required to prescribe in advance a fixed end date for the entry restrictions. . . . Like its predecessors, the Proclamation makes clear that its "conditional restrictions" will remain in force only so long as necessary to "address" the identified "inadequacies and risks" within the covered nations. To that end, the Proclamation establishes an ongoing process to engage covered nations and assess every 180 days whether the entry restrictions should be modified or terminated. Indeed, after the initial review period, the President determined that Chad had made sufficient improvements to its identity-management protocols, and he accordingly lifted the entry suspension on its nationals.

. . . We may assume that § 1182(f) does not allow the President to expressly override particular provisions of the INA. But plaintiffs have not identified any conflict between the statute and the Proclamation that would implicitly bar the President from addressing deficiencies in the Nation's vetting system.

To the contrary, the Proclamation supports Congress's individualized approach for determining admissibility. The INA sets forth various inadmissibility grounds based on connections to terrorism and criminal history, but those provisions can only work when the consular officer has sufficient (and sufficiently reliable) information to make that determination. The Proclamation promotes the effectiveness of the vetting process by helping to ensure the availability of such information. . . . Nor is there a conflict between the Proclamation and the Visa Waiver Program [which] allows travel without a visa for short-term visitors from 38 countries that have entered into a "rigorous security partnership" with the United States. Congress's decision to authorize a benefit for "many of America's closest allies," did not implicitly foreclose the Executive from imposing tighter restrictions on nationals of certain high-risk countries. . . . Fairly read, [§ 1182(f)] vests authority in the President to impose additional limitations on entry beyond the grounds for exclusion set forth in the INA—including in response to circumstances that might affect the vetting system or other "interests of the United States." . . . [Moreover,] Presidents have repeatedly suspended entry not because the covered nationals themselves engaged in harmful acts but instead to retaliate for conduct by their governments that conflicted with U.S. foreign policy interests. . . .

Plaintiffs' final statutory argument is that the President's entry suspension violates § 1152(a)(1)(A), which provides that "no person shall . . . be discriminated against in the issuance of an immigrant visa because of the person's race, sex, nationality, place of birth, or place of residence." . . . [T]his argument challenges only the validity of the entry restrictions on *immigrant* travel. . . . [P]laintiffs' reading would not affect any of the limitations on nonimmigrant travel in the Proclamation.

In any event, we reject plaintiffs' interpretation because it ignores the basic distinction between admissibility determinations and visa issuance that runs throughout the INA. Section 1182 defines the pool of individuals who are admissible to the United States. [For example,] any alien who is inadmissible under § 1182 (based on, for example, health risks, criminal history, or foreign policy consequences) is screened out as "ineligible to receive a visa." . . . Once § 1182

sets the boundaries of admissibility into the United States, § 1152(a)(1)(A) prohibits discrimination in the allocation of immigrant visas based on nationality
and other traits. . . . Had Congress instead intended in § 1152(a)(1)(A) to constrain the President's power to determine who may enter the country, it could easily have chosen language directed to that end. . . . Common sense and historical
practice confirm [that] [§]1152(a)(1)(A) has never been treated as a constraint on
the criteria for admissibility in § 1182. Presidents have repeatedly exercised their
authority to suspend entry on the basis of nationality. . . . President Reagan relied
on § 1182(f) to suspend entry "as immigrants by all Cuban nationals," subject to
exceptions. Likewise, President Carter invoked § 1185(a)(1) to deny and revoke
visas to all Iranian nationals.

On plaintiffs' reading, those orders were beyond the President's authority.
The entry restrictions in the Proclamation on North Korea (which plaintiffs do
not challenge in this litigation) would also be unlawful. Nor would the President
be permitted to suspend entry from particular foreign states in response to an epidemic confined to a single region, or a verified terrorist threat involving nationals of a specific foreign nation, or even if the United States were on the brink of
war. . . .

IV

We now turn to plaintiffs' claim that the Proclamation was issued for the
unconstitutional purpose of excluding Muslims. . . . [T]he individual plaintiffs
have Article III standing to challenge the exclusion of their relatives under the
Establishment Clause.

[O]ur cases recognize that "[t]he clearest command of the Establishment
Clause is that one religious denomination cannot be officially preferred over
another." *Larson v. Valente,* 456 U.S. 228, 244 (1982). Plaintiffs believe that the
Proclamation violates this prohibition by singling out Muslims for disfavored
treatment. The entry suspension, they contend, operates as a "religious gerrymander," in part because most of the countries covered by the Proclamation have
Muslim-majority populations. . . . [P]laintiffs allege that the primary purpose of
the Proclamation was religious animus and that the President's stated concerns
about vetting protocols and national security were but pretexts for discriminating
against Muslims.

At the heart of plaintiffs' case is a series of statements by the President and his
advisers casting doubt on the official objective of the Proclamation. For example,
while a candidate on the campaign trail, the President published a "Statement on
Preventing Muslim Immigration" that called for a "total and complete shutdown
of Muslims entering the United States until our country's representatives can
figure out what is going on." That statement remained on his campaign website
until May 2017. Then-candidate Trump also stated that "Islam hates us" and
asserted that the United States was "having problems with Muslims coming into
the country." Shortly after being elected, when asked whether violence in Europe
had affected his plans to "ban Muslim immigration," the President replied, "You
know my plans. All along, I've been proven to be right."

One week after his inauguration, the President issued EO-1. In a television interview, one of the President's campaign advisers explained that when the President "first announced it, he said, 'Muslim ban.' He called me up. He said, 'Put a commission together. Show me the right way to do it legally.'" The adviser said he assembled a group of Members of Congress and lawyers that "focused on, instead of religion, danger. . . . [The order] is based on places where there [is] substantial evidence that people are sending terrorists into our country."

Plaintiffs also note that after issuing EO-2 to replace EO-1, the President expressed regret that his prior order had been "watered down" and called for a "much tougher version" of his "Travel Ban." Shortly before the release of the Proclamation, he stated that the "travel ban . . . should be far larger, tougher, and more specific," but "stupidly that would not be politically correct." More recently, on November 29, 2017, the President retweeted links to three anti-Muslim propaganda videos. In response to questions about those videos, the President's deputy press secretary denied that the President thinks Muslims are a threat to the United States, explaining that "the President has been talking about these security issues for years now, from the campaign trail to the White House" and "has addressed these issues with the travel order that he issued earlier this year and the companion proclamation."

The President of the United States possesses an extraordinary power to speak to his fellow citizens and on their behalf. Our Presidents have frequently used that power to espouse the principles of religious freedom and tolerance on which this Nation was founded. In 1790 George Washington reassured the Hebrew Congregation of Newport, Rhode Island that "happily the Government of the United States . . . gives to bigotry no sanction, to persecution no assistance [and] requires only that they who live under its protection should demean themselves as good citizens." President Eisenhower, at the opening of the Islamic Center of Washington, similarly pledged to a Muslim audience that "America would fight with her whole strength for your right to have here your own church," declaring that "[t]his concept is indeed a part of America." And just days after the attacks of September 11, 2001, President George W. Bush returned to the same Islamic Center to implore his fellow Americans—Muslims and non-Muslims alike—to remember during their time of grief that "[t]he face of terror is not the true faith of Islam," and that America is "a great country because we share the same values of respect and dignity and human worth." Yet it cannot be denied that the Federal Government and the Presidents who have carried its laws into effect have—from the Nation's earliest days—performed unevenly in living up to those inspiring words.

Plaintiffs argue that this President's words strike at fundamental standards of respect and tolerance, in violation of our constitutional tradition. But the issue before us is not whether to denounce the statements. It is instead the significance of those statements in reviewing a Presidential directive, neutral on its face, addressing a matter within the core of executive responsibility. In doing so, we must consider not only the statements of a particular President, but also the authority of the Presidency itself.

The case before us differs in numerous respects from the conventional Establishment Clause claim. Unlike the typical suit involving religious displays or school prayer, plaintiffs seek to invalidate a national security directive regulating the entry of aliens abroad. Their claim accordingly raises a number of delicate issues regarding the scope of the constitutional right and the manner of proof. The Proclamation, moreover, is facially neutral toward religion. Plaintiffs therefore ask the Court to probe the sincerity of the stated justifications for the policy by reference to extrinsic statements—many of which were made before the President took the oath of office. These various aspects of plaintiffs' challenge inform our standard of review.

For more than a century, this Court has recognized that the admission and exclusion of foreign nationals is a "fundamental sovereign attribute exercised by the Government's political departments largely immune from judicial control." *Fiallo v. Bell,* 430 U.S. 787 (1977); see *Harisiades v. Shaughnessy,* 342 U.S. 580, 588–589 (1952) ("[A]ny policy toward aliens is vitally and intricately interwoven with contemporaneous policies in regard to the conduct of foreign relations [and] the war power."). Because decisions in these matters may implicate "relations with foreign powers," or involve "classifications defined in the light of changing political and economic circumstances," such judgments "are frequently of a character more appropriate to either the Legislature or the Executive." *Mathews v. Diaz,* 426 U.S. 67, 81 (1976).

Nonetheless, although foreign nationals seeking admission have no constitutional right to entry, this Court has engaged in a circumscribed judicial inquiry when the denial of a visa allegedly burdens the constitutional rights of a U.S. citizen. In *Kleindienst v. Mandel,* 408 U.S. 753 (1972), the Attorney General denied admission to a Belgian journalist and self-described "revolutionary Marxist," Ernest Mandel, who had been invited to speak at a conference at Stanford University. The professors who wished to hear Mandel speak challenged that decision under the First Amendment, and we acknowledged that their constitutional "right to receive information" was implicated. But we limited our review to whether the Executive gave a "facially legitimate and bona fide" reason for its action. Given the authority of the political branches over admission, we held that "when the Executive exercises this [delegated] power negatively on the basis of a facially legitimate and bona fide reason, the courts will neither look behind the exercise of that discretion, nor test it by balancing its justification" against the asserted constitutional interests of U.S. citizens.

The principal dissent [by Justice Sotomayor] suggests that *Mandel* has no bearing on this case, but our opinions have reaffirmed and applied its deferential standard of review across different contexts and constitutional claims. In *Din,* Justice Kennedy reiterated that "respect for the political branches' broad power over the creation and administration of the immigration system" meant that the Government need provide only a statutory citation to explain a visa denial. Likewise in *Fiallo,* we applied *Mandel* to a "broad congressional policy" giving immigration preferences to mothers of illegitimate children. Even though the statute created a "categorical" entry classification that discriminated on the basis of sex and legitimacy, the Court concluded that "it is not the judicial role in cases of this sort to probe and test the justifications" of immigration policies. . . .

Mandel's narrow standard of review "has particular force" in admission and immigration cases that overlap with "the area of national security." For one, "[j]udicial inquiry into the national-security realm raises concerns for the separation of powers" by intruding on the President's constitutional responsibilities in the area of foreign affairs. *Ziglar v. Abbasi*, 582 U.S. _____ (2017). For another, "when it comes to collecting evidence and drawing inferences" on questions of national security, "the lack of competence on the part of the courts is marked." *Humanitarian Law Project*.

The upshot of our cases in this context is clear: "Any rule of constitutional law that would inhibit the flexibility" of the President "to respond to changing world conditions should be adopted only with the greatest caution," and our inquiry into matters of entry and national security is highly constrained. *Mathews*. We need not define the precise contours of that inquiry in this case. A conventional application of *Mandel*, asking only whether the policy is facially legitimate and bona fide, would put an end to our review. But the Government has suggested that it may be appropriate here for the inquiry to extend beyond the facial neutrality of the order. For our purposes today, we assume that we may look behind the face of the Proclamation to the extent of applying rational basis review. That standard of review considers whether the entry policy is plausibly related to the Government's stated objective to protect the country and improve vetting processes. See *Railroad Retirement Bd. v. Fritz*, 449 U.S. 166, 179 (1980). As a result, we may consider plaintiffs' extrinsic evidence, but will uphold the policy so long as it can reasonably be understood to result from a justification independent of unconstitutional grounds.

The dissent finds "perplexing" the application of rational basis review in this context. But what is far more problematic is the dissent's assumption that courts should review immigration policies, diplomatic sanctions, and military actions under the *de novo* "reasonable observer" inquiry applicable to cases involving holiday displays and graduation ceremonies. [A] circumscribed inquiry applies to any constitutional claim concerning the entry of foreign nationals. The dissent can cite no authority for its proposition that the more free-ranging inquiry it proposes is appropriate in the national security and foreign affairs context. [relocated footnote — eds.]

Given the standard of review, it should come as no surprise that the Court hardly ever strikes down a policy as illegitimate under rational basis scrutiny. On the few occasions where we have done so, a common thread has been that the laws at issue lack any purpose other than a "bare . . . desire to harm a politically unpopular group." *Department of Agriculture v. Moreno*, 413 U.S. 528, 534 (1973). In one case, we invalidated a local zoning ordinance that required a special permit for group homes for the intellectually disabled, but not for other facilities such as fraternity houses or hospitals. We did so on the ground that the city's stated concerns about (among other things) "legal responsibility" and "crowded conditions" rested on "an irrational prejudice" against the intellectually disabled. *Cleburne v. Cleburne Living Center, Inc.*, 473 U.S. 432, 448-450

(1985). And in another case, this Court overturned a state constitutional amendment that denied gays and lesbians access to the protection of antidiscrimination laws. The amendment, we held, was "divorced from any factual context from which we could discern a relationship to legitimate state interests," and "its sheer breadth [was] so discontinuous with the reasons offered for it" that the initiative seemed "inexplicable by anything but animus." *Romer v. Evans,* 517 U.S. 620, 632, 635 (1996).

The Proclamation does not fit this pattern. It cannot be said that it is impossible to "discern a relationship to legitimate state interests" or that the policy is "inexplicable by anything but animus." Indeed, the dissent can only attempt to argue otherwise by refusing to apply anything resembling rational basis review. But because there is persuasive evidence that the entry suspension has a legitimate grounding in national security concerns, quite apart from any religious hostility, we must accept that independent justification.

The Proclamation is expressly premised on legitimate purposes: preventing entry of nationals who cannot be adequately vetted and inducing other nations to improve their practices. The text says nothing about religion. Plaintiffs and the dissent nonetheless emphasize that five of the seven nations currently included in the Proclamation have Muslim-majority populations. Yet that fact alone does not support an inference of religious hostility, given that the policy covers just 8% of the world's Muslim population and is limited to countries that were previously designated by Congress or prior administrations as posing national security risks.

The Proclamation, moreover, reflects the results of a worldwide review process undertaken by multiple Cabinet officials and their agencies. Plaintiffs seek to discredit the findings of the review, pointing to deviations from the review's baseline criteria resulting in the inclusion of Somalia and omission of Iraq. But as the Proclamation explains, in each case the determinations were justified by the distinct conditions in each country. . . . The dissent likewise doubts the thoroughness of the multi-agency review because a recent Freedom of Information Act request shows that the final DHS report "was a mere 17 pages." Yet a simple page count offers little insight into the actual substance of the final report, much less pre-decisional materials underlying it.

More fundamentally, plaintiffs and the dissent challenge the entry suspension based on their perception of its effectiveness and wisdom. They suggest that the policy is overbroad and does little to serve national security interests. But we cannot substitute our own assessment for the Executive's predictive judgments on such matters, all of which "are delicate, complex, and involve large elements of prophecy." While we of course "do not defer to the Government's reading of the First Amendment," the Executive's evaluation of the underlying facts is entitled to appropriate weight, particularly in the context of litigation involving "sensitive and weighty interests of national security and foreign affairs." *Humanitarian Law Project.*

Three additional features of the entry policy support the Government's claim of a legitimate national security interest. First, since the President introduced entry restrictions in January 2017, three Muslim-majority countries — Iraq, Sudan, and Chad — have been removed from the list of covered countries. . . . Second, for those countries that remain subject to entry restrictions, the Proclamation includes significant exceptions for various categories of foreign nationals. The policy permits nationals from nearly every covered country to travel to the United States on a variety of nonimmigrant visas. . . . These carveouts for nonimmigrant visas are substantial: Over the last three fiscal years — before the Proclamation was in effect — the majority of visas issued to nationals from the covered countries were nonimmigrant visas. The Proclamation also exempts permanent residents and individuals who have been granted asylum. Third, the Proclamation creates a waiver program open to all covered foreign nationals seeking entry as immigrants or nonimmigrants. According to the Proclamation, consular officers are to consider in each admissibility determination whether the alien demonstrates that (1) denying entry would cause undue hardship; (2) entry would not pose a threat to public safety; and (3) entry would be in the interest of the United States. . . .

Finally, the dissent invokes *Korematsu v. United States,* 323 U.S. 214 (1944). Whatever rhetorical advantage the dissent may see in doing so, *Korematsu* has nothing to do with this case. The forcible relocation of U.S. citizens to concentration camps, solely and explicitly on the basis of race, is objectively unlawful and outside the scope of Presidential authority. But it is wholly inapt to liken that morally repugnant order to a facially neutral policy denying certain foreign nationals the privilege of admission. The entry suspension is an act that is well within executive authority and could have been taken by any other President — the only question is evaluating the actions of this particular President in promulgating an otherwise valid Proclamation.

The dissent's reference to *Korematsu,* however, affords this Court the opportunity to make express what is already obvious: *Korematsu* was gravely wrong the day it was decided, has been overruled in the court of history, and — to be clear — "has no place in law under the Constitution."

Under these circumstances, the Government has set forth a sufficient national security justification to survive rational basis review. We express no view on the soundness of the policy. We simply hold today that plaintiffs have not demonstrated a likelihood of success on the merits of their constitutional claim.

V

Because plaintiffs have not shown that they are likely to succeed on the merits of their claims, we reverse the grant of the preliminary injunction as an abuse of discretion. The case now returns to the lower courts for such further proceedings as may be appropriate. Our disposition of the case makes it unnecessary to consider the propriety of the nationwide scope of the injunction issued by the District Court.

The judgment of the Court of Appeals is reversed, and the case is remanded for further proceedings consistent with this opinion.

It is so ordered.

Justice KENNEDY, concurring.

I join the Court's opinion in full.

There may be some common ground between the opinions in this case, in that the Court does acknowledge that in some instances, governmental action may be subject to judicial review to determine whether or not it is "inexplicable by anything but animus," *Romer v. Evans*, which in this case would be animosity to a religion. Whether judicial proceedings may properly continue in this case, in light of the substantial deference that is and must be accorded to the Executive in the conduct of foreign affairs, and in light of today's decision, is a matter to be addressed in the first instance on remand. And even if further proceedings are permitted, it would be necessary to determine that any discovery and other preliminary matters would not themselves intrude on the foreign affairs power of the Executive.

In all events, it is appropriate to make this further observation. There are numerous instances in which the statements and actions of Government officials are not subject to judicial scrutiny or intervention. That does not mean those officials are free to disregard the Constitution and the rights it proclaims and protects. The oath that all officials take to adhere to the Constitution is not confined to those spheres in which the Judiciary can correct or even comment upon what those officials say or do. Indeed, the very fact that an official may have broad discretion, discretion free from judicial scrutiny, makes it all the more imperative for him or her to adhere to the Constitution and to its meaning and its promise.

The First Amendment prohibits the establishment of religion and promises the free exercise of religion. From these safeguards, and from the guarantee of freedom of speech, it follows there is freedom of belief and expression. It is an urgent necessity that officials adhere to these constitutional guarantees and mandates in all their actions, even in the sphere of foreign affairs. An anxious world must know that our Government remains committed always to the liberties the Constitution seeks to preserve and protect, so that freedom extends outward, and lasts.

[Justice Thomas concurred, arguing that he was "skeptical that district courts have the authority to enter universal injunctions" covering the entire nation.]

[Justice Breyer, joined by Justice Kagan, dissented. He argued that there was evidence that the government was not serious about providing case-by-case waivers to provide visas for people — including especially Muslims — who had strong reasons for a visa and who posed no security threats. Such people included, among others, lawful permanent residents, asylum seekers, refugees, students, and children. Because the waiver requirement appeared to be a sham, it raised an inference that the Proclamation was motivated by animus toward Muslims rather than genuine security needs. Accordingly, Justice Breyer argued for a remand to the lower courts for further fact finding. "If this Court must decide the question without this further litigation, I would, on balance, find the evidence of antireligious bias . . . a sufficient basis to set the Proclamation aside."]

Justice SOTOMAYOR, with whom Justice GINSBURG joins, dissenting.

The United States of America is a Nation built upon the promise of religious liberty. Our Founders honored that core promise by embedding the principle of religious neutrality in the First Amendment. The Court's decision today fails to safeguard that fundamental principle. It leaves undisturbed a policy first advertised openly and unequivocally as a "total and complete shutdown of Muslims entering the United States" because the policy now masquerades behind a facade of national-security concerns. But this repackaging does little to cleanse Presidential Proclamation No. 9645 of the appearance of discrimination that the President's words have created. Based on the evidence in the record, a reasonable observer would conclude that the Proclamation was motivated by anti-Muslim animus. That alone suffices to show that plaintiffs are likely to succeed on the merits of their Establishment Clause claim. The majority holds otherwise by ignoring the facts, misconstruing our legal precedent, and turning a blind eye to the pain and suffering the Proclamation inflicts upon countless families and individuals, many of whom are United States citizens. Because that troubling result runs contrary to the Constitution and our precedent, I dissent.

I

[T]he "clearest command" of the Establishment Clause is that the Government cannot favor or disfavor one religion over another. *Larson v. Valente,* 456 U.S. 228, 244 (1982). . . . "When the government acts with the ostensible and predominant purpose" of disfavoring a particular religion, "it violates that central Establishment Clause value of official religious neutrality, there being no neutrality when the government's ostensible object is to take sides." *McCreary County v. American Civil Liberties Union of Ky.,* 545 U.S. 844, 860 (2005). To determine whether plaintiffs have proved an Establishment Clause violation, the Court asks whether a reasonable observer would view the government action as enacted for the purpose of disfavoring a religion.

In answering that question, this Court has generally considered the text of the government policy, its operation, and any available evidence regarding "the historical background of the decision under challenge, the specific series of events leading to the enactment or official policy in question, and the legislative or administrative history, including contemporaneous statements made by" the decisionmaker. At the same time, however, courts must take care not to engage in "any judicial psychoanalysis of a drafter's heart of hearts."

Although the majority briefly recounts a few of the statements and background events that form the basis of plaintiffs' constitutional challenge, *ante,* at 27-28, that highly abridged account does not tell even half of the story. The full record paints a far more harrowing picture, from which a reasonable observer would readily conclude that the Proclamation was motivated by hostility and animus toward the Muslim faith.

During his Presidential campaign, then-candidate Donald Trump pledged that, if elected, he would ban Muslims from entering the United States. Specifically, on December 7, 2015, he issued a formal statement "calling for a total and complete shutdown of Muslims entering the United States." That statement, which remained on his campaign website until May 2017 (several months into his Presidency), read in full:

> "Donald J. Trump is calling for a total and complete shutdown of Muslims entering the United States until our country's representatives can figure out what is going on. According to Pew Research, among others, there is great hatred towards Americans by large segments of the Muslim population. Most recently, a poll from the Center for Security Policy released data showing '25% of those polled agreed that violence against Americans here in the United States is justified as a part of the global jihad' and 51% of those polled 'agreed that Muslims in America should have the choice of being governed according to Shariah.' Shariah authorizes such atrocities as murder against nonbelievers who won't convert, beheadings and more unthinkable acts that pose great harm to Americans, especially women.
>
> "Mr. Trum[p] stated, 'Without looking at the various polling data, it is obvious to anybody the hatred is beyond comprehension. Where this hatred comes from and why we will have to determine. Until we are able to determine and understand this problem and the dangerous threat it poses, our country cannot be the victims of the horrendous attacks by people that believe only in Jihad, and have no sense of reason or respect of human life. If I win the election for President, we are going to Make America Great Again.' — Donald J. Trump."

On December 8, 2015, Trump justified his proposal during a television interview by noting that President Franklin D. Roosevelt "did the same thing" with respect to the internment of Japanese Americans during World War II. In January 2016, during a Republican primary debate, Trump was asked whether he wanted to "rethink [his] position" on "banning Muslims from entering the country." He answered, "No." A month later, at a rally in South Carolina, Trump told an apocryphal story about United States General John J. Pershing killing a large group of Muslim insurgents in the Philippines with bullets dipped in pigs' blood in the early 1900's. In March 2016, he expressed his belief that "Islam hates us. . . . [W]e can't allow people coming into this country who have this hatred of the United States . . . [a]nd of people that are not Muslim." That same month, Trump asserted that "[w]e're having problems with the Muslims, and we're having problems with Muslims coming into the country." He therefore called for surveillance of mosques in the United States, blaming terrorist attacks on Muslims' lack of "assimilation" and their commitment to "sharia law." A day later, he opined that Muslims "do not respect us at all" and "don't respect a lot of the things that are happening throughout not only our country, but they don't respect other things."

As Trump's presidential campaign progressed, he began to describe his policy proposal in slightly different terms. In June 2016, for instance, he characterized the policy proposal as a suspension of immigration from countries "where there's a proven history of terrorism." He also described the proposal as rooted in the need to stop "importing radical Islamic terrorism to the West through a failed immigration system." Asked in July 2016 whether he was "pull[ing] back from" his pledged Muslim ban, Trump responded, "I actually don't think it's a rollback. In fact, you could say it's an expansion." He then explained that he used different terminology because "[p]eople were so upset when [he] used the word Muslim."

A month before the 2016 election, Trump reiterated that his proposed "Muslim ban" had "morphed into a[n] extreme vetting from certain areas of the world." Then, on December 21, 2016, President-elect Trump was asked whether he would "rethink" his previous "plans to create a Muslim registry or ban Muslim immigration." He replied: "You know my plans. All along, I've proven to be right."

On January 27, 2017, one week after taking office, President Trump signed Executive Order No. 13769, 82 Fed. Reg. 8977 (2017) (EO-1), entitled "Protecting the Nation From Foreign Terrorist Entry Into the United States." As he signed it, President Trump read the title, looked up, and said "We all know what that means." That same day, President Trump explained to the media that, under EO-1, Christians would be given priority for entry as refugees into the United States. In particular, he bemoaned the fact that in the past, "[i]f you were a Muslim [refugee from Syria] you could come in, but if you were a Christian, it was almost impossible." Considering that past policy "very unfair," President Trump explained that EO-1 was designed "to help" the Christians in Syria. The following day, one of President Trump's key advisers candidly drew the connection between EO-1 and the "Muslim ban" that the President had pledged to implement if elected. According to that adviser, "[W]hen [Donald Trump] first announced it, he said, 'Muslim ban.' He called me up. He said, 'Put a commission together. Show me the right way to do it legally.'"

[After the 9th Circuit upheld a district court's injunction of EO-1], the Government declined to continue defending EO-1 in court and instead announced that the President intended to issue a new executive order. . . . One of the President's senior advisers publicly explained that EO-2 would "have the same basic policy outcome" as EO-1, and that any changes would address "very technical issues that were brought up by the court." After EO-2 was issued, the White House Press Secretary told reporters that, by issuing EO-2, President Trump "continue[d] to deliver on . . . his most significant campaign promises." That statement was consistent with President Trump's own declaration that "I keep my campaign promises, and our citizens will be very happy when they see the result." . . .

While litigation over EO-2 was ongoing, President Trump repeatedly made statements alluding to a desire to keep Muslims out of the country. For instance, he said at a rally of his supporters that EO-2 was just a "watered down version of the first one" and had been "tailor[ed]" at the behest of "the lawyers." He further added that he would prefer "to go back to the first [executive order] and go all the way" and reiterated his belief that it was "very hard" for Muslims to assimilate into Western culture. During a rally in April 2017, President Trump recited the lyrics to a song called "The Snake," a song about a woman who nurses a sick snake back to health but then is attacked by the snake, as a warning about Syrian refugees entering the country. And in June

2017, the President stated on Twitter that the Justice Department had submitted a "watered down, politically correct version" of the "original Travel Ban" "to S[upreme] C[ourt]."

According to the White House, President Trump's statements on Twitter are "official statements." [relocated footnote — eds.]

The President went on to tweet: "People, the lawyers and the courts can call it whatever they want, but I am calling it what we need and what it is, a TRAVEL BAN!" He added: "That's right, we need a TRAVEL BAN for certain DANGEROUS countries, not some politically correct term that won't help us protect our people!" Then, on August 17, 2017, President Trump issued yet another tweet about Islam, once more referencing the story about General Pershing's massacre of Muslims in the Philippines: "Study what General Pershing . . . did to terrorists when caught. There was no more Radical Islamic Terror for 35 years!"

In September 2017, President Trump tweeted that "[t]he travel ban into the United States should be far larger, tougher and more specific — but stupidly, that would not be politically correct!" Later that month, on September 24, 2017, President Trump issued [the current] Presidential Proclamation . . . , which restricts entry of certain nationals from six Muslim-majority countries. On November 29, 2017, President Trump "retweeted" three anti-Muslim videos, entitled "Muslim Destroys a Statue of Virgin Mary!", "Islamist mob pushes teenage boy off roof and beats him to death!", and "Muslim migrant beats up Dutch boy on crutches!" The content of these videos is highly inflammatory, and their titles are arguably misleading. [relocated footnote — eds.] Those videos were initially tweeted by a British political party whose mission is to oppose "all alien and destructive politic[al] or religious doctrines, including . . . Islam." When asked about these videos, the White House Deputy Press Secretary connected them to the Proclamation, responding that the "President has been talking about these security issues for years now, from the campaign trail to the White House" and "has addressed these issues with the travel order that he issued earlier this year and the companion proclamation."

As the majority correctly notes, "the issue before us is not whether to denounce" these offensive statements. Rather, the dispositive and narrow question here is whether a reasonable observer, presented with all "openly available data," the text and "historical context" of the Proclamation, and the "specific sequence of events" leading to it, would conclude that the primary purpose of the Proclamation is to disfavor Islam and its adherents by excluding them from the country. The answer is unquestionably yes.

Taking all the relevant evidence together, a reasonable observer would conclude that the Proclamation was driven primarily by anti-Muslim animus, rather than by the Government's asserted national-security justifications. Even before being sworn into office, then-candidate Trump stated that "Islam hates us," warned that "[w]e're having problems with the Muslims, and we're having problems with Muslims coming into the country," promised to enact a "total and complete shutdown of Muslims entering the United States," and instructed one of his advisers to find a "lega [l]" way to enact a Muslim ban, *id.,* at 125. The

President continued to make similar statements well after his inauguration, as detailed above.

The Government urges us to disregard the President's campaign statements. . . . To the contrary, courts must consider "the historical background of the decision under challenge, the specific series of events leading to the enactment or official policy in question, and the legislative or administrative history." *Church of Lukumi Babalu Aye, Inc. v. Hialeah,* 508 U.S. 520, 540 (1993) (opinion of Kennedy, J.). Moreover, President Trump and his advisers have repeatedly acknowledged that the Proclamation and its predecessors are an outgrowth of the President's campaign statements. For example, just last November, the Deputy White House Press Secretary reminded the media that the Proclamation addresses "issues" the President has been talking about "for years," including on "the campaign trail." In any case, as the Fourth Circuit correctly recognized, even without relying on any of the President's campaign statements, a reasonable observer would conclude that the Proclamation was enacted for the impermissible purpose of disfavoring Muslims. [relocated footnote—eds.]

Moreover, despite several opportunities to do so, President Trump has never disavowed any of his prior statements about Islam. Instead, he has continued to make remarks that a reasonable observer would view as an unrelenting attack on the Muslim religion and its followers. Given President Trump's failure to correct the reasonable perception of his apparent hostility toward the Islamic faith, it is unsurprising that the President's lawyers have, at every step in the lower courts, failed in their attempts to launder the Proclamation of its discriminatory taint. Notably, the Court recently found less pervasive official expressions of hostility and the failure to disavow them to be constitutionally significant. Cf. *Masterpiece Cakeshop, Ltd. v. Colorado Civil Rights Comm'n,* 584 U.S. ____, ____ (2018) (slip op., at 18) ("The official expressions of hostility to religion in some of the commissioners' comments—comments that were not disavowed at the Commission or by the State at any point in the proceedings that led to the affirmance of the order—were inconsistent with what the Free Exercise Clause requires"). It should find the same here.

Ultimately, what began as a policy explicitly "calling for a total and complete shutdown of Muslims entering the United States" has since morphed into a "Proclamation" putatively based on national-security concerns. But this new window dressing cannot conceal an unassailable fact: the words of the President and his advisers create the strong perception that the Proclamation is contaminated by impermissible discriminatory animus against Islam and its followers.

II

[T]he majority accepts that invitation and incorrectly applies a watered-down legal standard in an effort to short circuit plaintiffs' Establishment Clause claim. . . .

[*Kleindienst v.*] *Mandel* held that when the Executive Branch provides "a facially legitimate and bona fide reason" for denying a visa, "courts will neither look behind the exercise of that discretion, nor test it by balancing its justification." In his controlling concurrence in *Kerry v. Din,* 576 U.S. _____ (2015), Justice Kennedy applied *Mandel* 's holding and elaborated that courts can " 'look behind' the Government's exclusion of" a foreign national if there is "an affirmative showing of bad faith on the part of the consular officer who denied [the] visa." The extent to which *Mandel* and *Din* apply at all to this case is unsettled, and there is good reason to think they do not.

Mandel and *Din* are readily distinguishable from this case for a number of reasons. First, *Mandel* and *Din* each involved a constitutional challenge to an Executive Branch decision to exclude a single foreign national under a specific statutory ground of inadmissibility. Here, by contrast, President Trump is not exercising his discretionary authority to determine the admission or exclusion of a particular foreign national. He promulgated an executive order affecting millions of individuals on a categorical basis. Second, *Mandel* and *Din* did not purport to establish the framework for adjudicating cases (like this one) involving claims that the Executive Branch violated the Establishment Clause by acting pursuant to an unconstitutional purpose. Applying *Mandel*'s narrow standard of review to such a claim would run contrary to this Court's repeated admonition that "[f]acial neutrality is not determinative" in the Establishment Clause context. *Lukumi.* [T]he majority's passing invocation of *Fiallo v. Bell,* 430 U.S. 787 (1977), is misplaced. *Fiallo,* unlike this case, addressed a constitutional challenge to a statute enacted by Congress, not an order of the President. *Fiallo*'s application of *Mandel* says little about whether *Mandel*'s narrow standard of review applies to the unilateral executive proclamation promulgated under the circumstances of this case. Finally, even assuming that *Mandel* and *Din* apply here, they would not preclude us from looking behind the face of the Proclamation because plaintiffs have made "an affirmative showing of bad faith," *Din*, by the President who, among other things, instructed his subordinates to find a "lega[l]" way to enact a Muslim ban. [relocated footnote — eds.]

Indeed, even the Government agreed at oral argument that where the Court confronts a situation involving "all kinds of denigrating comments about" a particular religion and a subsequent policy that is designed with the purpose of disfavoring that religion but that "dot[s] all the i's and . . . cross[es] all the t's," *Mandel* would not "pu[t] an end to judicial review of that set of facts."

In light of the Government's suggestion "that it may be appropriate here for the inquiry to extend beyond the facial neutrality of the order," the majority rightly declines to apply *Mandel*'s "narrow standard of review" and "assume[s] that we may look behind the face of the Proclamation." In doing so, however, the Court, without explanation or precedential support, limits its review of the Proclamation to rational-basis scrutiny. [But] in other Establishment Clause cases, including those involving claims of religious animus or discrimination, this Court has applied a more stringent standard of review.[6] As explained above, the Proclamation is plainly unconstitutional under that heightened standard. See *supra,* at 10-13.

The majority [argues that] this Court's Establishment Clause precedents do not apply to cases involving "immigration policies, diplomatic sanctions, and military actions." But just because the Court has not confronted the precise situation at hand does not render these cases (or the principles they announced) inapplicable. Moreover, . . . the majority itself fails to cite any "authority for its proposition" that a more probing review is inappropriate in a case like this one, where United States citizens allege that the Executive has violated the Establishment Clause by issuing a sweeping executive order motivated by animus. In any event, even if there is no prior case directly on point, it is clear from our precedent that "[w]hatever power the United States Constitution envisions for the Executive" in the context of national security and foreign affairs, "it most assuredly envisions a role for all three branches when individual liberties are at stake." *Hamdi v. Rumsfeld,* 542 U.S. 507, 536 (2004) (plurality opinion). This Court's Establishment Clause precedents require that, if a reasonable observer would understand an executive action to be driven by discriminatory animus, the action be invalidated. *McCreary.* That reasonable-observer inquiry includes consideration of the Government's asserted justifications for its actions. The Government's invocation of a national-security justification, however, does not mean that the Court should close its eyes to other relevant information. Deference is different from unquestioning acceptance. Thus, what is "far more problematic" in this case is the majority's apparent willingness to throw the Establishment Clause out the window and forgo any meaningful constitutional review at the mere mention of a national-security concern. [relocated footnote — eds.]

But even under rational-basis review, the Proclamation must fall. That is so because the Proclamation is " 'divorced from any factual context from which we could discern a relationship to legitimate state interests,' and 'its sheer breadth [is] so discontinuous with the reasons offered for it'" that the policy is " 'inexplicable by anything but animus.'" *Romer*; see also *Cleburne* (recognizing that classifications predicated on discriminatory animus can never be legitimate because the Government has no legitimate interest in exploiting "mere negative attitudes, or fear" toward a disfavored group). The President's statements, which the majority utterly fails to address in its legal analysis, strongly support the conclusion that the Proclamation was issued to express hostility toward Muslims and exclude them from the country. Given the overwhelming record evidence of anti-Muslim animus, it simply cannot be said that the Proclamation has a legitimate basis.

The majority insists that the Proclamation furthers two interrelated national-security interests: "preventing entry of nationals who cannot be adequately vetted and inducing other nations to improve their practices." But the Court offers insufficient support for its view "that the entry suspension has a legitimate grounding in [those] national security concerns, quite apart from any religious hostility." Indeed, even a cursory review of the Government's asserted national-security rationale reveals that the Proclamation is nothing more than a " 'religious gerrymander.'" *Lukumi.*

[T]he Proclamation, just like its predecessors, overwhelmingly targets Muslim-majority nations. Given the record here, including all the President's statements linking the Proclamation to his apparent hostility toward Muslims, it is of no moment that the Proclamation also includes minor restrictions on two non-Muslim majority countries, North Korea and Venezuela, or that the Government has removed a few Muslim-majority countries from the list of covered countries since EO-1 was issued. Consideration of the entire record supports the conclusion that the inclusion of North Korea and Venezuela, and the removal of other countries, simply reflect subtle efforts to start "talking territory instead of Muslim," precisely so the Executive Branch could evade criticism or legal consequences for the Proclamation's otherwise clear targeting of Muslims. The Proclamation's effect on North Korea and Venezuela, for example, is insubstantial, if not entirely symbolic. A prior sanctions order already restricts entry of North Korean nationals, and the Proclamation targets only a handful of Venezuelan government officials and their immediate family members. As such, the President's inclusion of North Korea and Venezuela does little to mitigate the anti-Muslim animus that permeates the Proclamation.

The majority next contends that the Proclamation "reflects the results of a worldwide review process undertaken by multiple Cabinet officials." [T]he worldwide review does little to break the clear connection between the Proclamation and the President's anti-Muslim statements. For "[n]o matter how many officials affix their names to it, the Proclamation rests on a rotten foundation." The President campaigned on a promise to implement a "total and complete shutdown of Muslims" entering the country, translated that campaign promise into a concrete policy, and made several statements linking that policy (in its various forms) to anti-Muslim animus.

Ignoring all this, the majority empowers the President to hide behind an administrative review process that the Government refuses to disclose to the public. Furthermore, evidence of which we can take judicial notice indicates that the multiagency review process could not have been very thorough. Ongoing litigation under the Freedom of Information Act shows that the September 2017 report the Government produced after its review process was a mere 17 pages. That the Government's analysis of the vetting practices of hundreds of countries boiled down to such a short document raises serious questions about the legitimacy of the President's proclaimed national-security rationale.

Beyond that, Congress has already addressed the national-security concerns supposedly undergirding the Proclamation through an "extensive and complex" framework governing "immigration and alien status." . . . In addition to vetting rigorously any individuals seeking admission to the United States, the Government also rigorously vets the information-sharing and identity-management systems of other countries. . . . Put simply, Congress has already erected a statutory scheme that fulfills the putative national-security interests the Government now puts forth to justify the Proclamation. Tellingly, the Government remains wholly unable to articulate any credible national-security interest that would go unaddressed by the current statutory scheme absent the Proclamation. The Government also offers no evidence that this current vetting scheme, which involves a highly searching consideration of individuals required to obtain visas for entry into the United States and a highly searching consideration of which countries are eligible for inclusion in the Visa Waiver

Program, is inadequate to achieve the Proclamation's proclaimed objectives of "preventing entry of nationals who cannot be adequately vetted and inducing other nations to improve their [vetting and information-sharing] practices."

For many of these reasons, several former national-security officials from both political parties — including former Secretary of State Madeleine Albright, former State Department Legal Adviser John Bellinger III, former Central Intelligence Agency Director John Brennan, and former Director of National Intelligence James Clapper — have advised that the Proclamation and its predecessor orders "do not advance the national-security or foreign policy interests of the United States, and in fact do serious harm to those interests."

Moreover, the Proclamation purports to mitigate national-security risks by excluding nationals of countries that provide insufficient information to vet their nationals. Yet, as plaintiffs explain, the Proclamation broadly denies immigrant visas to all nationals of those countries, including those whose admission would likely not implicate these information deficiencies (*e.g.,* infants, or nationals of countries included in the Proclamation who are long-term residents of and traveling from a country not covered by the Proclamation). In addition, the Proclamation permits certain nationals from the countries named in the Proclamation to obtain nonimmigrant visas, which undermines the Government's assertion that it does not already have the capacity and sufficient information to vet these individuals adequately.

Equally unavailing is the majority's reliance on the Proclamation's waiver program. As several *amici* thoroughly explain, there is reason to suspect that the Proclamation's waiver program is nothing more than a sham. The remote possibility of obtaining a waiver pursuant to an ad hoc, discretionary, and seemingly arbitrary process scarcely demonstrates that the Proclamation is rooted in a genuine concern for national security.

In sum, none of the features of the Proclamation highlighted by the majority supports the Government's claim that the Proclamation is genuinely and primarily rooted in a legitimate national-security interest. What the unrebutted evidence actually shows is that a reasonable observer would conclude, quite easily, that the primary purpose and function of the Proclamation is to disfavor Islam by banning Muslims from entering our country.

III

[P]laintiffs are likely to succeed on the merits of their Establishment Clause claim. [They have also shown] that they are "likely to suffer irreparable harm in the absence of preliminary relief," that "the balance of equities tips in [their] favor," and that "an injunction is in the public interest."

First, . . . plaintiffs have adduced substantial evidence showing that the Proclamation will result in "a multitude of harms that are not compensable with monetary damages and that are irreparable — among them, prolonged separation from family members, constraints to recruiting and retaining students and faculty members to foster diversity and quality within the University community, and the diminished membership of the [Muslim] Association."

Second, plaintiffs have demonstrated that the balance of the equities tips in their favor. Against plaintiffs' concrete allegations of serious harm, the Government advances only nebulous national-security concerns. Although national security is unquestionably an issue of paramount public importance, it is not "a talisman" that the Government can use "to ward off inconvenient claims—a 'label' used to 'cover a multitude of sins.'" That is especially true here, because, as noted, the Government's other statutory tools, including the existing rigorous individualized vetting process, already address the Proclamation's purported national-security concerns.

Finally, plaintiffs and their *amici* have convincingly established that "an injunction is in the public interest." As explained by the scores of *amici* who have filed briefs in support of plaintiffs, the Proclamation has deleterious effects on our higher education system; national security; healthcare; artistic culture; and the Nation's technology industry and overall economy. Accordingly, the Court of Appeals correctly affirmed, in part, the District Court's preliminary injunction.

IV

The First Amendment stands as a bulwark against official religious prejudice and embodies our Nation's deep commitment to religious plurality and tolerance. . . . Instead of vindicating those principles, today's decision tosses them aside. In holding that the First Amendment gives way to an executive policy that a reasonable observer would view as motivated by animus against Muslims, the majority opinion upends this Court's precedent, repeats tragic mistakes of the past, and denies countless individuals the fundamental right of religious liberty.

Just weeks ago, the Court rendered its decision in *Masterpiece Cakeshop*, 584 U.S. ____, [involving a baker who refused to bake a wedding cake for a gay couple,] which applied the bedrock principles of religious neutrality and tolerance in considering a First Amendment challenge to government action. See *id.*, at ____ (slip op., at 17) ("The Constitution 'commits government itself to religious tolerance, and upon even slight suspicion that proposals for state intervention stem from animosity to religion or distrust of its practices, all officials must pause to remember their own high duty to the Constitution and to the rights it secures'". Those principles should apply equally here. In both instances, the question is whether a government actor exhibited tolerance and neutrality in reaching a decision that affects individuals' fundamental religious freedom. But unlike in *Masterpiece,* where a state civil rights commission was found to have acted without "the neutrality that the Free Exercise Clause requires," *id.*, at ____ (slip op., at 17), the government actors in this case will not be held accountable for breaching the First Amendment's guarantee of religious neutrality and tolerance. Unlike in *Masterpiece,* where the majority considered the state commissioners' statements about religion to be persuasive evidence of unconstitutional government action, the majority here completely sets aside the President's charged statements about Muslims as irrelevant. That holding erodes the foundational principles of religious tolerance that the Court elsewhere has so emphatically protected, and it tells members of minority religions in our country " 'that they are outsiders, not full members of the political community.' "

Today's holding is all the more troubling given the stark parallels between the reasoning of this case and that of *Korematsu v. United States,* 323 U.S. 214 (1944). In *Korematsu,* the Court gave "a pass [to] an odious, gravely injurious racial classification" authorized by an executive order. As here, the Government invoked an ill-defined national-security threat to justify an exclusionary policy of sweeping proportion. As here, the exclusion order was rooted in dangerous stereotypes about, *inter alia,* a particular group's supposed inability to assimilate and desire to harm the United States. As here, the Government was unwilling to reveal its own intelligence agencies' views of the alleged security concerns to the very citizens it purported to protect. And as here, there was strong evidence that impermissible hostility and animus motivated the Government's policy.

Although a majority of the Court in *Korematsu* was willing to uphold the Government's actions based on a barren invocation of national security, dissenting Justices warned of that decision's harm to our constitutional fabric. Justice Murphy recognized that there is a need for great deference to the Executive Branch in the context of national security, but cautioned that "it is essential that there be definite limits to [the government's] discretion," as "[i]ndividuals must not be left impoverished of their constitutional rights on a plea of military necessity that has neither substance nor support." Justice Jackson lamented that the Court's decision upholding the Government's policy would prove to be "a far more subtle blow to liberty than the promulgation of the order itself," for although the executive order was not likely to be long lasting, the Court's willingness to tolerate it would endure.

In the intervening years since *Korematsu,* our Nation has done much to leave its sordid legacy behind. See, *e.g.,* Civil Liberties Act of 1988, 50 U.S.C. App. § 4211 *et seq.* (setting forth remedies to individuals affected by the executive order at issue in *Korematsu*); Non–Detention Act of 1971, 18 U.S.C. § 4001(a) (forbidding the imprisonment or detention by the United States of any citizen absent an Act of Congress). Today, the Court takes the important step of finally overruling *Korematsu,* denouncing it as "gravely wrong the day it was decided." This formal repudiation of a shameful precedent is laudable and long overdue. But it does not make the majority's decision here acceptable or right. By blindly accepting the Government's misguided invitation to sanction a discriminatory policy motivated by animosity toward a disfavored group, all in the name of a superficial claim of national security, the Court redeploys the same dangerous logic underlying *Korematsu* and merely replaces one "gravely wrong" decision with another.

Our Constitution demands, and our country deserves, a Judiciary willing to hold the coordinate branches to account when they defy our most sacred legal commitments. Because the Court's decision today has failed in that respect, with profound regret, I dissent.

Discussion

1. *The plenary power doctrine and immigration exceptionalism.* One cannot understand the issues in *Trump v. Hawaii* apart from immigration law's unique status in the constitutional order. The current understanding of the federal government's power to regulate immigration stems from the plenary power doctrine that originated in the 19th century Chinese Exclusion Case, Chae Chan Ping v. United States, 130 U.S. 581, 609 (1889). This doctrine emerged only in the late 19th century; in the first hundred years of the country's history, the states played a much greater role in immigration regulation. See, e.g., Mayor of the City of New York v. Miln, 36 U.S. (11 Pet.) 102 (1837) (Casebook, p. 223). For an explanation of the rise of the plenary power doctrine, see Sarah H. Cleveland, Powers Inherent in Sovereignty: Indians, Aliens, Territories, and the Nineteenth Century Origins of Plenary Power Over Foreign Affairs, 81 Tex. L. Rev. 1 (2002).

The plenary power doctrine is associated with two different ideas. The first is that Congress's power to regulate immigration does not come from any enumerated power in Article I, but rather is an "an incident of sovereignty belonging to the government of the United States." *Chae Chan Ping*, 130 U.S. at 609. This theory suggests that, notwithstanding the theory of limited and enumerated powers, the federal government of the United States is like that of any other nation, with the right to protect national sovereignty by enforcing its borders. (It is perhaps no accident that the plenary power doctrine emerges after the Civil War). This theory views the plenary power doctrine as a matter of *sovereignty*.

The second idea is that—with a few notable exceptions—courts have largely refrained from enforcing constitutional constraints on the federal government's enactment and enforcement of immigration laws. See, e.g., Fiallo v. Bell, 430 U.S. 787, 792 (1977) ("Our cases have long recognized the power to expel or exclude aliens as a fundamental sovereign attribute exercised by the Government's political departments largely immune from judicial control.") This theory of the plenary power doctrine is premised on the superior *competence* of the political branches over that of the judiciary in questions of immigration and foreign affairs.

Federal courts have often allowed the political branches to make classifications and distinctions in immigration enforcement that would almost certainly be unconstitutional if made by the states, or even if made by the federal government outside of the immigration context. As a result, standard-form equal protection doctrine does not apply. See generally Gabriel J. Chin, Segregation's Last Stronghold: Race Discrimination and the Constitutional Law of Immigration, 46 UCLA L. Rev. 1 (1998). In addition, the Court has not generally used the Bill of Rights to protect the rights of noncitizens who live *outside* the United States. See United States v. Verdugo-Urquidez, 494 U.S. 259, 269 (1990) (holding that the Fifth Amendment's protections do not extend to aliens outside the territorial boundaries of the United States). *Trump v. Hawaii* arises in this difficult context for the protection of the rights of aliens.

2. *The scope of the plenary power doctrine and the role of judicial scrutiny in immigration law.* There are at least two different explanations for judicial deference in immigration law. The stronger version holds that the Constitution's equality norms simply do not constrain the distinctions the political branches use in deciding who can enter the country. The federal government has broad power to make virtually any distinctions it wants about who gains entry to the country and who must leave—including, for example, on the basis of religion, race, or national origin. The Justice Department did not adopt this position in the travel ban litigation. In oral arguments before the courts of appeals, DOJ lawyers conceded that it would be unconstitutional for the government to exclude Muslims, as such, from entering the United States. And in the Supreme Court opinion itself, Chief Justice Roberts (and Justice Kennedy's concurrence) assumed that the government could violate the Establishment Clause.

The second version of the "plenary power" doctrine focuses on the role of courts: Although the Constitution may impose substantive constraints on the immigration power, the judiciary should not attempt to oversee the political branches or decide whether the political branches have violated the Constitution. This norm is very strong but it is not insuperable. See, e.g., Sessions v. Morales-Santana, 137 S.Ct. 1678 (2017) (upholding an equal protection challenge in the face of a plenary power objection).[1] When courts consider claims of plenary power in the context of immigration law, courts generally apply a "presumption of regularity" and they accept at face value the Executive's representations of the basis for immigration restrictions. In the words of *Kleindienst v. Mandel,* "when the Executive exercises th[e] power [to exclude an alien] on the basis of a facially legitimate and bona fide reason, the courts will [not] look behind the exercise of that discretion."

3. *Litigation strategies for getting around the plenary power doctrine.* Although the plenary power doctrine is still very much alive, social change, political mobilization, globalization, and litigation strategies have put it under increasing pressure. The travel ban cases exemplify how constitutional doctrine in this area is being contested and reshaped in an era of globalization.

Plaintiffs attempting to chip away at the plenary power doctrine have tried two different strategies. First, they have used federal statutory claims and procedural objections to protect constitutional norms. Second, plaintiffs have tried to protect the rights of aliens through protecting the constitutional rights of *citizens and permanent resident aliens* who are affected by the immigration laws. This

1. In *Morales-Santana,* a federal statute made it more difficult for American fathers—as compared with American mothers—to transmit citizenship to their children born out of wedlock on foreign soil. In this case, which involved an explicit classification based on sex, the Court found an equal protection violation. But it remedied the constitutional inequality not by making it easier for American fathers to transmit citizenship, but by making it equally difficult for American mothers. Thus, it decided the case in a way that interfered as little as possible with Congress's political prerogatives. See Casebook at pp. 1323-26; cf. Kristin A. Collins, Equality, Sovereignty, and the Family in Morales-Santana, The Supreme Court—Comments, 131 Harv. L. Rev. 170, 204-208, 221 (2017).

avoids having to argue that the Constitution applies outside the territory of the United States. We see both of these strategies in *Trump v. Hawaii*: an argument that the President has not made appropriate findings for the Proclamation and that the Proclamation violates the Establishment Clause because it evidences government disapproval of Islam and discriminates against Muslims in the United States.

Because, as noted above, courts do not apply standard-form equal protection doctrine to immigration restrictions, the plaintiffs in the travel ban litigation also tried to use various workarounds to bring equality ideas into the analysis.

The statutory argument was based on the antidiscrimination rule of § 1152(a)(1)(A) of the 1965 Immigration and Naturalization Act, which was passed contemporaneously with the 1964 Civil Rights Act and the 1965 Voting Act.[2] The plaintiffs also argued that the Trump Administration had not offered factual findings to justify its Executive Order, and that the process by which the decision was made was procedurally irregular. Demonstrating a poor fit between means and ends, noting lack of adequate explanation, and emphasizing procedural irregularities are standard ways that courts show invidious motivation, or otherwise establish impermissible distinctions, in equal protection doctrine.

The plaintiffs' constitutional argument was based on the Establishment Clause, which has important overlaps with equality doctrines under the Fourteenth and Fifth Amendments. First, it forbids the government from preferring one religion over another, or religion over nonreligion; it also forbids signaling that some people are disfavored because of their religious identity, beliefs or practices. Second, as in equal protection law, one can show a violation of these norms by showing an intent to discriminate on the basis of religion. Third, modern Establishment Clause doctrine often focuses on the social meaning of government action, by asking whether a reasonable observer would view the government as endorsing (or disfavoring) a particular religion or religion in general. This inquiry is similar to the way the Court has treated animus doctrine in gay rights cases such as *Romer v. Evans* and *United States v. Windsor*.

4. *Taking Trump seriously but not literally.* Chief Justice Roberts well recognizes that President Trump had made many hostile remarks about Muslims in public both before and after his election. So it was not possible for the Court to pretend that there was no evidence of prejudice. Note carefully how Roberts deals with that problem in resolving the issues in the case.

Consider how Roberts states the facts of the case: he begins with the third of President Trump's executive orders, offering only a brief mention of the two earlier orders. The dissent, by contrast, begins the story with the 2016 campaign.

---

2. See Cristina M. Rodriguez, Immigration and the Civil Rights Agenda, 6 Stan. J. C.R. & C.L. 125, 127 (2010) ("The 1965 reforms of the INA that finally abolished [racially discriminatory immigration] quotas emerged from the political and cultural milieu that produced the Civil Rights Act of 1964 and the Voting Rights Act of 1965 and were defended by members of Congress as realizations of the anti-discrimination aspirations of the era.").

Roberts' framing focuses on an order that had been drafted and revised as a result of consultation among many different government actors. (Ironically, the reason why the third executive order appeared more professional than the earlier two was that the lower courts repeatedly forced the Executive Branch to respond to their objections.) The dissent's story, by contrast, suggests that the travel ban's origins were in demagogic politics; the original Executive order, EO-1, was hastily drafted with little professional advice, no inter-agency consultation, and no serious attempt at discovering the facts. Roberts' version of the facts focuses on a history of consultation, agency findings, and professional opinions which informed the President's judgment. The dissent's version of the facts focuses on a continuous pattern of provocative statements and tweets by the head of the Executive Branch, the President of the United States, who did not seem to care how the order was drafted as long as it achieved its original purpose.

How does the majority deal with the problem of these statements and tweets? Several lower courts judges and legal commentators argued that Trump's campaign statements could simply be disregarded because they were not made in his official capacity as President. Consider why this might make sense from the standpoint of constitutional law. One possibility is that campaign statements are unreliable evidence of intentions. Perhaps candidates will say things they don't really believe to get power but once they take office they will reveal their actual beliefs. A second possibility is that campaign statements do not reflect the views of the Administration as a whole. (Why is this relevant if the President is the head of the Executive Branch?) A third possibility has nothing to do with the reliability of the evidence. Instead, it argues that campaigns are often messy, dirty affairs, and politicians should get a fresh start once they take office, so that they are not hamstrung by what they had to say to get into office. One of the problems with these arguments is that Trump didn't seem to change his behavior very much after he became President. Instead, he understood that his supporters liked his blunt views about Muslims and he played to his base repeatedly once in office.

Roberts takes a different approach to the problem. He begins by asserting that "the issue before us is not whether to denounce the statements." What does he mean by this? (Note that the Court has no problem denouncing the Japanese internment later in the opinion. Is the difference that these events are safely in the past and do not involve a sitting president?)

Next, Roberts remarks that "we must consider not only the statements of a particular President, but also the authority of the Presidency itself." Thus, Roberts seems to be saying, there cannot be a "Trump discount" in construing the policies of this Administration, with judges offering less deference to Trump than they would to other presidents. Do you agree that courts should not decide cases based on their estimate of whether a given president is markedly different from other presidents in terms of competence, public-spiritedness, venality, rationality, or intelligence?

Roberts believes that whatever rule the Court applies, it cannot be one specially crafted for Trump, but must be a rule that could apply to any President, and, more important, to the entire Executive Branch—which is composed of many people, including diplomatic, military, and legal professionals.

One reason for not focusing on Trump's own statements, or applying a "Trump discount" to his administration's decisions, is that Trump is the head of a large bureaucracy that forms the Executive Branch of government. What conception of executive decision making does Roberts presuppose here? Does he assume that President Trump was not actually the primary mover and final decider with respect to the travel ban? Does he assume that professionals in his Administration reached a similar judgment about the need for the policy free from any bias towards Muslims? Suppose the President ordered his employees to come up with an exclusion policy because he harbors a prejudice against Muslims, or because he found that it was a winning issue during the election and believed that it would play well with elements of his political base who are hostile to Muslims. Nevertheless, he told his employees to eliminate any facial discrimination against Muslims so that the travel ban would appear legally innocuous. Should this be sufficient for the policy to pass muster?

At oral argument, the Solicitor General Noel Francisco emphasized that the travel ban arose out of routine and professional Executive branch deliberation rather than from the arbitrary decision of a rogue President. Consider this remarkable exchange with Justice Kagan:

> JUSTICE KAGAN: [L]et's say in some future time a . . . President gets elected who is a vehement anti-Semite . . . and says all kinds of denigrating comments about Jews and provokes a lot of resentment and hatred over the course of a campaign and in his presidency and, in the course of that, asks his staff or his cabinet members . . . to issue recommendations so that he can issue a proclamation of this kind, and they dot all the i's and they cross all the t's. And what emerges . . . is a proclamation that says no one shall enter from Israel. . . . Do you say [*Kleindienst v.*] *Mandel* puts an end to judicial review of that set of facts?
>
> GENERAL FRANCISCO: No, Your Honor, I don't say *Mandel* puts an end to it. . . . *Mandel* would be the starting point of the analysis, because it does involve the exclusion of aliens. . . . [I]f his cabinet were to actually come to him and say, Mr. President, there is honestly a national security risk here and you have to act, I think then that the President would be allowed to follow that advice even if in his private heart of hearts he also harbored animus. . . .
>
> Given that Israel happens to be one of the country's closest allies in the war against terrorism, it's not clear to me that you actually could satisfy. . . *Mandel*'s rational basis standard on that, unless it truly were based . . . on a cabinet-level recommendation that was about national security.
>
> JUSTICE KAGAN: General . . . this is a[n] out-of-the-box kind of President in my hypothetical. . . . (Laughter.)
>
> GENERAL FRANCISCO: We—we—we don't have those, Your Honor.[3]

Should the result be any different if the President is "out-of-the-box"?

---

3. *Trump v. Hawaii*, Oral Argument Transcript at 16-18.

5. *From facial validity to rational basis?* Note how Roberts deals with *Kleindienst v. Mandel.* He does not simply apply its test of whether there is a "facially legitimate and bona fide" explanation for the Proclamation. Instead, he accepts (as did the Solicitor General) that the Court may have to look behind the face of the policy. Why concede this point? One possibility is that Roberts felt constrained by the factual record in the case. This is not a situation in which the Justices might merely *suspect* that the President is prejudiced; rather the record provides evidence that he is prejudiced against Muslims and that he traded on prejudice against Muslims (and other minority groups) to get elected.

Having conceded that the Court should look behind the policy and engage in judicial scrutiny, Roberts chooses the very lowest level of scrutiny, the rational basis test of *Williamson v. Lee Optical*, which makes no inquiry into actual motivations, postulates public-spirited purposes even for suspicions legislation passed in suspicious circumstances, and asks if there is any conceivable set of facts that might justify the choices the government has made. What justifies this choice of the standard of review? (Note Chief Justice Roberts' citation to *Railroad Retirement Board v. Fritz* (Casebook, p. 567), a case in which Congress had been bamboozled into voting for a bill whose consequences it did not fully understand; the Court nevertheless held that the statute passed the rational basis test.) Rational basis used this way effectively eliminates any inquiry into *actual* motivations, which, of course, is the central issue that plaintiffs were trying to raise. Thus, modifying *Kleindienst* to include a rational basis inquiry doesn't change the result.

Of course, standard-form Establishment Clause doctrine does not apply rational basis. Instead it asks whether a government policy has the purpose or effect of endorsing or disfavoring a particular religion or religion in general. Thus, it focuses on actual motivations. Moreover, the government's purpose must be "genuine, not a sham, and not merely secondary to a religious objective." McCreary County v. ACLU of Ky., 545 U.S. 844 (2005).

Roberts explains that such judicial scrutiny is best designed for cases involving domestic laws and policies, and not decisions about "immigration policies, diplomatic sanctions, and military actions." What justifies this distinction? Remember that a classic justification for heightened scrutiny (elaborated in footnote four of *Carolene Products*) is democratic legitimacy. If government officials have acted with prejudice toward discrete and insular minorities, their actions lack democratic legitimacy. Are concerns of democratic legitimacy less relevant or important where the subject matter is "immigration policies, diplomatic sanctions, and military actions"? Or is Roberts' point that courts are simply less competent to pass on these questions?

6. *Rational basis, no bite.* Roberts recognizes that there is another version of the rational basis test, "rational basis with a bite," that *does* focus on whether a policy is based on irrational prejudice (*Cleburne*) or animus (*Romer v. Evans*). However, Roberts does not apply this test in the way it was applied in United States v. Windsor, 133 S.Ct. 2675 (2013), which struck down the Defense of Marriage Act (see Casebook pp. 1570-74). Roberts says that the Proclamation

is constitutional because "[i]t cannot be said that it is impossible to 'discern a relationship to legitimate state interests' or that the policy is 'inexplicable by anything but animus.'" Yet *Windsor* struck down a ban on federal benefits for same-sex marriages even though the government had identified a series of legitimate state interests; rather the case turned on the majority's belief that the law was motivated by anti-gay animus.

7. *Justice Kennedy washes his hands.* Note Justice Kennedy's concurrence, which provides the crucial fifth vote. He argues that although courts will not interfere with Executive Branch foreign policy decisions, Executive Branch officials also take an oath to uphold the Constitution, and they have a duty not to make decisions based on unconstitutional motives. In fact, Kennedy says, it is precisely because courts will not second-guess government officials' decisions in the area of foreign policy that they must be especially careful not to violate the Constitution. Does Kennedy offer any way of reining in Presidents who do not take their oaths seriously? Or is his point that this must be left to electoral politics?

What do you make of Justice Kennedy's citation to *Romer v. Evans* and his statement that "Whether judicial proceedings may properly continue in this case, in light of the substantial deference that is and must be accorded to the Executive in the conduct of foreign affairs, and in light of today's decision, is a matter to be addressed in the first instance on remand"? Does this leave the door open to further litigation and discovery on the question of the President's "animosity to a religion"?[4]

Justice Kennedy announced his retirement at the end of June 2018, and was replaced by Justice Brett Kavanaugh. It is not yet clear what the newly constituted Court will do with the animus doctrine, as developed in his decisions in *Romer* and *Windsor.*

8. *What does it mean to overrule* Korematsu*?* Both the majority and the dissent compare the travel ban decision to *Korematsu.* Justice Sotomayor's dissent argues that the Court in *Hawaii v. Trump* failed to stand up to prejudice, and was cowed by claims of national security, just as it had been in *Korematsu.* Thus, through the very act of overruling *Korematsu,* the Court was legitimating new forms of racial and religious discrimination.

Chief Justice Roberts makes two points. First, he denounces *Korematsu,* which he says, "has been overruled in the court of history, and — to be clear — has no place in law under the Constitution."

Second, and perhaps more important, he distinguishes *Korematsu,* arguing that it "has nothing to do with this case." *Korematsu* involved "[t]he forcible relocation of U.S. citizens to concentration camps, solely and explicitly on the basis of race," whereas Trump's Proclamation is "a facially neutral policy denying certain foreign nationals the privilege of admission. The entry suspension is

---

4. For an argument to this effect, see Noah Feldman, Take Trump's Travel Ban Back to Court, Bloomberg News, June 29, 2018, https://www.bloomberg.com/view/articles/2018-06-29/take-trump-s- travel-ban-back-to-court (discussing arguments by Owen Fiss).

an act that is well within executive authority and could have been taken by any other President." And because "the Government has set forth a sufficient national security justification to survive rational basis review," the Court will uphold the suspension.

President Roosevelt's Executive Order 9066 was facially neutral as to race and nationality: it simply gave the military the authority to designate areas "from which any or all persons may be excluded." However, General DeWitt's proclamations based on that order were directed at "all persons of Japanese ancestry."

Note that *Korematsu* involved both the detention of both Japanese-American citizens *and* Japanese-American resident aliens. Roberts' description of the vice of *Korematsu* only refers to citizens. Does this mean that *Korematsu* is still good law if the government decides to round up and detain Muslim non-citizens present in the United States?

One of the ironies of Roberts' dual move—denouncing *Korematsu* and distinguishing it—is that the "overruling" of *Korematsu* is purely dicta, because, according to Roberts, the case is legally irrelevant to the issues presented in *Trump v. Hawaii.*

9. *The court of history.* Roberts says that *Korematsu* "has been overruled by the court of history." What is the relationship between the "court of history" and the Supreme Court of the United States? The theory of interpretation presupposed by this metaphor is that, in the long run, later generations decide whether earlier generations have correctly interpreted the Constitution. Yet Roberts also says that *Korematsu* was "wrong the day it was decided," so, presumably, it was not necessary to wait for history's judgment.

10. "Korematsu *has nothing to do with this case.*" Why does *Korematsu* "ha[ve] nothing to do" with *Trump v. Hawaii?*[5] Consider the following possibilities:

1. *Korematsu* (and related decisions such as Hirabayashi v. United States, 320 U.S. 81 (1943)) involved race, whereas *Trump* involves religion.

2. *Korematsu* and *Hirabayashi* involved Japanese-American citizens and resident aliens, whereas *Trump* involved aliens seeking to enter the United States.

3. *Korematsu* and *Hirabayashi* involved curfews and detention, whereas *Trump* involves exclusion from the United States and the separation of families.

4. *Korematsu* and *Hirabayashi* were justified on national security grounds but the military orders in question involved an explicit categorization based on race, whereas *Trump* is justified on national security grounds but it involves a facially neutral rule that survives rational basis scrutiny. It is true that the Court generally treat invidious motivation as being as unconstitutional as facial classification (See *Washington v. Davis*, which requires a showing of intention, and *Masterpiece Cakeshop*, decided this Term, in which the Court held that Colorado had violated religious neutrality.) However, in *Trump*, Justice

5. See Joseph Fishkin, Why Was Korematsu Wrong, Balkinization, June 26, 2018, https://balkin.blogspot.com/2018/06/why-was-korematsu-wrong.html; Richard Primus, The Travel Ban and Inter-Branch Conflict, Take Care, June 26, 2018, https://takecareblog.com/blog/the-travel-ban-and-inter-branch-conflict.

Roberts argues that the Court should not inquire into unconstitutional motivation because "[i]t cannot be said that it is impossible to 'discern a relationship to legitimate state interests' or that the policy is 'inexplicable by anything but animus.'"

What do you make of these possible distinctions?

One may assume that a well-trained lawyer can demonstrate that almost any contemporary government action defended on grounds of national security these days is distinguishable from *Korematsu* and *Hirabayashi*. (Consider, as examples, the actions of the Bush and Obama administrations in dealing with terrorist suspects: the establishment of Guantanamo Bay as (in effect) a law-free zone, the use of waterboarding and other "enhanced interrogation techniques," and the use of drones.) That said, do *Korematsu* and *Hirabayashi* have any other lessons for contemporary decisionmakers about national security and constitutional values?

DEPARTMENT OF HOMELAND SECURITY V. REGENTS OF THE UNIVERSITY OF CALIFORNIA, 140 S.Ct. 1891 (2020): [In 2012, the Department of Homeland Security (DHS) under the Obama Administration issued a memorandum announcing an immigration relief program known as Deferred Action for Childhood Arrivals (DACA), which allows certain unauthorized aliens who arrived in the United States as children to apply for a two-year forbearance of removal. Those granted such relief become eligible for work authorization and various federal benefits. Some 700,000 aliens have availed themselves of this opportunity.

Two years later, the Obama DHS expanded DACA eligibility and created a related program known as Deferred Action for Parents of Americans and Lawful Permanent Residents (DAPA). If implemented, that program would have made 4.3 million parents of U.S. citizens or lawful permanent residents eligible for the same forbearance from removal, work eligibility, and other benefits as DACA recipients. Texas, joined by 25 other states, secured a nationwide preliminary injunction barring implementation of both the DACA expansion and DAPA. The Fifth Circuit upheld the injunction, concluding that the program violated the Immigration and Nationality Act (INA), which carefully defines eligibility for benefits. The Supreme Court, with only eight members following the death of Justice Scalia, affirmed by an equally divided vote, and the litigation then continued in the District Court.

In June 2017, after President Trump succeeded President Obama, the Trump DHS rescinded the DAPA program, citing, among other reasons, the ongoing suit by Texas and new policy priorities. That September, the Attorney General advised Acting Secretary of Homeland Security Elaine C. Duke that DACA shared DAPA's legal flaws and should also be rescinded. The next day, Duke acted on that advice. Taking into consideration the Fifth Circuit and Supreme Court rulings and the Attorney General's letter, Duke decided to terminate the program. She explained that DHS would no longer accept new applications, but that existing DACA recipients whose benefits were set to expire within six months could apply for a two-year renewal. For all other DACA recipients, previously issued grants of relief would expire on their own terms, with no prospect for renewal.

In June 2017, the Trump Administration rescinded the DACA program. Several groups of plaintiffs challenged the decision under the Administrative Procedure Act. They also argued that the rescission of DACA was done out of animus against Latinos and therefore violated the Equal Protection Component of the Fifth Amendment's Due Process Clause.

The Court held 5-4 that the rescission was arbitrary and capricious and therefore unlawful under the APA. It also dismissed the plaintiffs' Due Process claims. Justice Roberts wrote the majority opinion, with Justice Sotomayor dissenting on the Due Process claims. Justices Thomas, Alito, Gorsuch, and Kavanaugh agreed that plaintiffs' Due Process claim should be dismissed, but dissented on the APA holding.]

ROBERTS, C.J.:

To plead animus, a plaintiff must raise a plausible inference that an "invidious discriminatory purpose was a motivating factor" in the relevant decision. *Arlington Heights.* Possible evidence includes disparate impact on a particular group, "[d]epartures from the normal procedural sequence," and "contemporary statements by members of the decisionmaking body." Tracking these factors, respondents allege that animus is evidenced by (1) the disparate impact of the rescission on Latinos from Mexico, who represent 78% of DACA recipients; (2) the unusual history behind the rescission; and (3) pre- and post-election statements by President Trump.

None of these points, either singly or in concert, establishes a plausible equal protection claim. First, because Latinos make up a large share of the unauthorized alien population, one would expect them to make up an outsized share of recipients of any cross-cutting immigration relief program. Were this fact sufficient to state a claim, virtually any generally applicable immigration policy could be challenged on equal protection grounds.

Second, there is nothing irregular about the history leading up to the September 2017 rescission. . . . [W]hen the Attorney General . . . determined that DACA shared DAPA's legal defects, DHS's decision to reevaluate DACA was not a "strange about-face." It was a natural response to a newly identified problem.

Finally, the cited statements are unilluminating. The relevant actors were most directly Acting [Department of Homeland Security] Secretary Duke and the Attorney General [Jefferson B. Sessions III]. . . . [R]espondents did not "identif[y] statements by [either] that would give rise to an inference of discriminatory motive." Instead, respondents contend that President Trump made critical statements about Latinos that evince discriminatory intent. But, even as interpreted by respondents, these statements — remote in time and made in unrelated contexts — do not qualify as "contemporary statements" probative of the decision at issue. *Arlington Heights.* Thus, like respondents' other points, the statements fail to raise a plausible inference that the rescission was motivated by animus.

Justice SOTOMAYOR, concurring in part, concurring in the judgment in part, and dissenting in part.

The majority rightly holds that the Department of Homeland Security (DHS) violated the Administrative Procedure Act in rescinding the Deferred Action for Childhood Arrivals (DACA) program. But the Court forecloses any challenge to the rescission under the Equal Protection Clause. I believe that determination is unwarranted on the existing record and premature at this stage of the litigation. I would instead permit respondents to develop their equal protection claims on remand.

The complaints each set forth particularized facts that plausibly allege discriminatory animus. . . .

First, the plurality dismisses the statements that President Trump made both before and after he assumed office. The *Batalla Vidal* complaints catalog then-candidate Trump's declarations that Mexican immigrants are "people that have lots of problems," "the bad ones," and "criminals, drug dealers, [and] rapists." The *Regents* complaints additionally quote President Trump's 2017 statement comparing undocumented immigrants to "animals" responsible for "the drugs, the gangs, the cartels, the crisis of smuggling and trafficking, [and] MS13." The plurality brushes these aside as "unilluminating," "remote in time," and having been "made in unrelated contexts."

But "nothing in our precedent supports [the] blinkered approach" of disregarding any of the campaign statements as remote in time from later-enacted policies. *Trump v. Hawaii*, 585 U.S. ____, ____, n.3, 138 S.Ct. 2392, 2438, n.3, (2018) (Sotomayor, J., dissenting). Nor did any of the statements arise in unrelated contexts. They bear on unlawful migration from Mexico — a keystone of President Trump's campaign and a policy priority of his administration — and, according to respondents, were an animating force behind the rescission of DACA. Taken together, "the words of the President" help to "create the strong perception" that the rescission decision was "contaminated by impermissible discriminatory animus." This perception provides respondents with grounds to litigate their equal protection claims further.

Next, the plurality minimizes the disproportionate impact of the rescission decision on Latinos after considering this point in isolation. But the impact of the policy decision must be viewed in the context of the President's public statements on and off the campaign trail. At the motion-to-dismiss stage, I would not so readily dismiss the allegation that an executive decision disproportionately harms the same racial group that the President branded as less desirable mere months earlier.

Finally, the plurality finds nothing untoward in the "specific sequence of events leading up to the challenged decision." I disagree. As late as June 2017, DHS insisted it remained committed to DACA, even while rescinding a related program, the Deferred Action for Parents of Americans and Lawful Permanent Residents. But a mere three months later, DHS terminated DACA without, as the plurality acknowledges, considering important aspects of the termination. The abrupt change in position plausibly suggests that something other than questions about the legality of DACA motivated the rescission decision. Accordingly, it raises the possibility of a "significant mismatch between the decision . . . made and the rationale . . . provided." *Department of Commerce v. New York*, 588 U.S. ____, ____, 139 S.Ct. 2551, 2575 (2019). Only by bypassing context does the plurality conclude otherwise.

The facts in respondents' complaints create more than a "sheer possibility that a defendant has acted unlawfully." Whether they ultimately amount to actionable discrimination should be determined only after factual development on remand. Because the Court prematurely disposes of respondents' equal protection claims by overlooking the strength of their complaints, I join all but Part IV of the opinion and do not concur in the corresponding part of the judgment.

Discussion

1. Compare the Court's treatment of the Due Process claims with its treatment of the Establishment Clause claims in *Trump v. Hawaii*. In both cases, the Court refused to impute Trump's personal prejudices to the operations of the federal government. And in both cases, the challenged decisions reflected the platform on which candidate Trump ran.

2. Can one avoid the question of Trump's animus, as the majority does, by arguing that the policies were carried out by Attorney General Sessions and DHS Secretary Duke, and there were no allegations that either of them acted out of animus? To what extent does it matter that Sessions and Duke were carrying out the President's policies as opposed to their own policies?

It may be difficult to tell where animus lies in a chain of command. Compare *Korematsu*, in which Executive Order 9066 was signed by President Roosevelt but the decision to implement the order broadly to intern Japanese-American citizens was carried out by General DeWitt, who historians argue was motivated by anti-Japanese animus. If respondents' claims fail because evidence of Trump's animus is not probative, and there were no allegations of animus by Sessions and Duke, does *Trump v. Hawaii* become an easy case, because the executive orders were written and prepared by persons other than the President and all he did was sign them?

3. Are there any circumstances in which a hypothetical President's racist, prejudiced, or bigoted statements could constitutionally invalidate a policy of his or her administration, as long as the policy can be defended by the Justice Department in terms unrelated to race, religion, or ethnicity? Should we conclude that the principle of *Washington v. Davis* does not apply to sitting presidents, or simply that courts will do everything possible to avoid suggesting that government policies are affected by the President's prejudices?

* * *

DEPARTMENT OF HOMELAND SECURITY V. THURAISSIGIAM, 140 S.Ct. 1959 (2020): The Illegal Immigration Reform and Immigrant Responsibility Act (IIRIRA) provides for the expedited removal of "applicants" seeking admission into the United States, whether at a designated port of entry or elsewhere. 8 U.S.C. § 1225(a)(1). An applicant may avoid expedited removal by demonstrating to an asylum officer a "credible fear of persecution," defined as "a significant possibility . . . that the alien could establish eligibility for asylum." § 1225(b)(1)(B)(v). An applicant who makes this showing is entitled to "full consideration" of an asylum claim in a standard removal hearing. 8 C.F.R. § 208.30(f). An asylum officer's rejection of a credible-fear claim is reviewed by a supervisor and may then be appealed to an immigration judge. But IIRIRA limits the review that a federal court may conduct on a petition for a writ of habeas corpus. 8 U.S.C. § 1252(e)(2). In particular, courts may not review "the determination" that an applicant lacks a credible fear of persecution. § 1252(a)(2)(A)(iii).

Respondent Vijayakumar Thuraissigiam is a Sri Lankan national who was stopped just 25 yards after crossing the southern border without inspection or an entry document. He was detained for expedited removal. An asylum officer rejected his claim that he had a credible fear of persecution, a supervising officer agreed, and an Immigration Judge affirmed.

Thuraissigiam then filed a federal habeas petition, asserting for the first time a fear of persecution based on his Tamil ethnicity and political views and requesting a new opportunity to apply for asylum. He argued that because the IIRIRA withdraws judicial review of an applicant's eligibility for asylum, it violates the Suspension Clause of Article I, section 9.

The Supreme Court, in an opinion by Justice Alito, joined by Chief Justice Roberts and Justices Thomas, Gorsuch, and Kavanaugh, held that the IIRIRA was constitutional: "The Suspension Clause provides that '[t]he Privilege of the Writ of Habeas Corpus shall not be suspended, unless when in Cases of Rebellion or Invasion the public Safety may require it.' U.S. Const., Art. I, § 9, cl. 2. In INS v. St. Cyr, 533 U.S. 289 (2001), we wrote that the Clause, at a minimum, 'protects the writ as it existed in 1789,' when the Constitution was adopted."

Nevertheless, Justice Alito argued that historically, the writ protected only against unlawful detention: "[N]either respondent nor his amici have shown that the writ of habeas corpus was understood at the time of the adoption of the Constitution to permit a petitioner to claim the right to enter or remain in a country or to obtain administrative review potentially leading to that result. The writ simply provided a means of contesting the lawfulness of restraint and securing release." "Not only did respondent fail to seek release, he does not dispute that confinement during the pendency of expedited asylum review, and even during the additional proceedings he seeks, is lawful."

Justice Alito distinguished *Boumediene v. Bush* (discussed in Chapter 6), which "is not about immigration at all." *Boumediene* "held that suspected foreign terrorists could challenge their detention at the naval base in Guantanamo Bay, Cuba. They had been 'apprehended on the battlefield in Afghanistan' and elsewhere, not while crossing the border. . . . [N]othing in the Court's discussion of the Suspension Clause suggested that they could have used habeas as a means of gaining entry." He distinguished *INS v. St. Cyr*, which interpreted the IIRIRA as not stripping habeas jurisdiction, because it too understood habeas to be about unlawful detention.

Justice Alito also concluded that Thuraissigiam had no independent Due Process right to a hearing: " 'the decisions of executive or administrative officers, acting within powers expressly conferred by Congress, are due process of law.' Nishimura Ekiu v. United States, 142 U.S. 651, 660 (1892). . . . [A]n alien in respondent's position has only those rights regarding admission that Congress has provided by statute. In respondent's case, Congress provided the right to a 'determin[ation]' whether he had 'a significant possibility' of 'establish[ing] eligibility for asylum,' and he was given that right. Because the Due Process Clause provides nothing more, it does not require review of that determination or how it was made."

Justice Thomas concurred: "The Founders appear to have understood '[t]he Privilege of the Writ of Habeas Corpus' to guarantee freedom from discretionary detention, and a 'suspen[sion]' of that privilege likely meant a statute granting the executive the power to detain without bail or trial based on mere suspicion of a crime or dangerousness. Thus, the expedited removal procedure in the Illegal Immigration Reform and Immigrant Responsibility Act of 1996, 110 Stat. 3009-546, is likely not a suspension."

Justices Breyer and Ginsburg concurred in the judgment, arguing that as applied to the facts of the case, the IIRIRA did not violate Thuraissigiam's right to habeas review. But the Court should not go further than this: "Addressing more broadly whether the Suspension Clause protects people challenging removal decisions may raise a host of difficult questions in the immigration context."

"What review might the Suspension Clause assure, say, a person apprehended years after she crossed our borders clandestinely and started a life in this country? Under current law, noncitizens who have lived in the United States for up to two years may be placed in expedited-removal proceedings, but Congress might decide to raise that 2-year cap (or remove it altogether). Does the Suspension Clause let Congress close the courthouse doors to a long-term permanent resident facing removal?" Or "[c]ould Congress, . . . deny habeas review to someone ordered removed despite claiming to be a natural-born U.S. citizen?. . . What about foreclosing habeas review of a claim that rogue immigration officials forged the record of a credible-fear interview that, in truth, never happened? Or that such officials denied a refugee asylum based on the dead-wrong legal interpretation that Judaism does not qualify as a 'religion' under governing law? Cf. Tod v. Waldman, 266 U.S. 113 (1924) (observing that immigration officials ignored a Jewish family's claim that they were 'refugees' fleeing 'religious persecution')."

Justice Sotomayor, joined by Justice Kagan, dissented: "Fairly characterized, respondent's claims allege legal error (for violations of governing asylum law and for violations of procedural due process) and an open-ended request for habeas relief. It is 'uncontroversial' that the writ encompasses such claims."

Chapter 8

Sex Equality

Insert on p. 1273 immediately before Note: The Nineteenth Amendment:

Note: Can the Equal Rights Amendment Be Ratified Today?

The Equal Rights Amendment (ERA), first proposed in Congress in 1923, was approved by both houses of Congress in 1972 and sent to the states. The text of the 1972 proposal reads:

Section 1. Equality of rights under the law shall not be denied or abridged by the United States or by any state on account of sex.

Section 2. The Congress shall have the power to enforce, by appropriate legislation, the provisions of this article.

Section 3. This amendment shall take effect two years after the date of ratification.

The joint Congressional resolution sending the proposal to the states placed a seven-year deadline on ratification. Between 1972 and 1977, 35 state legislatures ratified the ERA. However, as discussed earlier in this Casebook (pp. 1267-68), the New Right, led by Phyllis Schlafly, made opposition to the ERA a signature issue, and the ratifications stalled. Congress extended the deadline to 1982, but no more states ratified during the extended period.

The ERA gathered renewed interest in during the 2010s. In 2008, a Facebook page dedicated to support for the ERA began discussing sexist responses to Hillary Clinton's candidacy for the Democratic nomination for President in 2008 and protesting the Supreme Court's pay equity decision in Lilly Ledbetter v. Goodyear Tire & Rubber Co., 550 U.S. 618 (2007).[1] After Donald Trump became President, prompting a national Women's March in January of 2017, focus on the ERA's ratification intensified.[2] Shortly thereafter, in March of 2017,

---

1. For the ERA Facebook page, see https://www.facebook.com/ERAusa/.

2. For a short history of the recent mobilization, see Dahlia Lithwick, The ERA Is Back: The '70s-era constitutional amendment could be the perfect remedy for the #MeToo era, Slate, April 23, 2018, https://slate.com/news-and-politics/2018/04/the-equal-rights-amendment-could-be-the-perfect-remedy-for-the-metoo-era.html; The Equal Rights Amendment: Unfinished Business for the Constitution, http://www.equalrightsamendment.org/; Jessica Newirth, Equal Means Equal: Why the Time for an Equal Rights Amendment Is Now (2015).

Nevada's Legislature ratified the 1972 proposal. Illinois followed in 2018, and on January 15, 2020, Virginia voted to ratify the ERA, bringing the total to 38 states who, at one point or another, have ratified the ERA since 1972. However, 5 states had rescinded their ratifications in the 1970s: Nebraska (1973), Tennessee (1974), Idaho (1977), Kentucky (1978), and South Dakota (1979).[3] This raises the question of whether Virginia's ratification counts as the thirty-eighth state needed to ratify.[4]

The day after Virginia ratified, the National Archives announced that it would not take any action to certify the ERA as part of the Constitution. It stated that it would follow the advice of the Department of Justice's Office of Legal Counsel (OLC), which had issued a memo arguing that it was too late for states to ratify the amendment because the deadline had passed.[5]

On February 13, 2020, the House of Representatives voted to lift the ratification deadline by a vote of 232-183.[6]

Virginia has filed suit in federal district court, asserting that the Constitution has been amended because the deadline in the joint resolution supporting the ERA as initially sent to the states was outside Congress's Article V powers. The state asks the court to order the archivist to publish the amendment.[7]

What is the legal effect of Virginia's action and the House's resolution? Has the Constitution been amended?

Discussion

1. *The role of time limits.* Can states disregard time limits set by Congress? One might distinguish between time limits which appear in the actual text of the proposal (call these textual time limits), and time limits which appear only in the congressional resolution that sends the proposed amendment to the states (call these proposal time limits). Amendments 18 and 20-22 have textual time limits; later amendments (with the notable exception of the Twenty-Seventh, to be discussed shortly) have included time limits in the congressional proposal.

One might argue that while states cannot ratify a proposed amendment which, by its own terms, expires on a certain date, they need not be bound by time limits that appear only in the congressional proposal that accompanies the text. "It was

3. Thomas H. Neale, Cong. Res. Serv., *The Proposed Equal Rights Amendment: Contemporary Ratification Issues*, (December 29, 2019), https://crsreports.congress.gov/product/pdf/R/R42979/19.

4. See Rachel Frank, Previewing the ERA Debates, Balkinization, https://balkin.blogspot.com/2018/06/previewing-era-debates.html, on which this discussion note is based.

5. Office of Legal Counsel, Ratification of the Equal Rights Amendment (January 6, 2020), https://www.justice.gov/olc/file/1235176/download; US Archives confirms it won't take steps to certify ERA, Associated Press, January 28, 2020, https://apnews.com/0b1f3d4cb590caab15e35d24c9997fd8.

6. H.J. Res. 79 (February 13, 2020), https://www.congress.gov/bill/116th-congress/house-joint-resolution/79/text.

7. For a discussion of the issues in the lawsuit, see Julie Suk, Who Decides the Future of the Equal Rights Amendment?, Take Care, July 6, 2020, https://takecareblog.com/blog/who-decides-the-future-of-the-equal-rights-amendment.

in the resolving clause, but it wasn't a part of the amendment that was proposed by Congress," the Nevada bill's chief sponsor observed. "That's why the time limit is irrelevant."[8]

Article V specifies that "The Congress, whenever two thirds of both houses shall deem it necessary, *shall propose amendments* to this Constitution." Such proposals "shall be valid to all intents and purposes, as part of this Constitution, when ratified by the legislatures of three fourths of the several states, or by conventions in three fourths thereof, *as the one or the other mode of ratification may be proposed by the Congress.*"

Defenders of Congressional prerogatives might argue that this language gives Congress complete power to decide both the nature of the proposal and the conditions under which ratification becomes effective.

Defenders of state prerogatives might respond that the language does no such thing: Congress merely has the power to decide whether ratifications will be by state legislatures or by state conventions; hence, it may not impose additional conditions. For this reason, the 1982 extension was completely unnecessary, and its expiration was irrelevant.

In Dillon v. Gloss, 256 U.S. 368 (1921), the Supreme Court held that Congress had the power to impose time limits on a proposed amendment to the Constitution, and that seven years was a reasonable requirement. (*Dillion* involved the Eighteenth Amendment, which included time limits in the text of the amendment itself). Conversely, the Supreme Court held in Coleman v. Miller, 307 U.S. 433 (1939), that if Congress chooses not to add time limits, proposals remain alive indefinitely. The Court argued that the question of whether ratification is timely is a political question, left to Congress's judgment. (See Casebook pp. 526-28) *Coleman* involved a proposed Child Labor Amendment (which would have given Congress the power to pass laws regulating child labor); both the Child Labor Amendment and the Nineteenth Amendment contained no time limits, unlike Amendments 18 and 20-26.

Note that if one accepts that Congress gets to make decisions about ratification, it might also follow that Congress has the power to extend the deadline if it chooses. That would mean that the 1982 extension was valid. But what if a state (such as Nevada and Illinois) ratifies after the extension has expired? Again, there are several possibilities. The ratifications after 1982 might be invalid. Or Congress may accept these ratifications as valid retroactively, if it passes a new joint resolution promulgating the ratification of the new amendment. (Query: would such a promulgating resolution require a two-thirds vote of both houses or only a simple majority? Note that the text of Article V says nothing about Congress's role in promulgation. From a structural perspective, does

---

8. Colin Dwyer & Carrie Kaufman, Nevada Ratifies The Equal Rights Amendment . . . 35 Years After The Deadline, Morning Edition, National Public Radio, March 21, 2017, https://www.npr.org/sections/thetwo-way/2017/03/21/520962541/nevada-on-cusp-of-ratifying-equal-rights-amendment-35-years-after-deadline.

it make better sense to hold a promulgating resolution to the supermajority standards of an Article V proposing resolution, or to ordinary majority standards?)

2. *Contemporaneous ratification: The problem of transgenerational amendments.* Behind these debates are larger questions of the purposes behind Article V.

One might argue that too much time has passed for the ERA to be ratified. Congressional amendments should reflect the will of a supermajority of Americans, which must be expressed within a bounded period of time — perhaps seven years (as *Dillon* suggested), or within a single generation.

On the other hand, consider the Twenty-Seventh Amendment, which was the second of the original twelve proposed by Congress in 1789. The third through twelfth proposals became Amendments 1 through 10, what we now call the Bill of Rights. The Madison Amendment, as it is sometimes called, was finally ratified in 1992, and became Amendment 27. The 200 years between proposal and ratification of the Twenty-Seventh Amendment are many times longer than the forty-some years that have elapsed since the ERA was sent to the states in 1972.

3. *Concurrent ratification: The problem of rescissions.* A different objection is that five states have rescinded their ratifications. That means that ratification requires six more states, not just one. The argument for this view is that a valid amendment to the Constitution requires the *concurrent* agreement of three quarters of the states, even if all of the states ratify at different points in time. The agreement of the states is not concurrent if one of the states withdraws consent before the finish line is reached.

On the other hand, the text of Article V only mentions ratifications, not rescissions. There is also some institutional precedent for not counting rescissions. Congress refused to accept rescissions of the Fourteenth and Nineteenth Amendments (although it is not clear that counting the rescissions would have brought the total under three quarters of the states, see Casebook p. 350 n. 30). The Attorneys General of the states that attempted to rescind the ERA expressed doubts about whether they were effective. Aside from text and precedent, are there good structural arguments for not counting rescissions? If a state may change its mind and vote for an amendment during the ratification process, why shouldn't it be able to change its mind and vote against?

4. *Promulgation: The problem of who decides and announces ratification.* The text of Article V does not make clear who decides when and whether an amendment has properly been ratified. One theory is that as soon as three quarters of the state legislatures ratify, the amendment is part of the Constitution. But this begs the question of what to do if there is a dispute about whether the requirements have been met. (Suppose that a state tries to rescind, or there is a dispute about whether both houses of a state legislature properly voted on the proposal.) *Coleman* seems to suggest that the issue is a political question that is left to Congress. If so, then Congress can resolve any disputes — and bestow a much needed dose of political legitimacy — by passing a joint resolution promulgating a new amendment.

The Twenty-Seventh Amendment offers an interesting example. After Michigan ratified the Twenty-Seventh Amendment in May 1992, the United States Archivist proclaimed that a new amendment had been added to the Constitution, operating on the advice of the Department of Justice, which took the position that contemporaneous ratification and congressional approval were both unnecessary. Congress, however, passed a joint resolution two days later proclaiming that the Twenty-Seventh Amendment was now (i.e., when Congress spoke) a valid part of the Constitution. Because of popular upset about a financial scandal involving the House bank, both the President and Congress were eager to pronounce the Twenty-Seventh Amendment ratified: this showed that they were responding to public outcry about government corruption. As a result, the case of the Twenty-Seventh Amendment did not provide a clear example of who would decide if there was disagreement between the political branches.

Whatever the answer to this question, congressional promulgation has an additional advantage: it bestows legitimacy on the ratification process, and may help silence concerns about whether the process was consistent with constitutional norms. The ERA presents a case in which the ratification process has been protracted, but the constitutional norm at issue has grown in authority and interpretive significance in the intervening decades. Even so, opponents might raise objections; hence, congressional promulgation might help quiet concerns about the legitimacy of the ratification process. Thus, although congressional ratification may not be necessary legally, it may be important politically. (How might this affect your views about the proper voting rules for promulgation, as discussed in note 1, supra?) Suppose that Congress passed a joint resolution promulgating the ERA, and a plaintiff brought suit under the amendment. How if at all, would or should congressional promulgation influence federal courts' judgment about whether the amendment was properly part of the Constitution?

5. *Interpretation: What would the new amendment mean?* Suppose that an additional state—or six additional states—ratifies the proposed ERA and Congress passes a joint resolution of promulgation. How should courts interpret the new amendment? Should they look to what people in the 1970s thought about what the ERA would do, or should they look to what people *today* think about what the ERA would do? Or are both of these irrelevant to its proper construction? Think about previous debates about originalism in this Casebook. Note that originalist arguments presuppose a bounded period of time that fixes original meaning or original understanding. But what if this assumption is lacking? Can originalism operate under these conditions?

Suppose that Congress prepares a legislative report accompanying its joint resolution offering its views about what the new amendment means. Should courts follow the views of this report? Suppose, for example, that the report says that the new amendment has nothing whatsoever to do with gay rights, or transgender rights. Should courts take this as binding or as very persuasive?

Suppose a judge concluded that (1) the long ratification history of the ERA supplied evidence of many deliberative agents operating in many times and places and espousing many different views; and (2) Congress lacked power to create a ratification history and a definitive meaning for the amendment as part of the promulgation process. How should the judge interpret the amendment?

6. *The difference an ERA makes — short term and long term effects.* What constitutional protections would an Equal Rights Amendment provide in addition to those already provided by the equality guarantees of the Fifth and Fourteenth Amendments? (Eagle Forum, through which Phyllis Schlafly led opposition to the ERA since its introduction in the 1970s, has complied a top ten list.[9])

Look at the text of the proposed ERA and consider its likely effects. Is there any reason why a judge who does not think that gay rights or transgender rights are protected by the Constitution would change his or her mind after the ratification of the ERA? What about a judge who believes that the Constitution should be interpreted in light of the contested and evolving views of the American people? Put another way, what difference will this particular piece of constitutional text make?

In what areas of law — if any — do you think adding an ERA to existing equal protection case law would be likely to make the most difference? Is the current Supreme Court likely to share this view?

Consider what laws Congress might enact under section two of the ERA, which provides that "The Congress shall have the power to enforce, by appropriate legislation, the provisions of this article." Given existing interpretations of the Commerce Clause and section five of the Fourteenth Amendment, what new kinds of legislation might the ERA's section two enable Congress to enact? Would the state action requirement announced in the *Civil Rights Cases* apply to Section two legislation enforcing the new amendment? Would the *Boerne* rule of congruence and proportionality?

Even if you think that the text would probably not change any current judge's mind, how might it affect political mobilization around constitutional norms? Put another way, what do you think a ratified ERA in 2018 would do — either now or in the future — in American politics, or in American constitutional law? What effect might the new text have in a generation?

---

9. Eagle Forum, Top ten cases that prove the Equal Rights Amendment would have been a disaster, http://eagleforum.org/era/2002/top-ten.shtml (listing *Rostker v. Goldberg, Harris v. McRae, Baehr v. Lewin, Ohio v. Akron Ctr. For Reproductive Health, Bob Jones University v. United States, United States v. Morrison, Boy Scouts of America v. Dale, Personnel Adm'r of Massachusetts v. Feeney, Parham v. Hughes,* and *Miller v. Albright*).

Chapter 9

Liberty, Equality, and Fundamental Rights: The Constitution, the Family, and the Body

Insert at the end of p. 1510:

JUNE MEDICAL SERVICES L.L.C. ET AL. v. RUSSO
2020 WL 3492640

Justice BREYER announced the judgment of the Court and delivered an opinion, in which Justice GINSBURG, Justice SOTOMAYOR, and Justice KAGAN join.

[A] Louisiana statute, Act 620, . . . is almost word-for-word identical to [the] Texas' admitting-privileges law [struck down in *Whole Woman's Health*. . . . [T]he District Court found that the statute offers no significant health benefit. It found that conditions on admitting privileges common to hospitals throughout the State have made and will continue to make it impossible for abortion providers to obtain conforming privileges for reasons that have nothing to do with the State's asserted interests in promoting women's health and safety. And it found that this inability places a substantial obstacle in the path of women seeking an abortion. . . . We have examined the extensive record carefully and conclude that it supports the District Court's findings of fact. Those findings mirror those made in *Whole Woman's Health* in every relevant respect and require the same result. We consequently hold that the Louisiana statute is unconstitutional. . . .

III

. . . In *Whole Woman's Health*, we quoted *Casey* in explaining that . . . " '*[u]nnecessary* health regulations'" impose an unconstitutional " '*undue burden*'" if they have " '*the purpose or effect of presenting a substantial obstacle to a woman seeking an abortion.*'" (quoting *Casey*; emphasis added). . . . [I]n applying these standards, courts must "consider the burdens a law imposes on abortion access together with the benefits those laws confer." We cautioned that courts "must review legislative 'factfinding under a deferential standard.'" But they "must not 'place dispositive weight' on those 'findings,'" for the courts " 'retai[n] an independent constitutional duty to review factual findings where constitutional rights are at stake.'" (quoting *Gonzales*).

We held in *Whole Woman's Health* that the trial court faithfully applied these standards. . . . The District Court in this suit did the same. The Court of Appeals disagreed with the District Court, not so much in respect to the legal standards that we have just set forth, but because it did not agree with the factual findings on which the District Court relied in assessing both the burdens that Act 620 imposes and the health-related benefits it might bring. . . . [But] a district court's findings of fact, "whether based on oral or other evidence, must not be set aside unless clearly erroneous, and the reviewing court must give due regard to the trial court's opportunity to judge the witnesses' credibility." Fed. Rule Civ. Proc. 52(a)(6). In " 'applying [this] standard to the findings of a district court sitting without a jury, appellate courts must constantly have in mind that their function is not to decide factual issues *de novo.*'" Where "the district court's account of the evidence is plausible in light of the record viewed in its entirety, the court of appeals may not reverse it even though convinced that had it been sitting as the trier of fact, it would have weighed the evidence differently." "A finding that is 'plausible' in light of the full record—even if another is equally or more so—must govern." . . .

Under that familiar standard, we find that the testimony and other evidence contained in the extensive record developed over the 6-day trial support the District Court's ultimate conclusion that, "[e]ven if Act 620 could be said to further women's health to some marginal degree, the burdens it imposes far outweigh any such benefit, and thus the Act imposes an unconstitutional undue burden."

IV

The District Court found that enforcing the admitting-privileges requirement would "result in a drastic reduction in the number and geographic distribution of abortion providers," . . . mak[ing] it impossible for "many women seeking a safe, legal abortion in Louisiana . . . to obtain one" and that it would impose "substantial obstacles" on those who could. . . . The evidence on which the District Court relied in this case is even stronger and more detailed [than in *Whole Woman's Health*]. The District Court supervised [the anonymous platintiff doctors in the case.] Does 1, 2, 5, and 6 for over a year and a half as they tried, and largely failed, to obtain conforming privileges from 13 relevant hospitals. The court heard direct evidence that some of the doctors' applications were denied for reasons that had nothing to do with their ability to perform abortions safely. It also compiled circumstantial evidence that explains why other applications were denied and explains why, given the costs of applying and the reputational risks that accompany rejection, some providers could have chosen in good faith *not* to apply to every qualifying hospital. The evidence also shows that opposition to abortion played a significant role in some hospitals' decisions to deny admitting privileges. . . . Just as in *Whole Woman's Health*, the experiences of the individual doctors in this case support the District Court's factual finding that Louisiana's admitting-privileges requirement, like that in Texas' law, serves no " 'relevant credentialing function.'" . . .

The Court of Appeals. . . . argued that Does 2, 5, and 6 had acted in bad faith. [But] the law requires appellate courts to review a trial court's findings under the deferential clear-error standard we have described. Our review of the record convinces us that the Court of Appeals misapplied that standard.

Justice Alito does not dispute that the District Court's findings are not "clearly erroneous." He argues instead that both the District Court and the Court of Appeals applied the wrong legal standard to the record in this case. By asking whether the doctors acted in "good faith," he contends, the courts below failed to account for the doctors' supposed "incentive to do as little as" possible to obtain conforming privileges. But that is not a legal argument at all. It is simply another way of saying that the doctors acted in *bad* faith. The District Court, after monitoring the doctors' efforts for a year and a half, found otherwise. And "[w]hen the record is examined in light of the appropriately deferential standard, it is apparent that it contains nothing that mandates a finding that the District Court's conclusion was clearly erroneous." . . .

The District Court drew from the record evidence . . . several conclusions in respect to the burden that Act 620 is likely to impose upon women's ability to access abortions in Louisiana. . . . [E]nforcing the admitting-privileges requirement would eliminate Does 1, 2, and 6. The District Court credited Doe 3's uncontradicted, in-court testimony that he would stop performing abortions if he was the last provider in northern Louisiana. . . . And Doe 5's inability to obtain privileges in the Baton Rouge area would leave Louisiana with just one clinic with one provider to serve the 10,000 women annually who seek abortions in the State. . . . Those women not altogether prevented from obtaining an abortion would face . . . "longer waiting times, and increased crowding." [D]elays in obtaining an abortion increase the risk that a woman will experience complications from the procedure and may make it impossible for her to choose a noninvasive medication abortion. . . . [B]oth experts and laypersons testified that the burdens of this increased travel would fall disproportionately on poor women, who are least able to absorb them. . . .

V

The District Court found that there was " 'no significant health-related problem that the new law helped to cure.' " It found that the admitting-privileges requirement "[d]oes [n]ot [p]rotect [w]omen's [h]ealth," provides "no significant health benefits," and makes no improvement to women's health "compared to prior law." Our examination of the record convinces us that these findings are not "clearly erroneous."

[T]he District Court found that the admitting-privileges requirement serves no "relevant credentialing function." [H]ospitals can, and do, deny admitting privileges for reasons unrelated to a doctor's ability safely to perform abortions. And Act 620's requirement that physicians obtain privileges at a hospital within 30 miles of the place where they perform abortions further constrains providers for reasons that bear no relationship to competence. Moreover, while "competency is a factor" in credentialing decisions, hospitals primarily focus upon a doctor's ability to perform the inpatient, hospital-based procedures for which the doctor seeks privileges — not outpatient abortions. . . . And nothing in the record indicates that the background vetting for admitting privileges adds significantly to the vetting that the State Board of Medical Examiners already provides.

[T]he District Court found that the admitting-privileges requirement "does not conform to prevailing medical standards and will not improve the safety of abortion in Louisiana." . . . As in *Whole Woman's Health*, the State introduced no evidence "showing that patients have better outcomes when their physicians have admitting privileges" or "of any instance in which an admitting privileges requirement would have helped even one woman obtain better treatment." . . .

We conclude, in light of the record, that the District Court's significant factual findings — both as to burdens and as to benefits — have ample evidentiary support. None is "clearly erroneous." Given the facts found, we must also uphold the District Court's related factual and legal determinations. These include its determination that Louisiana's law poses a "substantial obstacle" to women seeking an abortion; its determination that the law offers no significant health-related benefits; and its determination that the law consequently imposes an "undue burden" on a woman's constitutional right to choose to have an abortion. We also agree with its ultimate legal conclusion that, in light of these findings and our precedents, Act 620 violates the Constitution. . . .

This case is similar to, nearly identical with, *Whole Woman's Health.* And the law must consequently reach a similar conclusion. Act 620 is unconstitutional. The Court of Appeals' judgment is erroneous. It is

Reversed.

CHIEF JUSTICE ROBERTS, concurring in the judgment.

. . . I joined the dissent in *Whole Woman's Health* and continue to believe that the case was wrongly decided. The question today however is not whether *Whole Woman's Health* was right or wrong, but whether to adhere to it in deciding the present case. . . .

Today's case is a challenge from several abortion clinics and providers to a Louisiana law nearly identical to the Texas law struck down four years ago in *Whole Woman's Health.* Just like the Texas law, the Louisiana law requires physicians performing abortions to have "active admitting privileges at a hospital . . . located not further than thirty miles from the location at which the abortion is performed." Following a six-day bench trial, the District Court found that Louisiana's law would "result in a drastic reduction in the number and geographic distribution of abortion providers." The law would reduce the number of clinics from three to "one, or at most two," and the number of physicians providing abortions from five to "one, or at most two," and "therefore cripple women's ability to have an abortion in Louisiana."

The legal doctrine of *stare decisis* requires us, absent special circumstances, to treat like cases alike. The Louisiana law imposes a burden on access to abortion just as severe as that imposed by the Texas law, for the same reasons. Therefore Louisiana's law cannot stand under our precedents. . . .

Both Louisiana and the providers agree that the undue burden standard announced in *Casey* provides the appropriate framework to analyze Louisiana's law. . . . Neither party has asked us to reassess the constitutional validity of that standard. . . .

Under *Casey*, the State may not impose an undue burden on the woman's ability to obtain an abortion. "A finding of an undue burden is a shorthand for the conclusion that a state regulation has the purpose or effect of placing a substantial obstacle in the path of a woman seeking an abortion of a nonviable fetus." Laws that do not pose a substantial obstacle to abortion access are permissible, so long as they are "reasonably related" to a legitimate state interest.

After faithfully reciting this standard, the Court in *Whole Woman's Health* added the following observation: "The rule announced in *Casey* . . . requires that courts consider the burdens a law imposes on abortion access together with the benefits those laws confer." The plurality repeats today that the undue burden standard requires courts "to weigh the law's asserted benefits against the burdens it imposes on abortion access."

Read in isolation from *Casey*, such an inquiry could invite a grand "balancing test in which unweighted factors mysteriously are weighed." Under such tests, "equality of treatment is . . . impossible to achieve; predictability is destroyed; judicial arbitrariness is facilitated; judicial courage is impaired."

In this context, courts applying a balancing test would be asked in essence to weigh the State's interests in "protecting the potentiality of human life" and the health of the woman, on the one hand, against the woman's liberty interest in defining her "own concept of existence, of meaning, of the universe, and of the mystery of human life" on the other. *Casey*. There is no plausible sense in which anyone, let alone this Court, could objectively assign weight to such imponderable values and no meaningful way to compare them if there were. Attempting to do so would be like "judging whether a particular line is longer than a particular rock is heavy," Pretending that we could pull that off would require us to act as legislators, not judges, and would result in nothing other than an "unanalyzed exercise of judicial will" in the guise of a "neutral utilitarian calculus."

Nothing about *Casey* suggested that a weighing of costs and benefits of an abortion regulation was a job for the courts. On the contrary, we have explained that the "traditional rule" that "state and federal legislatures [have] wide discretion to pass legislation in areas where there is medical and scientific uncertainty" is "consistent with *Casey*." *Gonzales v. Carhart*. *Casey* instead focuses on the existence of a substantial obstacle, the sort of inquiry familiar to judges across a variety of contexts. . . .

The only restriction *Casey* found unconstitutional was Pennsylvania's spousal notification requirement. On that score, the Court recited a bevy of social science evidence demonstrating that "millions of women in this country . . . may have justifiable fears of physical abuse" or "devastating forms of psychological abuse from their husbands." In addition to "physical violence" and "child abuse," women justifiably feared "verbal harassment, threats of future violence, the destruction of possessions, physical confinement to the home, the withdrawal of financial support, or the disclosure of the abortion to family and friends." *Ibid.* The spousal notification requirement was "thus likely to prevent a significant number of women from obtaining an abortion." It did not "merely make abortions a little more difficult or expensive to obtain; for many women, it [imposed] a substantial obstacle." The Court emphasized that it would not "blind [itself] to the fact that the significant number of women who fear for their safety and the safety of their children are likely to be deterred from procuring an abortion as surely as if the Commonwealth had outlawed abortion in all cases."

The upshot of *Casey* is clear: The several restrictions that did not impose a substantial obstacle were constitutional, while the restriction that did impose a substantial obstacle was unconstitutional.

To be sure, the Court at times discussed the benefits of the regulations, including when it distinguished spousal notification from parental consent. But in the context of *Casey*'s governing standard, these benefits were not placed on a scale opposite the law's burdens. Rather, *Casey* discussed benefits in considering the threshold requirement that the State have a "legitimate purpose" and that the law be "reasonably related to that goal."

So long as that showing is made, the only question for a court is whether a law has the "effect of placing a substantial obstacle in the path of a woman seeking an abortion of a nonviable fetus." . . .

Mazurek v. Armstrong [520 U.S. 968 (1997) (*per curiam*)] places this understanding of *Casey*'s undue burden standard beyond doubt. *Mazurek* involved a challenge to a Montana law restricting the performance of abortions to licensed physicians. It was "uncontested that there was insufficient evidence of a 'substantial obstacle' to abortion." Therefore, once the Court found that the Montana Legislature had not acted with an "unlawful motive," the Court's work was complete. In fact, the Court found the challengers' argument — that the law was invalid because "all health evidence contradicts the [State's] claim that there is any health basis for the law" — to be "*squarely foreclosed* by *Casey* itself."

We should respect the statement in *Whole Woman's Health* that it was applying the undue burden standard of *Casey*. . . .

Here the plurality expressly acknowledges that we are not considering how to analyze an abortion regulation that does not present a substantial obstacle. . . . In this case, *Casey*'s requirement of finding a substantial obstacle before invalidating an abortion regulation is therefore a sufficient basis for the decision, as it was in *Whole Woman's Health*. In neither case, nor in *Casey* itself, was there call for consideration of a regulation's benefits, and nothing in *Casey* commands such consideration. . . . [T]he discussion of benefits in *Whole Woman's Health* was not necessary to its holding. [relocated footnote — eds.] . . .

Under principles of *stare decisis*, I agree with the plurality that the determination in *Whole Woman's Health* that Texas's law imposed a substantial obstacle requires the same determination about Louisiana's law. Under those same principles, I would adhere to the holding of *Casey*, requiring a substantial obstacle before striking down an abortion regulation. . . .

[T]he District Court found that "since the passage of [the Louisiana law], all five remaining doctors have attempted *in good faith* to comply" with the law by applying for admitting privileges, yet have had very little success. This finding was necessary to ensure that the physicians' inability to obtain admitting privileges was attributable to the new law rather than a halfhearted attempt to obtain privileges. Only then could the District Court accurately identify the Louisiana law's burden on abortion access.

The question is not whether we would reach the same findings from the same record. These District Court findings "entail[ed] primarily . . . factual work" and therefore are "review[ed] only for clear error." Clear error review follows from a candid appraisal of the comparative advantages of trial courts and appellate courts. "While we review transcripts for a living, they listen to witnesses for a living. While we largely read briefs for a living, they largely assess the credibility of parties and witnesses for a living."

We accordingly will not disturb the factual conclusions of the trial court unless we are "left with the definite and firm conviction that a mistake has been committed." In my view, the District Court's work reveals no such clear error, for the reasons the plurality explains. The District Court findings therefore bind us in this case.

Stare decisis instructs us to treat like cases alike. The result in this case is controlled by our decision four years ago invalidating a nearly identical Texas law. The Louisiana law burdens women seeking previability abortions to the same extent as the Texas law, according to factual findings that are not clearly erroneous. For that reason, I concur in the judgment of the Court that the Louisiana law is unconstitutional.

Justice THOMAS, dissenting.

Today a majority of the Court perpetuates its ill-founded abortion jurisprudence by enjoining a perfectly legitimate state law and doing so without jurisdiction. As is often the case with legal challenges to abortion regulations, this suit was brought by abortionists and abortion clinics. Their sole claim before this Court is that Louisiana's law violates the purported substantive due process right of a woman to abort her unborn child. But they concede that this right does not belong to them, and they seek to vindicate no private rights of their own. Under a proper understanding of Article III, these plaintiffs lack standing to invoke our jurisdiction. . . . I agree with Justice Alito that Louisiana did not waive its standing challenge below. But even if there were a waiver, it would not be relevant. Louisiana argues that the abortionists and abortion clinics lack standing under Article III to assert the putative rights of their potential clients. No waiver, however explicit, could relieve us of our independent obligation to ensure that we have jurisdiction before addressing the merits of a case. And under a proper understanding of Article III's case-or-controversy requirement, plaintiffs lack standing to invoke our jurisdiction because they assert no private rights of their own, seeking only to vindicate the putative constitutional rights of individuals not before the Court. . . .

Even if the plaintiffs had standing, the Court would still lack the authority to enjoin Louisiana's law, which represents a constitutionally valid exercise of the State's traditional police powers. . . . The Constitution does not constrain the States' ability to regulate or even prohibit abortion. . . . *Roe* is grievously wrong for many reasons, but the most fundamental is that its core holding — that the Constitution protects a woman's right to abort her unborn child — finds no support in the text of the Fourteenth Amendment. . . . More specifically, the idea that the Framers of the Fourteenth Amendment understood the Due Process Clause to protect a right to abortion is farcical. . . .

The Court's current "formulation of the *stare decisis* standard does not comport with our judicial duty under Article III," which requires us to faithfully interpret the Constitution. Rather, when our prior decisions clearly conflict with the text of the Constitution, we are required to "privilege [the] text over our own precedents." Because *Roe* and its progeny are premised on a "demonstrably erroneous interpretation of the Constitution," we should not apply them here. . . . [W]e exceed our constitutional authority whenever we "appl[y] demonstrably erroneous precedent instead of the relevant law's text." Because we can reconcile neither *Roe* nor its progeny with the text of our Constitution, those decisions should be overruled. . . .

Justice Alito, with whom Justice Gorsuch joins, with whom Justice Thomas joins except as to [the instructions on remand], and with whom Justice Kavanaugh joins as to Parts I, II, and III, dissenting.

[T]he plurality eschews the constitutional test set out in *Casey* and instead employs the balancing test adopted in *Whole Woman's Health.* The plurality concludes that the Louisiana law does nothing to protect the health of women, but that is disproved by substantial evidence in the record. And the plurality upholds the District Court's finding that the Louisiana law would cause a drastic reduction in the number of abortion providers in the State even though this finding was based on an erroneous legal standard and a thoroughly inadequate factual inquiry.

The Chief Justice stresses the importance of *stare decisis* and thinks that precedent, namely *Whole Woman's Health,* dooms the Louisiana law. But at the same time, he votes to overrule *Whole Woman's Health* insofar as it changed the *Casey* test.

Both the plurality and The Chief Justice hold that abortion providers can invoke a woman's abortion right when they attack state laws that are enacted to protect a woman's health. Neither waiver nor *stare decisis* can justify this holding, which clashes with our general rule on third-party standing. And the idea that a regulated party can invoke the right of a third party for the purpose of attacking legislation enacted to protect the third party is stunning. Given the apparent conflict of interest, that concept would be rejected out of hand in a case not involving abortion.

For these reasons, I cannot join the decision of the Court. I would remand the case to the District Court and instruct that court, before proceeding any further, to require the joinder of a plaintiff with standing. If a proper plaintiff is added, the District Court should conduct a new trial and determine, based on proper evidence, whether enforcement of Act 620 would diminish the number of abortion providers in the State to such a degree that women's access to abortions would be substantially impaired. In making that determination, the court should jettison the nebulous "good faith" test that it used in judging whether the physicians who currently lack admitting privileges would be able to obtain privileges and thus continue to perform abortions if Act 620 were permitted to take effect. Because the doctors in question (many of whom are or were plaintiffs in this case) stand to lose, not gain, by obtaining privileges, the court should require the plaintiffs to show that these doctors sought admitting privileges with the degree of effort that they would expend if their personal interests were at stake. . . .

IV

This case features a blatant conflict of interest between an abortion provider and its patients. Like any other regulated entity, an abortion provider has a financial interest in avoiding burdensome regulations such as Act 620's admitting privileges requirement. Applying for privileges takes time and energy, and maintaining privileges may impose additional burdens. Women seeking abortions, on the other hand, have an interest in the preservation of regulations that protect their health. The conflict inherent in such a situation is glaring.

Some may not see the conflict in this case because they are convinced that the admitting privileges requirement does nothing to promote safety and is really just a ploy. But an abortion provider's ability to assert the rights of women when it challenges ostensible safety regulations should not turn on the merits of its claim.

The problem with the rule that the majority embraces is highlighted if we consider challenges to other safety regulations. Suppose, for example, that a clinic in a State that allows certified non-physicians to perform abortions claims that the State's certification requirements are too onerous and that they imperil the clinic's continued operation. Should the clinic be able to assert the rights of women in attacking this regulation, which the state lawmakers thought was important to protect women's health?

When an abortion regulation is enacted for the asserted purpose of protecting the health of women, an abortion provider seeking to strike down that law should not be able to rely on the constitutional rights of women. Like any other party unhappy with burdensome regulation, the provider should be limited to its own rights. . . .

Justice GORSUCH, dissenting.
. . .

When it comes to the factual record, litigants normally start the case on a clean slate. While a previous case's legal rules can create precedent binding in the current dispute, earlier "fact-bound" decisions typically "provide only minimal help when other courts consider" later cases with different factual "circumstances." . . .

No hint of these rules can be found in today's decision. From beginning to end, the plurality treats *Whole Woman's Health*'s fact-laden predictions about how a Texas law would impact the availability of abortion in that State in 2016 as if they obviously and necessarily applied to Louisiana in 2020. Most notably, the plurality cites *Whole Woman's Health* for the proposition that admitting privileges requirements offer no benefit when it comes to patient safety or otherwise. But *Whole Woman's Health* found an absence of benefit based only on the particular factual record before it. Nothing in the decision suggested that its conclusions about the costs and benefits of the Texas statute were universal principles of law, medicine, or economics true in all places and at all times. Yet that is exactly how the plurality treats those conclusions—all while leaving unmentioned the facts Louisiana amassed in an effort to show that its law promises patient benefits in this place at this time.

Not only does today's decision treat factual questions as if they were legal ones, it treats legal questions as if they were facts. We have previously explained that it would "be inconsistent with the idea of a unitary system of law" for the Supreme Court to defer to lower court legal holdings. Yet, the plurality today reviews for clear error not only the district court's findings about how the law will affect abortion access, but also the lower court's judgment that the law's effects impose a "substantial obstacle." The plurality defers not only to the district court's findings about the extent of the law's benefits, but also to the lower court's judgment that the benefits are so limited that the law's burden on abortion access is "undue." By declining to apply our normal *de novo* standard of review to questions of law like these, today's decision proceeds on the remarkable premise that, even if the district court was wrong on the law, a duly enacted statute must fall because the lower court wasn't *clearly* wrong. . . .

[A]s today's concurrence recognizes, the legal standard the plurality applies when it comes to admitting privileges for abortion clinics turns out to be exactly the sort of all-things-considered balancing of benefits and burdens this Court has long rejected. Really, it's little more than the judicial version of a hunter's stew: Throw in anything that looks interesting, stir, and season to taste. . . . The plurality sides with the district court in concluding that the time and cost some women might have to endure to obtain an abortion outweighs the benefits of Act 620. Perhaps the plurality sees that answer as obvious, given its apparent conclusion that the Act would offer the public no benefits of any kind. But for its test to provide any helpful guidance, it must be capable of resolving cases the plurality can't so easily dismiss. Suppose, for example, a factfinder credited the State's evidence of medical benefit, finding that a small number of women would obtain safer medical care if the law went into effect. But suppose the same factfinder *also* credited a plaintiff's evidence of burden, finding that a large number of women would have to endure longer wait times and farther drives, and that a very small number of women would be unable to obtain an abortion at all. How is a judge supposed to balance, say, a few women's emergency hysterectomies against many women spending extra hours travelling to a clinic? The plurality's test offers no guidance. Nor can it. The benefits and burdens are incommensurable, and they do not teach such things in law school.

When judges take it upon themselves to assess the raw costs and benefits of a new law or regulation, it can come as no surprise that "[s]ome courts wind up attaching the same significance to opposite facts," and even attaching the opposite significance to the same facts. *Ibid.* It can come as no surprise, either, that judges retreat to their underlying assumptions or moral intuitions when deciding whether a burden is undue. For what else is left?

Some judges have thrown up their hands at the task put to them by the Court in this area. If everything comes down to balancing costs against benefits, they have observed, "the only institution that can give an authoritative answer" is this Court, because the question isn't one of law at all and the only "balance" that matters is the one this Court strikes. The lament is understandable. Missing here is exactly what judges usually depend on when asked to make tough calls: an administrable legal rule to follow, a neutral principle, something outside themselves to guide their decision. . . .

[T]he concurrence suggests [that] [w]e don't need to resort to a raw balancing test to resolve today's dispute. A deeper respect for *stare decisis* and existing precedents, the concurrence assures us, supplies the key to a safe way out. Unfortunately, however, the reality proves more complicated.

Start with the concurrence's discussion of *Whole Woman's Health*. Immediately after paying homage to *stare decisis*, the concurrence *refuses* to follow the all-things-considered balancing test that decision employed when striking down Texas's admitting privileges law. In the process, the concurrence rightly recounts many of the problems with raw balancing tests. But then, switching directions again, the concurrence insists we are bound by an *alternative* holding in *Whole Woman's Health*. According to the concurrence, this alternative holding declared that the Texas law imposed an impermissible "substantial obstacle" to abortion access in light *only* of the burdens the law imposed—"independent of [any] discussion of [the law's] benefits." And, the concurrence concludes, because the facts of this suit look like those in *Whole Woman's Health*, we must find an impermissible substantial obstacle here too.

But in this footwork lie at least two missteps. For one, the facts of this suit cannot be so neatly reduced to *Whole Woman's Health* redux. For another, *Whole Woman's Health* nowhere issued the alternative holding on which the concurrence pins its argument. At no point did the Court hold that the burdens imposed by the Texas law alone—divorced from any consideration of the law's benefits—could suffice to establish a substantial obstacle. To the contrary, *Whole Woman's Health* insisted that the substantial obstacle test "*requires* that courts consider the burdens a law imposes on abortion access together with the benefits th[e] la[w] confer[s]." And whatever else respect for *stare decisis* might suggest, it cannot demand allegiance to a nonexistent ruling inconsistent with the approach actually taken by the Court.

The concurrence's fallback argument doesn't solve the problem either. So what if *Whole Woman's Health* rejected the benefits-free version of the "substantial obstacle" test the concurrence endorses? The concurrence assures us that *Planned Parenthood of Southeastern Pa. v. Casey*, specified this form of the test, so we must (or at least may) do the same, whatever *Whole Woman's Health* says.

But here again, the concurrence rests on at least one mistaken premise. In the context of laws implicating only the State's interest in fetal life previability, the *Casey* plurality did describe its "undue burden" test as asking whether the law in question poses a substantial obstacle to abortion access. But when a State enacts a law "to further the health or safety of a woman seeking an abortion," the *Casey* plurality added a key qualification: Only "[*u*]*nnecessary* health regulations that have the purpose or effect of presenting a substantial obstacle to a woman seeking an abortion impose an undue burden on the right." *Ibid.* (emphasis added). That qualification is clearly applicable here, yet the concurrence nowhere addresses it, applying instead a new test of its own creation. In the context of medical regulations, too, the concurrence's new test might even prove stricter than strict scrutiny. After all, it's possible for a regulation to survive strict scrutiny if it is narrowly tailored to advance a compelling state interest. And no one doubts that women's health can be such an interest. Yet, under the concurrence's test it seems possible that even the most compelling and narrowly tailored medical regulation would have to fail if it placed a substantial obstacle in the way of abortion access. Such a result would appear to create yet another discontinuity with *Casey*, which expressly disavowed any test as strict as strict scrutiny.

To arrive at today's result, rules must be brushed aside and shortcuts taken. While the concurrence parts ways with the plurality at the last turn, the road both travel leads us to a strangely open space, unconstrained by many of the neutral principles that normally govern the judicial process. The temptation to proceed this direction, closer with each step toward an unobstructed exercise of will, may be always with us, a danger inherent in judicial review. But it is an impulse this Court normally strives mightily to resist. Today, in a highly politicized and contentious arena, we prove unwilling, or perhaps unable, to resist that temptation. Either way, respectfully, it is a sign we have lost our way.

Justice KAVANAUGH, dissenting.

I join Parts I, II, and III of Justice Alito's dissent. A threshold question in this case concerns the proper standard for evaluating state abortion laws. The Louisiana law at issue here requires doctors who perform abortions to have admitting privileges at a hospital within 30 miles of the abortion clinic. The State asks us to assess the law by applying the undue burden standard of *Planned Parenthood of Southeastern Pa. v. Casey*. . . . The State has not asked the Court to depart from the *Casey* standard. [relocated footnote — eds.] . . . . The plaintiffs ask us to apply the cost-benefit standard of *Whole Woman's Health v. Hellerstedt*.

Today, five Members of the Court reject the *Whole Woman's Health* cost-benefit standard. (Roberts, C.J., concurring in judgment); (Thomas, J., dissenting); (Alito, J., joined by Thomas, Gorsuch, and Kavanaugh, JJ., dissenting); (Gorsuch, J., dissenting). A different five Members of the Court conclude that Louisiana's admitting-privileges law is unconstitutional because it "would restrict women's access to abortion to the same degree as" the Texas law in *Whole Woman's Health*. (opinion of Roberts, C.J.); see also (opinion of Breyer, J., joined by Ginsburg, Sotomayor, and Kagan, JJ.).

I agree with the first of those two conclusions. But I respectfully dissent from the second because, in my view, additional factfinding is necessary to properly evaluate Louisiana's law. As Justice Alito thoroughly and carefully explains, the factual record at this stage of plaintiffs' facial, pre-enforcement challenge does not adequately demonstrate that the three relevant doctors (Does 2, 5, and 6) cannot obtain admitting privileges or, therefore, that any of the three Louisiana abortion clinics would close as a result of the admitting-privileges law. I expressed the same concern about the incomplete factual record more than a year ago during the stay proceedings, and the factual record has not changed since then. In short, I agree with Justice Alito that the Court should remand the case for a new trial and additional factfinding under the appropriate legal standards. . . . In my view, the District Court on remand should also address the State's new argument (raised for the first time in this Court) that these doctors and clinics lack third-party standing. [relocated footnote — eds.]

Discussion

1. *Stare decisis or chipping away?* In *June Medical*, the Fifth Circuit appeared to defy the Court's 2016 decision in *Whole Woman's Health*, upholding a Louisiana TRAP law that was essentially the same as the Texas law struck down four years previously. When the Supreme Court took the case following Justice Kennedy's retirement, it was the first time there was a majority of clearly pro-life Justices in many years. The question was whether a Court with a new pro-life majority would greatly weaken *Casey* by upholding Louisiana's TRAP law, whose obvious purpose was to practically foreclose the availability of abortion in the state. (The Justices, however, did not ask the litigants to brief whether *Casey* itself should be overruled.)

The Court could have weakened *Casey* in several ways. It could have rejected the idea that the Louisiana statute burdens women's abilities to get an abortion, because it was possible that some doctors could meet the statute's requirements. This approach was taken by several of the dissenters, who cast doubt on the lower court's factual findings.

Another approach, promoted by Justice Thomas and Justice Alito, was to alter the doctrines of standing, and hold that abortion providers do not have standing to raise the Due Process claims of pregnant women seeking abortions. Justice Alito argued that where Louisiana justified its regulation in terms of protecting women's health, pregnant women and abortion providers had an inherent conflict of interest: Abortion providers might sacrifice women's health for lower regulation and higher profits. And although "[s]ome may not see the conflict in this case because they are convinced that the admitting privileges requirement does nothing to promote safety and is really just a ploy . . . an abortion provider's ability to assert the rights of women when it challenges ostensible safety regulations should not turn on the merits of its claim." The effect of eliminating third-party standing would be to make it somewhat harder to challenge abortion laws. Why do you think that would be?

What actually happened was that Chief Justice Roberts joined the Court's liberals to strike down the law. But in the process, he wrote a limiting concurrence that significantly altered the test of *Whole Woman's Health*.

Whole Woman's Health held that where the state justifies an abortion restriction in terms of benefits to women's health, courts must "consider the burdens a law imposes on abortion access together with the benefits those laws confer." In other words, what constitutes an *undue* burden depends on how much the regulation actually furthers women's health. That is because pro-life states had moved to using health regulations (as opposed to fetal protection laws) to eliminate abortion services. The more the regulation burdens the right to abortion, the greater the actual health benefits for women the state must demonstrate. Conversely, where the regulation does almost nothing to benefit health, as in Texas's and Louisiana's laws, the court should strike the law down if it makes it more difficult for women to get abortions.

This test was designed to meet the structure of most post-*Casey* TRAP laws—which piled regulatory burdens onto abortion clinics in the hopes of shutting down most or all of them. The test of *Whole Woman's Health* also sidestepped an inquiry into purpose—even though it was well understood by judges, lawyers, politicians, and their constituents alike that the point of the laws was to restrict access to abortion.

Chief Justice Roberts responds that *Casey* does not focus on the balancing of costs and benefits. Its only concern is whether there is an undue burden, i.e., "the purpose or effect of placing a substantial obstacle in the path of a woman seeking an abortion of a nonviable fetus." He argues that this question should be decided in isolation from the presence or absence of a challenged law's benefits for women's health.

The result of Roberts' test is that where a law does little to advance women's health, but judges do not think it creates a substantial obstacle to abortion, they should uphold it. This will make it easier for courts who doubt that TRAP laws really do very much to inhibit women's access to abortion to uphold these laws. The dissenters in this case, for example, do not believe that the admitting privileges requirements really will stop doctors from performing abortions, and Justice Alito suggests the doctors are not really trying to meet the state's requirements.

On the other hand, Roberts' test has a strange consequence, as Justice Gorsuch points out: If law places a substantial obstacle in the way of women seeking abortion, it should be struck down even if it genuinely advances women's health: "it seems possible that even the most compelling and narrowly tailored medical regulation would have to fail if it placed a substantial obstacle in the way of abortion access." This result is inconsistent both with *Casey* and *Whole Woman's Health*. Hence Gorsuch argues that although Roberts makes much of the need to follow precedent, Roberts is actually rejecting previous precedent.

To be sure, it is unlikely that future courts will hold that regulations that actually advance women's health create an undue burden. Instead, they will argue that the burden the regulation imposes is not "substantial." Thus, after *June Medical*, judges and Justices will continue to balance costs and benefits—they will simply not say so openly. And they will likely do this hidden balancing in ways that conform to their basic views about the importance—or the illegiti-macy—of constitutional rights to abortion.

Insert on p. 1607 immediately before Note: The Right to Die and Other Implied Fundamental Rights:

BOSTOCK v. CLAYTON COUNTY, GEORGIA
140 S.Ct. 1731 (2020)

Justice GORSUCH delivered the opinion of the Court.

Sometimes small gestures can have unexpected consequences. Major initiatives practically guarantee them. In our time, few pieces of federal legislation rank in sig-nificance with the Civil Rights Act of 1964. There, in Title VII, Congress outlawed discrimination in the workplace on the basis of race, color, religion, sex, or national origin. Today, we must decide whether an employer can fire someone simply for being homosexual or transgender. The answer is clear. An employer who fires an individual for being homosexual or transgender fires that person for traits or actions it would not have questioned in members of a different sex. Sex plays a necessary and undisguisable role in the decision, exactly what Title VII forbids.

Those who adopted the Civil Rights Act might not have anticipated their work would lead to this particular result. Likely, they weren't thinking about many of the Act's consequences that have become apparent over the years, including its prohibition against discrimination on the basis of motherhood or its ban on the sexual harassment of male employees. But the limits of the drafters' imagina-tion supply no reason to ignore the law's demands. When the express terms of a statute give us one answer and extratextual considerations suggest another, it's no contest. Only the written word is the law, and all persons are entitled to its benefit.

I

[In each of these cases,] [a] n employer fired a long-time employee shortly after the employee revealed that he or she is homosexual or transgender—and allegedly for no reason other than the employee's homosexuality or transgender status.

Gerald Bostock worked for Clayton County, Georgia, as a child welfare advo-cate. . . . After a decade with the county, Mr. Bostock began participating in a gay recreational softball league. . . . Soon, he was fired for conduct "unbecom-ing" a county employee.

Donald Zarda worked as a skydiving instructor at Altitude Express in New York. After several seasons with the company, Mr. Zarda mentioned that he was gay and, days later, was fired.

Aimee Stephens worked at R.G. & G.R. Harris Funeral Homes in Garden City, Michigan. When she got the job, Ms. Stephens presented as a male. . . . In her sixth year with the company, Ms. Stephens wrote a letter to her employer explaining that she planned to "live and work full-time as a woman" after she returned from an upcoming vacation. The funeral home fired her before she left, telling her "this is not going to work out." . . .

II

This Court normally interprets a statute in accord with the ordinary public meaning of its terms at the time of its enactment. After all, only the words on the page constitute the law adopted by Congress and approved by the President. . . . We must determine the ordinary public meaning of Title VII's command that it is "unlawful . . . for an employer to fail or refuse to hire or to discharge any individual, or otherwise to discriminate against any individual with respect to his compensation, terms, conditions, or privileges of employment, because of such individual's race, color, religion, sex, or national origin." § 2000e–2(a)(1). . . .

Appealing to roughly contemporaneous dictionaries, the employers say that, as used here, the term "sex" in 1964 referred to "status as either male or female [as] determined by reproductive biology." The employees counter by submitting that, even in 1964, the term bore a broader scope, capturing more than anatomy and reaching at least some norms concerning gender identity and sexual orientation. But because nothing in our approach to these cases turns on the outcome of the parties' debate, and because the employees concede the point for argument's sake, we proceed on the assumption that "sex" signified what the employers suggest, referring only to biological distinctions between male and female. . . .

[T]he statute prohibits employers from taking certain actions "because of" sex. And, as this Court has previously explained, "the ordinary meaning of 'because of' is 'by reason of' or 'on account of.'" In the language of law, this means that Title VII's "because of" test incorporates the "'simple'" and "traditional" standard of but-for causation. That form of causation is established whenever a particular outcome would not have happened "but for" the purported cause. In other words, a but-for test directs us to change one thing at a time and see if the outcome changes. If it does, we have found a but-for cause. . . .

Often, events have multiple but-for causes. . . . When it comes to Title VII, the adoption of the traditional but-for causation standard means a defendant cannot avoid liability just by citing some *other* factor that contributed to its challenged employment decision. So long as the plaintiff 's sex was one but-for cause of that decision, that is enough to trigger the law.

No doubt, Congress could have taken a more parsimonious approach. As it has in other statutes, it could have added "solely" to indicate that actions taken "because of" the confluence of multiple factors do not violate the law. Or it could have written "primarily because of" to indicate that the prohibited factor had to be the main cause of the defendant's challenged employment decision. But none of this is the law we have. If anything, Congress has moved in the opposite direction, supplementing Title VII in 1991 to allow a plaintiff to prevail merely by showing that a protected trait like sex was a "motivating factor" in a defendant's challenged employment practice. Civil Rights Act of 1991, § 107,

105 Stat. 1075, codified at 42 U.S.C. § 2000e–2(m). Under this more forgiving standard, liability can sometimes follow even if sex *wasn't* a but-for cause of the employer's challenged decision. Still, because nothing in our analysis depends on the motivating factor test, we focus on the more traditional but-for causation standard that continues to afford a viable, if no longer exclusive, path to relief under Title VII. § 2000e–2(a)(1).

As sweeping as even the but-for causation standard can be, Title VII does not concern itself with everything that happens "because of" sex. The statute imposes liability on employers only when they "fail or refuse to hire," "discharge," "or otherwise . . . discriminate against" someone because of a statutorily protected characteristic like sex. *Ibid.* The employers acknowledge that they discharged the plaintiffs in today's cases, but assert that the statute's list of verbs is qualified by the last item on it: "otherwise . . . discriminate against." By virtue of the word *otherwise*, the employers suggest, Title VII concerns itself not with every discharge, only with those discharges that involve discrimination.

Accepting this point, too, for argument's sake, the question becomes: What did "discriminate" mean in 1964? As it turns out, it meant then roughly what it means today: "To make a difference in treatment or favor (of one as compared with others)." Webster's New International Dictionary 745 (2d ed. 1954). To "discriminate against" a person, then, would seem to mean treating that individual worse than others who are similarly situated. In so-called "disparate treatment" cases like today's, this Court has also held that the difference in treatment based on sex must be intentional. So, taken together, an employer who intentionally treats a person worse because of sex — such as by firing the person for actions or attributes it would tolerate in an individual of another sex — discriminates against that person in violation of Title VII.

At first glance, another interpretation might seem possible. Discrimination sometimes involves "the act, practice, or an instance of discriminating categorically rather than individually." On that understanding, the statute would require us to consider the employer's treatment of groups rather than individuals, to see how a policy affects one sex as a whole versus the other as a whole. That idea holds some intuitive appeal too. Maybe the law concerns itself simply with ensuring that employers don't treat women generally less favorably than they do men. So how can we tell which sense, individual or group, "discriminate" carries in Title VII?

The statute answers that question directly. It tells us three times — including immediately after the words "discriminate against" — that our focus should be on individuals, not groups: Employers may not "fail or refuse to hire or . . . discharge any *individual*, or otherwise . . . discriminate against any *individual* with respect to his compensation, terms, conditions, or privileges of employment, because of such *individual's* . . . sex." § 2000e–2(a)(1) (emphasis added). And the meaning of "individual" was as uncontroversial in 1964 as it is today: "A particular being as distinguished from a class, species, or collection." Webster's New International Dictionary, at 1267. Here, again, Congress could have written the law differently. It might have said that "it shall be an unlawful employment practice to prefer one sex to the other in hiring, firing, or the terms or conditions of employment." It might have said that there should be no "sex discrimination," perhaps implying a focus on differential treatment between the two sexes as groups. More narrowly still, it could have forbidden only "sexist policies" against women as a class. But, once again, that is not the law we have.

The consequences of the law's focus on individuals rather than groups are anything but academic. Suppose an employer fires a woman for refusing his sexual advances. It's no defense for the employer to note that, while he treated that individual woman worse than he would have treated a man, he gives preferential treatment to female employees overall. The employer is liable for treating *this* woman worse in part because of her sex. Nor is it a defense for an employer to say it discriminates against both men and women because of sex. This statute works to protect individuals of both sexes from discrimination, and does so equally. So an employer who fires a woman, Hannah, because she is insufficiently feminine and also fires a man, Bob, for being insufficiently masculine may treat men and women as groups more or less equally. But in *both* cases the employer fires an individual in part because of sex. Instead of avoiding Title VII exposure, this employer doubles it.

From the ordinary public meaning of the statute's language at the time of the law's adoption, a straightforward rule emerges: An employer violates Title VII when it intentionally fires an individual employee based in part on sex. It doesn't matter if other factors besides the plaintiff 's sex contributed to the decision. And it doesn't matter if the employer treated women as a group the same when compared to men as a group. If the employer intentionally relies in part on an individual employee's sex when deciding to discharge the employee—put differently, if changing the employee's sex would have yielded a different choice by the employer—a statutory violation has occurred. Title VII's message is "simple but momentous": An individual employee's sex is "not relevant to the selection, evaluation, or compensation of employees." *Price Waterhouse v. Hopkins*, 490 U.S. 228, 239 (1989) (plurality opinion).

The statute's message for our cases is equally simple and momentous: An individual's homosexuality or transgender status is not relevant to employment decisions. That's because it is impossible to discriminate against a person for being homosexual or transgender without discriminating against that individual based on sex. Consider, for example, an employer with two employees, both of whom are attracted to men. The two individuals are, to the employer's mind, materially identical in all respects, except that one is a man and the other a woman. If the employer fires the male employee for no reason other than the fact he is attracted to men, the employer discriminates against him for traits or actions it tolerates in his female colleague. Put differently, the employer intentionally singles out an employee to fire based in part on the employee's sex, and the affected employee's sex is a but-for cause of his discharge. Or take an employer who fires a transgender person who was identified as a male at birth but who now identifies as a female. If the employer retains an otherwise identical employee who was identified as female at birth, the employer intentionally penalizes a person identified as male at birth for traits or actions that it tolerates in an employee identified as female at birth. Again, the individual employee's sex plays an unmistakable and impermissible role in the discharge decision.

That distinguishes these cases from countless others where Title VII has nothing to say. Take an employer who fires a female employee for tardiness or incompetence or simply supporting the wrong sports team. Assuming the employer would not have tolerated the same trait in a man, Title VII stands silent. But unlike any of these other traits or actions, homosexuality and transgender status are inextricably bound up with sex. Not because homosexuality or transgender status are related to sex in some vague sense or because discrimination on these bases has some disparate impact on one sex or another, but because to discriminate on these grounds requires an employer to intentionally treat individual employees differently because of their sex.

Nor does it matter that, when an employer treats one employee worse because of that individual's sex, other factors may contribute to the decision. Consider an employer with a policy of firing any woman he discovers to be a Yankees fan. Carrying out that rule because an employee is a woman *and* a fan of the Yankees is a firing "because of sex" if the employer would have tolerated the same allegiance in a male employee. Likewise here. When an employer fires an employee because she is homosexual or transgender, two causal factors may be in play — *both* the individual's sex *and* something else (the sex to which the individual is attracted or with which the individual identifies). But Title VII doesn't care. If an employer would not have discharged an employee but for that individual's sex, the statute's causation standard is met, and liability may attach.

Reframing the additional causes in today's cases as additional intentions can do no more to insulate the employers from liability. Intentionally burning down a neighbor's house is arson, even if the perpetrator's ultimate intention (or motivation) is only to improve the view. No less, intentional discrimination based on sex violates Title VII, even if it is intended only as a means to achieving the employer's ultimate goal of discriminating against homosexual or transgender employees. There is simply no escaping the role intent plays here: Just as sex is necessarily a but-for *cause* when an employer discriminates against homosexual or transgender employees, an employer who discriminates on these grounds inescapably *intends* to rely on sex in its decisionmaking. Imagine an employer who has a policy of firing any employee known to be homosexual. The employer hosts an office holiday party and invites employees to bring their spouses. A model employee arrives and introduces a manager to Susan, the employee's wife. Will that employee be fired? If the policy works as the employer intends, the answer depends entirely on whether the model employee is a man or a woman. To be sure, that employer's ultimate goal might be to discriminate on the basis of sexual orientation. But to achieve that purpose the employer must, along the way, intentionally treat an employee worse based in part on that individual's sex.

An employer musters no better a defense by responding that it is equally happy to fire male *and* female employees who are homosexual or transgender. Title VII liability is not limited to employers who, through the sum of all of their employment actions, treat the class of men differently than the class of women. Instead, the law makes each instance of discriminating against an individual employee because of that individual's sex an independent violation of Title VII. So just as an employer who fires both Hannah and Bob for failing to fulfill traditional sex stereotypes doubles rather than eliminates Title VII liability, an employer who fires both Hannah and Bob for being gay or transgender does the same. . . .

In *Phillips v. Martin Marietta Corp.*, 400 U.S. 542 (1971) (*per curiam*), a company allegedly refused to hire women with young children, but did hire men with children the same age. Because its discrimination depended not only on the employee's sex as a female but also on the presence of another criterion — namely, being a parent of young children — the company contended it hadn't engaged in discrimination "because of " sex. The company maintained, too, that it hadn't violated the law because, as a whole, it tended to favor hiring women over men. Unsurprisingly by now, these submissions did not sway the Court. That an employer discriminates intentionally against an individual only in part because of sex supplies no defense to Title VII. Nor does the fact an employer may happen to favor women as a class.

In *Los Angeles Dept. of Water and Power v. Manhart*, 435 U.S. 702 (1978), an employer required women to make larger pension fund contributions than men. The employer sought to justify its disparate treatment on the ground that women tend to live longer than men, and thus are likely to receive more from the pension fund over time. By everyone's admission, the employer was not guilty of animosity against women or a "purely habitual assumptio[n] about a woman's inability to perform certain kinds of work"; instead, it relied on what appeared to be a statistically accurate statement about life expectancy. Even so, the Court recognized, a rule that appears evenhanded at the group level can prove discriminatory at the level of individuals. True, women as a class may live longer than men as a class. But "[t]he statute's focus on the individual is unambiguous," and any individual woman might make the larger pension contributions and still die as early as a man. Likewise, the Court dismissed as irrelevant the employer's insistence that its actions were motivated by a wish to achieve classwide equality between the sexes: An employer's intentional discrimination on the basis of sex is no more permissible when it is prompted by some further intention (or motivation), even one as prosaic as seeking to account for actuarial tables. The employer violated Title VII because, when its policy worked exactly as planned, it could not "pass the simple test" asking whether an individual female employee would have been treated the same regardless of her sex.

In *Oncale v. Sundowner Offshore Services, Inc.*, 523 U.S. 75 (1998), a male plaintiff alleged that he was singled out by his male co-workers for sexual harassment. The Court held it was immaterial that members of the same sex as the victim committed the alleged discrimination. Nor did the Court concern itself with whether men as a group were subject to discrimination or whether something in addition to sex contributed to the discrimination, like the plaintiff's conduct or personal attributes. "[A]ssuredly," the case didn't involve "the principal evil Congress was concerned with when it enacted Title VII." But, the Court unanimously explained, it is "the provisions of our laws rather than the principal concerns of our legislators by which we are governed." Because the plaintiff alleged that the harassment would not have taken place but for his sex — that is, the plaintiff would not have suffered similar treatment if he were female — a triable Title VII claim existed.

The lessons these cases hold for ours are by now familiar.

First, it's irrelevant what an employer might call its discriminatory practice, how others might label it, or what else might motivate it. . . . When an employer fires an employee for being homosexual or transgender, it necessarily and intentionally discriminates against that individual in part because of sex. And that is all Title VII has ever demanded to establish liability.

Second, the plaintiff 's sex need not be the sole or primary cause of the employer's adverse action. . . . [I]t has no significance here if another factor — such as the sex the plaintiff is attracted to or presents as — might also be at work, or even play a more important role in the employer's decision.

Finally, an employer cannot escape liability by demonstrating that it treats males and females comparably as groups. . . . [A]n employer who intentionally fires an individual homosexual or transgender employee in part because of that individual's sex violates the law even if the employer is willing to subject all male and female homosexual or transgender employees to the same rule. . . .

[T]he employers assert that discrimination on the basis of homosexuality and transgender status aren't referred to as sex discrimination in ordinary conversation. If asked by a friend (rather than a judge) why they were fired, even today's plaintiffs would likely respond that it was because they were gay or transgender, not because of sex. According to the employers, that conversational answer, not the statute's strict terms, should guide our thinking and suffice to defeat any suggestion that the employees now before us were fired because of sex.

But this submission rests on a mistaken understanding of what kind of cause the law is looking for in a Title VII case. In conversation, a speaker is likely to focus on what seems most relevant or informative to the listener. So an employee who has just been fired is likely to identify the primary or most direct cause rather than list literally every but-for cause. To do otherwise would be tiring at best. But these conversational conventions do not control Title VII's legal analysis, which asks simply whether sex was a but-for cause. . . .

Trying another angle, the defendants before us suggest that an employer who discriminates based on homosexuality or transgender status doesn't *intentionally* discriminate based on sex, as a disparate treatment claim requires. But, as we've seen, an employer who discriminates against homosexual or transgender employees necessarily and intentionally applies sex-based rules. An employer that announces it will not employ anyone who is homosexual, for example, intends to penalize male employees for being attracted to men and female employees for being attracted to women. . . .

Maybe the employers mean they don't intend to harm one sex or the other as a class. But as should be clear by now, the statute focuses on discrimination against individuals, not groups. Alternatively, the employers may mean that they don't perceive themselves as motivated by a desire to discriminate based on sex. But nothing in Title VII turns on the employer's labels or any further intentions (or motivations) for its conduct beyond sex discrimination. . . .

Aren't these cases different, the employers ask, given that an employer could refuse to hire a gay or transgender individual without ever learning the applicant's sex? . . . Suppose an employer's application form offered a single box to check if the applicant is either black or Catholic. If the employer refuses to hire anyone who checks that box, would we conclude the employer has complied with Title VII, so long as it studiously avoids learning any particular applicant's race or religion? Of course not: By intentionally setting out a rule that makes hiring turn on race or religion, the employer violates the law, whatever he might know or not know about individual applicants.

The same holds here. There is no way for an applicant to decide whether to check the homosexual or transgender box without considering sex. To see why, imagine an applicant doesn't know what the words homosexual or transgender mean. Then try writing out instructions for who should check the box without using the words man, woman, or sex (or some synonym). It can't be done. Likewise, there is no way an employer can discriminate against those who check the homosexual or transgender box without discriminating in part because of an applicant's sex. By discriminating against homosexuals, the employer intentionally penalizes men for being attracted to men and women for being attracted to women. By discriminating against transgender persons, the employer unavoidably discriminates against persons with one sex identified at birth and another today. Any way you slice it, the employer intentionally refuses to hire applicants in part because of the affected individuals' sex, even if it never learns any applicant's sex.

Next, the employers turn to Title VII's list of protected characteristics — race, color, religion, sex, and national origin. Because homosexuality and transgender status can't be found on that list and because they are conceptually distinct from sex, the employers reason, they are implicitly excluded from Title VII's reach. Put another way, if Congress had wanted to address these matters in Title VII, it would have referenced them specifically.

But that much does not follow. We agree that homosexuality and transgender status are distinct concepts from sex. But, as we've seen, discrimination based on homosexuality or transgender status necessarily entails discrimination based on sex; the first cannot happen without the second. Nor is there any such thing as a "canon of donut holes," in which Congress's failure to speak directly to a specific case that falls within a more general statutory rule creates a tacit exception. Instead, when Congress chooses not to include any exceptions to a broad rule, courts apply the broad rule. And that is exactly how this Court has always approached Title VII. "Sexual harassment" is conceptually distinct from sex discrimination, but it can fall within Title VII's sweep. *Oncale.* Same with "motherhood discrimination." See *Phillips.* Would the employers have us reverse those cases on the theory that Congress could have spoken to those problems more specifically? Of course not. As enacted, Title VII prohibits all forms of discrimination because of sex, however they may manifest themselves or whatever other labels might attach to them.

The employers try the same point another way. Since 1964, they observe, Congress has considered several proposals to add sexual orientation to Title VII's list of protected characteristics, but no such amendment has become law. Meanwhile, Congress has enacted other statutes addressing other topics that do discuss sexual orientation. This postenactment legislative history, they urge, should tell us something.

But what? There's no authoritative evidence explaining why later Congresses adopted other laws referencing sexual orientation but didn't amend this one. Maybe some in the later legislatures understood the impact Title VII's broad language already promised for cases like ours and didn't think a revision needed. Maybe others knew about its impact but hoped no one else would notice. Maybe still others, occupied by other concerns, didn't consider the issue at all. All we can know for certain is that speculation about why a later Congress declined to adopt new legislation offers a "particularly dangerous" basis on which to rest an interpretation of an existing law a different and earlier Congress did adopt. *Sullivan v. Finkelstein*, 496 U.S. 617, 632 (1990) (Scalia, J., concurring) ("Arguments based on subsequent legislative history . . . should not be taken seriously, not even in a footnote"). . . .

Ultimately, the employers are forced to abandon the statutory text and precedent altogether and appeal to assumptions and policy. Most pointedly, they contend that few in 1964 would have expected Title VII to apply to discrimination against homosexual and transgender persons. And whatever the text and our precedent indicate, they say, shouldn't this fact cause us to pause before recognizing liability?

It might be tempting to reject this argument out of hand. This Court has explained many times over many years that, when the meaning of the statute's terms is plain, our job is at an end. The people are entitled to rely on the law as written, without fearing that courts might disregard its plain terms based on some extratextual consideration. Of course, some Members of this Court have consulted legislative history when interpreting *ambiguous* statutory language. But that has no bearing here. "Legislative history, for those who take it into account, is meant to clear up ambiguity, not create it." And as we have seen, no ambiguity exists about how Title VII's terms apply to the facts before us. To be sure, the statute's application in these cases reaches "beyond the principal evil" legislators may have intended or expected to address. *Oncale*. But " 'the fact that [a statute] has been applied in situations not expressly anticipated by Congress' " does not demonstrate ambiguity; instead, it simply " 'demonstrates [the] breadth' " of a legislative command. And "it is ultimately the provisions of" those legislative commands "rather than the principal concerns of our legislators by which we are governed." *Oncale*; see also A. Scalia & B. Garner, Reading Law: The Interpretation of Legal Texts 101 (2012) (noting that unexpected applications of broad language reflect only Congress's "presumed point [to] produce general coverage—not to leave room for courts to recognize ad hoc exceptions").

Still, while legislative history can never defeat unambiguous statutory text, historical sources can be useful for a different purpose: Because the law's ordinary meaning at the time of enactment usually governs, we must be sensitive to the possibility a statutory term that means one thing today or in one context might have meant something else at the time of its adoption or might mean something different in another context. And we must be attuned to the possibility that a statutory phrase ordinarily bears a different meaning than the terms do when viewed individually or literally. To ferret out such shifts in linguistic usage or subtle distinctions between literal and ordinary meaning, this Court has sometimes consulted the understandings of the law's drafters as some (not always conclusive) evidence. . . .

The employers, however, advocate nothing like that here. They do not seek to use historical sources to illustrate that the meaning of any of Title VII's language has changed since 1964 or that the statute's terms, whether viewed individually or as a whole, ordinarily carried some message we have missed. To the contrary, as we have seen, the employers *agree* with our understanding of all the statutory language—"discriminate against any individual . . . because of such individual's . . . sex." Nor do the competing dissents offer an alternative account about what these terms mean either when viewed individually or in the aggregate. Rather than suggesting that the statutory language bears some other *meaning*, the employers and dissents merely suggest that, because few in 1964 expected today's *result*, we should not dare to admit that it follows ineluctably from the statutory text. When a new application emerges that is both unexpected and important, they would seemingly have us merely point out the question, refer the subject back to Congress, and decline to enforce the plain terms of the law in the meantime. That is exactly the sort of reasoning this Court has long rejected. Admittedly, the employers take pains to couch their argument in terms of seeking to honor the statute's "expected applications" rather than vindicate its "legislative intent." But the concepts are closely related. One could easily contend that legislators only intended expected applications or that a statute's purpose is limited to achieving applications foreseen at the time of enactment. However framed, the employer's logic impermissibly seeks to displace the plain meaning of the law in favor of something lying beyond it.

If anything, the employers' new framing may only add new problems. The employers assert that "no one" in 1964 or for some time after would have anticipated today's result. But is that really true? Not long after the law's passage, gay and transgender employees began filing Title VII complaints, so at least *some* people foresaw this potential application. . . . And less than a decade after Title VII's passage, during debates over the Equal Rights Amendment, others counseled that its language—which was strikingly similar to Title VII's—might also protect homosexuals from discrimination.

Why isn't that enough to demonstrate that today's result isn't totally unexpected? How many people have to foresee the application for it to qualify as "expected"? Do we look only at the moment the statute was enacted, or do we allow some time for the implications of a new statute to be worked out? Should we consider the expectations of those who had no reason to give a particular application any thought or only those with reason to think about the question? How do we account for those who change their minds over time, after learning new facts or hearing a new argument? How specifically or generally should we frame the "application" at issue? None of these questions have obvious answers, and the employers don't propose any.

One could also reasonably fear that objections about unexpected applications will not be deployed neutrally. Often lurking just behind such objections resides a cynicism that Congress could not *possibly* have meant to protect a disfavored group. Take this Court's encounter with the Americans with Disabilities Act's directive that no " 'public entity' " can discriminate against any " 'qualified individual with a disability.' " *Pennsylvania Dept. of Corrections v. Yeskey*, 524 U.S. 206, 208 (1998). Congress, of course, didn't list every public entity the statute would apply to. And no one batted an eye at its application to, say, post offices. But when the statute was applied to *prisons*, curiously, some demanded a closer look: Pennsylvania argued that "Congress did not 'envisio[n] that the ADA would be applied to state prisoners.' " This Court emphatically rejected that view, explaining that, "in the context of an unambiguous statutory text," whether a specific application was anticipated by Congress "is irrelevant." As *Yeskey* and today's cases exemplify, applying protective laws to groups that were politically unpopular at the time of the law's passage — whether prisoners in the 1990s or homosexual and transgender employees in the 1960s — often may be seen as unexpected. But to refuse enforcement just because of that, because the parties before us happened to be unpopular at the time of the law's passage, would not only require us to abandon our role as interpreters of statutes; it would tilt the scales of justice in favor of the strong or popular and neglect the promise that all persons are entitled to the benefit of the law's terms.

The employer's position also proves too much. If we applied Title VII's plain text only to applications some (yet-to-be-determined) group expected in 1964, we'd have more than a little law to overturn. . . .

As one Equal Employment Opportunity Commission (EEOC) Commissioner observed shortly after the law's passage, the words of " 'the sex provision of Title VII [are] difficult to . . . control.' " The "difficult[y]" may owe something to the initial proponent of the sex discrimination rule in Title VII, Representative Howard Smith. On some accounts, the congressman may have wanted (or at least was indifferent to the possibility of) broad language with wide-ranging effect. Not necessarily because he was interested in rooting out sex discrimination in all its forms, but because he may have hoped to scuttle the whole Civil Rights Act and thought that adding language covering sex discrimination would serve as a poison pill. Certainly nothing in the meager legislative history of this provision suggests it was meant to be read narrowly.

Whatever his reasons, thanks to the broad language Representative Smith introduced, many, maybe most, applications of Title VII's sex provision were "unanticipated" at the time of the law's adoption. In fact, many now-obvious applications met with heated opposition early on, even among those tasked with enforcing the law. In the years immediately following Title VII's passage, the EEOC officially opined that listing men's positions and women's positions separately in job postings was simply helpful rather than discriminatory. Some courts held that Title VII did not prevent an employer from firing an employee for refusing his sexual advances. And courts held that a policy against hiring mothers but not fathers of young children wasn't discrimination because of sex.

Over time, though, the breadth of the statutory language proved too difficult to deny. By the end of the 1960s, the EEOC reversed its stance on sex-segregated job advertising. In 1971, this Court held that treating women with children differently from men with children violated Title VII. And by the late 1970s, courts began to recognize that sexual harassment can sometimes amount to sex discrimination. While to the modern eye each of these examples may seem "plainly [to] constitut[e] discrimination because of biological sex," all were hotly contested for years following Title VII's enactment. And as with the discrimination we consider today, many federal judges long accepted interpretations of Title VII that excluded these situations. Would the employers have us undo every one of these unexpected applications too?

[T]he employers are left to abandon their concern for expected applications and fall back to the last line of defense for all failing statutory interpretation arguments: naked policy appeals. If we were to apply the statute's plain language, they complain, any number of undesirable policy consequences would follow. Gone here is any pretense of statutory interpretation; all that's left is a suggestion we should proceed without the law's guidance to do as we think best. But that's an invitation no court should ever take up. The place to make new legislation, or address unwanted consequences of old legislation, lies in Congress. When it comes to statutory interpretation, our role is limited to applying the law's demands as faithfully as we can in the cases that come before us. As judges we possess no special expertise or authority to declare for ourselves what a self-governing people should consider just or wise. And the same judicial humility that requires us to refrain from adding to statutes requires us to refrain from diminishing them.

What are these consequences anyway? The employers worry that our decision will sweep beyond Title VII to other federal or state laws that prohibit sex discrimination. And, under Title VII itself, they say sex-segregated bathrooms, locker rooms, and dress codes will prove unsustainable after our decision today. But none of these other laws are before us; we have not had the benefit of adversarial testing about the meaning of their terms, and we do not prejudge any such question today. Under Title VII, too, we do not purport to address bathrooms, locker rooms, or anything else of the kind. The only question before us is whether an employer who fires someone simply for being homosexual or transgender has discharged or otherwise discriminated against that individual "because of such individual's sex." As used in Title VII, the term " 'discriminate against' " refers to "distinctions or differences in treatment that injure protected individuals." Firing employees because of a statutorily protected trait surely counts. Whether other policies and practices might or might not qualify as unlawful discrimination or find justifications under other provisions of Title VII are questions for future cases, not these.

Separately, the employers fear that complying with Title VII's requirement in cases like ours may require some employers to violate their religious convictions. We are also deeply concerned with preserving the promise of the free exercise of religion enshrined in our Constitution; that guarantee lies at the heart of our pluralistic society. But worries about how Title VII may intersect with religious liberties are nothing new; they even predate the statute's passage. As a result of its deliberations in adopting the law, Congress included an express statutory exception for religious organizations. § 2000e–1(a). This Court has also recognized that the First Amendment can bar the application of employment discrimination laws "to claims concerning the employment relationship between a religious institution and its ministers." *Hosanna-Tabor Evangelical Lutheran Church and School v. EEOC*, 565 U.S. 171, 188 (2012). And Congress has gone a step further yet in the Religious Freedom Restoration Act of 1993 (RFRA), 107 Stat. 1488, codified at 42 U.S.C. § 2000bb *et seq.* That statute prohibits the federal government from substantially burdening a person's exercise of religion unless it demonstrates that doing so both furthers a compelling governmental interest and represents the least restrictive means of furthering that interest. § 2000bb–1. Because RFRA operates as a kind of super statute, displacing the normal operation of other federal laws, it might supersede Title VII's commands in appropriate cases. See § 2000bb–3.

But how these doctrines protecting religious liberty interact with Title VII are questions for future cases too. . . . [W]hile other employers in other cases may raise free exercise arguments that merit careful consideration, none of the employers before us today represent in this Court that compliance with Title VII will infringe their own religious liberties in any way.

Some of those who supported adding language to Title VII to ban sex discrimination may have hoped it would derail the entire Civil Rights Act. Yet, contrary to those intentions, the bill became law. Since then, Title VII's effects have unfolded with far-reaching consequences, some likely beyond what many in Congress or elsewhere expected.

But none of this helps decide today's cases. Ours is a society of written laws. Judges are not free to overlook plain statutory commands on the strength of nothing more than suppositions about intentions or guesswork about expectations. In Title VII, Congress adopted broad language making it illegal for an employer to rely on an employee's sex when deciding to fire that employee. We do not hesitate to recognize today a necessary consequence of that legislative choice: An employer who fires an individual merely for being gay or transgender defies the law.

The judgments of the Second and Sixth Circuits in Nos. 17–1623 and 18–107 are affirmed. The judgment of the Eleventh Circuit in No. 17–1618 is reversed, and the case is remanded for further proceedings consistent with this opinion.

It is so ordered.

Justice ALITO, with whom Justice THOMAS joins, dissenting.

There is only one word for what the Court has done today: legislation. The document that the Court releases is in the form of a judicial opinion interpreting a statute, but that is deceptive.

Title VII of the Civil Rights Act of 1964 prohibits employment discrimination on any of five specified grounds: "race, color, religion, sex, [and] national origin." 42 U.S.C. § 2000e–2(a)(1). Neither "sexual orientation" nor "gender identity" appears on that list. For the past 45 years, bills have been introduced in Congress to add "sexual orientation" to the list, and in recent years, bills have included "gender identity" as well. But to date, none has passed both Houses. . . .

Because no such amendment of Title VII has been enacted in accordance with the requirements in the Constitution (passage in both Houses and presentment to the President, Art. I, § 7, cl. 2), Title VII's prohibition of discrimination because of "sex" still means what it has always meant. But the Court is not deterred by these constitutional niceties. Usurping the constitutional authority of the other branches, the Court has essentially taken H.R. 5's provision on employment discrimination and issued it under the guise of statutory interpretation.[4] A more brazen abuse of our authority to interpret statutes is hard to recall.

The Court tries to convince readers that it is merely enforcing the terms of the statute, but that is preposterous. Even as understood today, the concept of discrimination because of "sex" is different from discrimination because of "sexual orientation" or "gender identity." And in any event, our duty is to interpret statutory terms to "mean what they conveyed to reasonable people *at the time they were written.*" A. Scalia & B. Garner, Reading Law: The Interpretation of Legal Texts 16 (2012) (emphasis added). If every single living American had been surveyed in 1964, it would have been hard to find any who thought that discrimination because of sex meant discrimination because of sexual orientation—not to mention gender identity, a concept that was essentially unknown at the time.

The Court attempts to pass off its decision as the inevitable product of the textualist school of statutory interpretation championed by our late colleague Justice Scalia, but no one should be fooled. The Court's opinion is like a pirate ship. It sails under a textualist flag, but what it actually represents is a theory of statutory interpretation that Justice Scalia excoriated—the theory that courts should "update" old statutes so that they better reflect the current values of society. See A. Scalia, A Matter of Interpretation 22 (1997). If the Court finds it appropriate to adopt this theory, it should own up to what it is doing.

Many will applaud today's decision because they agree on policy grounds with the Court's updating of Title VII. But the question in these cases is not whether discrimination because of sexual orientation or gender identity *should be* outlawed. The question is *whether Congress did that in 1964.*

It indisputably did not.

[I]t should be perfectly clear that Title VII does not reach discrimination because of sexual orientation or gender identity. If "sex" in Title VII means biologically male or female, then discrimination because of sex means discrimination because the person in question is biologically male or biologically female, not because that person is sexually attracted to members of the same sex or identifies as a member of a particular gender.

How then does the Court claim to avoid that conclusion? The Court tries to cloud the issue by spending many pages discussing matters that are beside the point. The Court observes that a Title VII plaintiff need not show that "sex" was the sole or primary motive for a challenged employment decision or its sole or primary cause; that Title VII is limited to discrimination with respect to a list of specified actions (such as hiring, firing, etc.); and that Title VII protects individual rights, not group rights.

All that is true, but so what? In cases like those before us, a plaintiff must show that sex was a "motivating factor" in the challenged employment action, 42 U.S.C. § 2000e–2(m), so the question we must decide comes down to this: if an individual employee or applicant for employment shows that his or her sexual orientation or gender identity was a "motivating factor" in a hiring or discharge decision, for example, is that enough to establish that the employer discriminated "because of . . . sex"? Or, to put the same question in different terms, if an employer takes an employment action solely because of the sexual orientation or gender identity of an employee or applicant, has that employer necessarily discriminated because of biological sex?

The answers to those questions must be no, unless discrimination because of sexual orientation or gender identity inherently constitutes discrimination because of sex. The Court attempts to prove that point, and it argues, not merely that the terms of Title VII *can* be interpreted that way but that they *cannot reasonably be interpreted any other way*. According to the Court, the text is unambiguous.

The arrogance of this argument is breathtaking. [T]here is not a shred of evidence that any Member of Congress interpreted the statutory text that way when Title VII was enacted. . . . [U]ntil 2017, every single Court of Appeals to consider the question interpreted Title VII's prohibition against sex discrimination to mean discrimination on the basis of biological sex. And for good measure, the Court's conclusion that Title VII unambiguously reaches discrimination on the basis of sexual orientation and gender identity necessarily means that the EEOC failed to see the obvious for the first 48 years after Title VII became law. Day in and day out, the Commission enforced Title VII but did not grasp what discrimination "because of . . . sex" unambiguously means.

The Court's argument is not only arrogant, it is wrong. It fails on its own terms. "Sex," "sexual orientation," and "gender identity" are different concepts, as the Court concedes. *Ante*, at _____ ("homosexuality and transgender status are distinct concepts from sex"). And neither "sexual orientation" nor "gender identity" is tied to either of the two biological sexes. See *ante*, at _____ (recognizing that "discrimination on these bases" does not have "some disparate impact on one sex or another"). Both men and women may be attracted to members of the opposite sex, members of the same sex, or members of both sexes. And individuals who are born with the genes and organs of either biological sex may identify with a different gender. . . .

Contrary to the Court's contention, discrimination because of sexual orientation or gender identity does not in and of itself entail discrimination because of sex. We can see this because it is quite possible for an employer to discriminate on those grounds without taking the sex of an individual applicant or employee into account. An employer can have a policy that says: "We do not hire gays, lesbians, or transgender individuals." And an employer can implement this policy without paying any attention to or even knowing the biological sex of gay, lesbian, and transgender applicants. In fact, at the time of the enactment of Title VII, the United States military had a blanket policy of refusing to enlist gays or lesbians, and under this policy for years thereafter, applicants for enlistment were required to complete a form that asked whether they were "homosexual."

At oral argument, the attorney representing the employees, a prominent professor of constitutional law, was asked if there would be discrimination because of sex if an employer with a blanket policy against hiring gays, lesbians, and transgender individuals implemented that policy without knowing the biological sex of any job applicants. Her candid answer was that this would "not" be sex discrimination. And she was right.

The attorney's concession was necessary, but it is fatal to the Court's interpretation, for if an employer discriminates against individual applicants or employees without even knowing whether they are male or female, it is impossible to argue that the employer intentionally discriminated because of sex. An employer cannot intentionally discriminate on the basis of a characteristic of which the employer has no knowledge. And if an employer does not violate Title VII by discriminating on the basis of sexual orientation or gender identity without knowing the sex of the affected individuals, there is no reason why the same employer could not lawfully implement the same policy even if it knows the sex of these individuals. If an employer takes an adverse employment action for a perfectly legitimate reason—for example, because an employee stole company property—that action is not converted into sex discrimination simply because the employer knows the employee's sex. As explained, a disparate treatment case requires proof of intent—*i.e.,* that the employee's sex motivated the firing. In short, what this example shows is that discrimination because of sexual orientation or gender identity does not inherently or necessarily entail discrimination because of sex, and for that reason, the Court's chief argument collapses.

. . .

Title VII prohibits discrimination because of *sex itself,* not everything that is related to, based on, or defined with reference to, "sex." Many things are related to sex. Think of all the nouns other than "orientation" that are commonly modified by the adjective "sexual." Some examples yielded by a quick computer search are "sexual harassment," "sexual assault," "sexual violence," "sexual intercourse," and "sexual content."

Does the Court really think that Title VII prohibits discrimination on all these grounds? Is it unlawful for an employer to refuse to hire an employee with a record of sexual harassment in prior jobs? Or a record of sexual assault or violence?

To be fair, the Court does not claim that Title VII prohibits discrimination because of *everything* that is related to sex. The Court draws a distinction between things that are "inextricably" related and those that are related in "some vague sense." Apparently the Court would graft onto Title VII some arbitrary line separating the things that are related closely enough and those that are not. And it would do this in the name of high textualism. An additional argument made in passing also fights the text of Title VII and the policy it reflects. The Court proclaims that "[a]n individual's homosexuality or transgender status is not relevant to employment decisions." That is the policy view of many people in 2020, and perhaps Congress would have amended Title VII to implement it if this Court had not intervened. But that is not the policy embodied in Title VII in its current form. Title VII prohibits discrimination based on five specified grounds, and neither sexual orientation nor gender identity is on the list. As long as an employer does not discriminate based on one of the listed grounds, the employer is free to decide for itself which characteristics are "relevant to [its] employment decisions." By proclaiming that sexual orientation and gender identity are "not relevant to employment decisions," the Court updates Title VII to reflect what it regards as 2020 values. . . .

In 1964, ordinary Americans reading the text of Title VII would not have dreamed that discrimination because of sex meant discrimination because of sexual orientation, much less gender identity. The *ordinary meaning* of discrimination because of "sex" was discrimination because of a person's biological sex, not sexual orientation or gender identity. The possibility that discrimination on either of these grounds might fit within some exotic understanding of sex discrimination would not have crossed their minds. . . .

In 1964, the concept of prohibiting discrimination "because of sex" was no novelty. It was a familiar and well-understood concept, and what it meant was equal treatment for men and women. . . .

Discrimination "because of sex" was not understood as having anything to do with discrimination because of sexual orientation or transgender status. Any such notion would have clashed in spectacular fashion with the societal norms of the day.

For most 21st-century Americans, it is painful to be reminded of the way our society once treated gays and lesbians, but any honest effort to understand what the terms of Title VII were understood to mean when enacted must take into account the societal norms of that time. And the plain truth is that in 1964 homosexuality was thought to be a mental disorder, and homosexual conduct was regarded as morally culpable and worthy of punishment. . . .

Society's treatment of homosexuality and homosexual conduct was consistent with this understanding. Sodomy was a crime in every State but Illinois, see W. Eskridge, Dishonorable Passions 387–407 (2008), and in the District of Columbia, a law enacted by Congress made sodomy a felony punishable by imprisonment for up to 10 years and permitted the indefinite civil commitment of "sexual psychopath[s]." . . .

To its credit, our society has now come to recognize the injustice of past practices, and this recognition provides the impetus to "update" Title VII. But that is not our job. Our duty is to understand what the terms of Title VII were understood to mean when enacted, and in doing so, we must take into account the societal norms of that time. We must therefore ask whether ordinary Americans in 1964 would have thought that discrimination because of "sex" carried some exotic meaning under which private-sector employers would be prohibited from engaging in a practice that represented the official policy of the Federal Government with respect to its own employees. We must ask whether Americans at that time would have thought that Title VII banned discrimination against an employee for engaging in conduct that Congress had made a felony and a ground for civil commitment.

The questions answer themselves. Even if discrimination based on sexual orientation or gender identity could be squeezed into some arcane understanding of sex discrimination, the context in which Title VII was enacted would tell us that this is not what the statute's terms were understood to mean at that time. To paraphrase something Justice Scalia once wrote, "our job is not to scavenge the world of English usage to discover whether there is any possible meaning" of discrimination because of sex that might be broad enough to encompass discrimination because of sexual orientation or gender identity. Without strong evidence to the contrary (and there is none here), our job is to ascertain and apply the *"ordinary* meaning" of the statute. And in 1964, ordinary Americans most certainly would not have understood Title VII to ban discrimination because of sexual orientation or gender identity. . . .

While Americans in 1964 would have been shocked to learn that Congress had enacted a law prohibiting sexual orientation discrimination, they would have been bewildered to hear that this law also forbids discrimination on the basis of "transgender status" or "gender identity," terms that would have left people at the time scratching their heads. The term "transgender" is said to have been coined "'in the early 1970s,'" and the term "gender identity," now understood to mean "[a]n internal sense of being male, female or something else," apparently first appeared in an academic article in 1964. Certainly, neither term was in common parlance; indeed, dictionaries of the time still primarily defined the word "gender" by reference to grammatical classifications. . . .

It defies belief to suggest that the public meaning of discrimination because of sex in 1964 encompassed discrimination on the basis of a concept that was essentially unknown to the public at that time.

The Court's main excuse for entirely ignoring the social context in which Title VII was enacted is that the meaning of Title VII's prohibition of discrimination because of sex is clear, and therefore it simply does not matter whether people in 1964 were "smart enough to realize" what its language means. According to the Court, an argument that looks to the societal norms of those times represents an impermissible attempt to displace the statutory language.

The Court's argument rests on a false premise. As already explained at length, the text of Title VII does not prohibit discrimination because of sexual orientation or gender identity. And what the public thought about those issues in 1964 is relevant and important, not because it provides a ground for departing from the statutory text, but because it helps to explain what the text was understood to mean when adopted. . . .

[I]t would be a wild understatement to say that discrimination because of sexual orientation and transgender status was not the "principal evil" on Congress's mind in 1964. Whether we like to admit it now or not, in the thinking of Congress and the public at that time, such discrimination would not have been evil at all. . . .

IV

What the Court has done today—interpreting discrimination because of "sex" to encompass discrimination because of sexual orientation or gender identity—is virtually certain to have far-reaching consequences. Over 100 federal statutes prohibit discrimination because of sex. . . . [T]he Court dismisses questions about "bathrooms, locker rooms, or anything else of the kind." And it declines to say anything about other statutes whose terms mirror Title VII's.

The Court's brusque refusal to consider the consequences of its reasoning is irresponsible. If the Court had allowed the legislative process to take its course, Congress would have had the opportunity to consider competing interests and might have found a way of accommodating at least some of them. In addition, Congress might have crafted special rules for some of the relevant statutes. But by intervening and proclaiming categorically that employment discrimination based on sexual orientation or gender identity is simply a form of discrimination because of sex, the Court has greatly impeded—and perhaps effectively ended—any chance of a bargained legislative resolution. Before issuing today's radical decision, the Court should have given some thought to where its decision would lead.

[T]he position that the Court now adopts will threaten freedom of religion, freedom of speech, and personal privacy and safety. No one should think that the Court's decision represents an unalloyed victory for individual liberty.

I will briefly note some of the potential consequences of the Court's decision, but I do not claim to provide a comprehensive survey or to suggest how any of these issues should necessarily play out under the Court's reasoning. . . .

"[B]athrooms, locker rooms, [and other things] of [that] kind." The Court may wish to avoid this subject, but it is a matter of concern to many people who are reticent about disrobing or using toilet facilities in the presence of individuals whom they regard as members of the opposite sex. For some, this may simply be a question of modesty, but for others, there is more at stake. For women who have been victimized by sexual assault or abuse, the experience of seeing an unclothed person with the anatomy of a male in a confined and sensitive location such as a bathroom or locker room can cause serious psychological harm.

Under the Court's decision, however, transgender persons will be able to argue that they are entitled to use a bathroom or locker room that is reserved for persons of the sex with which they identify, and while the Court does not define what it means by a transgender person, the term may apply to individuals who are "gender fluid," that is, individuals whose gender identity is mixed or changes over time. Thus, a person who has not undertaken any physical transitioning may claim the right to use the bathroom or locker room assigned to the sex with which the individual identifies at that particular time. The Court provides no clue why a transgender person's claim to such bathroom or locker room access might not succeed.

A similar issue has arisen under Title IX, which prohibits sex discrimination by any elementary or secondary school and any college or university that receives federal financial assistance. In 2016, a Department of Justice advisory warned that barring a student from a bathroom assigned to individuals of the gender with which the student identifies constitutes unlawful sex discrimination, and some lower court decisions have agreed. . . .

Women's sports. Another issue that may come up under both Title VII and Title IX is the right of a transgender individual to participate on a sports team or in an athletic competition previously reserved for members of one biological sex. This issue has already arisen under Title IX, where it threatens to undermine one of that law's major achievements, giving young women an equal opportunity to participate in sports. The effect of the Court's reasoning may be to force young women to compete against students who have a very significant biological advantage, including students who have the size and strength of a male but identify as female and students who are taking male hormones in order to transition from female to male. Students in these latter categories have found success in athletic competitions reserved for females.

The logic of the Court's decision could even affect professional sports. Under the Court's holding that Title VII prohibits employment discrimination because of transgender status, an athlete who has the physique of a man but identifies as a woman could claim the right to play on a women's professional sports team. The owners of the team might try to claim that biological sex is a bona fide occupational qualification (BFOQ) under 42 U.S.C. § 2000e–2(e), but the BFOQ exception has been read very narrowly. See *Dothard v. Rawlinson*, 433 U.S. 321, 334 (1977).

Housing. The Court's decision may lead to Title IX cases against any college that resists assigning students of the opposite biological sex as roommates. A provision of Title IX, 20 U.S.C. § 1686, allows schools to maintain "separate living facilities for the different sexes," but it may be argued that a student's "sex" is the gender with which the student identifies. Similar claims may be brought under the Fair Housing Act.

Employment by religious organizations. Briefs filed by a wide range of religious groups—Christian, Jewish, and Muslim—express deep concern that the position now adopted by the Court "will trigger open conflict with faithbased employment practices of numerous churches, synagogues, mosques, and other religious institutions." They argue that "[r]eligious organizations need employees who actually live the faith," and that compelling a religious organization to employ individuals whose conduct flouts the tenets of the organization's faith forces the group to communicate an objectionable message.

This problem is perhaps most acute when it comes to the employment of teachers. A school's standards for its faculty "communicate a particular way of life to its students," and a "violation by the faculty of those precepts" may undermine the school's "moral teaching." Thus, if a religious school teaches that sex outside marriage and sex reassignment procedures are immoral, the message may be lost if the school employs a teacher who is in a same-sex relationship or has undergone or is undergoing sex reassignment. Yet today's decision may lead to Title VII claims by such teachers and applicants for employment.

At least some teachers and applicants for teaching positions may be blocked from recovering on such claims by the "ministerial exception" recognized in *Hosanna-Tabor Evangelical Lutheran Church and School v. EEOC*, 565 U.S. 171 (2012). . . . But even if teachers with those responsibilities qualify, what about other very visible school employees who may not qualify for the ministerial exception? Provisions of Title VII provide exemptions for certain religious organizations and schools "with respect to the employment of individuals of a particular religion to perform work connected with the carrying on" of the "activities" of the organization or school, 42 U.S.C. § 2000e–1(a); see also § 2000e–2(e)(2), but the scope of these provisions is disputed, and as interpreted by some lower courts, they provide only narrow protection.

Healthcare. Healthcare benefits may emerge as an intense battleground under the Court's holding. Transgender employees have brought suit under Title VII to challenge employer-provided health insurance plans that do not cover costly sex reassignment surgery. Similar claims have been brought under the Affordable Care Act (ACA), which broadly prohibits sex discrimination in the provision of healthcare.

Such claims present difficult religious liberty issues because some employers and healthcare providers have strong religious objections to sex reassignment procedures, and therefore requiring them to pay for or to perform these procedures will have a severe impact on their ability to honor their deeply held religious beliefs.

Freedom of speech. The Court's decision may even affect the way employers address their employees and the way teachers and school officials address students. Under established English usage, two sets of sex-specific singular personal pronouns are used to refer to someone in the third person (he, him, and his for males; she, her, and hers for females). But several different sets of gender-neutral pronouns have now been created and are preferred by some individuals who do not identify as falling into either of the two traditional categories. Some jurisdictions, such as New York City, have ordinances making the failure to use an individual's preferred pronoun a punishable offense, and some colleges have similar rules. After today's decision, plaintiffs may claim that the failure to use their preferred pronoun violates one of the federal laws prohibiting sex discrimination.

The Court's decision may also pressure employers to suppress any statements by employees expressing disapproval of same-sex relationships and sex reassignment procedures. Employers are already imposing such restrictions voluntarily, and after today's decisions employers will fear that allowing employees to express their religious views on these subjects may give rise to Title VII harassment claims.

Constitutional claims. Finally, despite the important differences between the Fourteenth Amendment and Title VII, the Court's decision may exert a gravitational pull in constitutional cases. Under our precedents, the Equal Protection Clause prohibits sex-based discrimination unless a "heightened" standard of review is met. *United States v. Virginia*, 518 U.S. 515 (1996). By equating discrimination because of sexual orientation or gender identity with discrimination because of sex, the Court's decision will be cited as a ground for subjecting all three forms of discrimination to the same exacting standard of review.

Under this logic, today's decision may have effects that extend well beyond the domain of federal antidiscrimination statutes. This potential is illustrated by pending and recent lower court cases in which transgender individuals have challenged a variety of federal, state, and local laws and policies on constitutional grounds. . . .

Although the Court does not want to think about the consequences of its decision, we will not be able to avoid those issues for long. The entire Federal Judiciary will be mired for years in disputes about the reach of the Court's reasoning. . . .

The updating desire to which the Court succumbs no doubt arises from humane and generous impulses. Today, many Americans know individuals who are gay, lesbian, or transgender and want them to be treated with the dignity, consideration, and fairness that everyone deserves. But the authority of this Court is limited to saying what the law *is*.

The Court itself recognizes this: "The place to make new legislation . . . lies in Congress. When it comes to statutory interpretation, our role is limited to applying the law's demands as faithfully as we can in the cases that come before us." *Ante*, at _____.

It is easy to utter such words. If only the Court would live by them.

I respectfully dissent.

Justice KAVANAUGH, dissenting.

Like many cases in this Court, this case boils down to one fundamental question: Who decides? Title VII of the Civil Rights Act of 1964 prohibits employment discrimination "because of" an individual's "race, color, religion, sex, or national origin." The question here is whether Title VII should be expanded to prohibit employment discrimination because of sexual orientation. Under the Constitution's separation of powers, the responsibility to amend Title VII belongs to Congress and the President in the legislative process, not to this Court.

The political branches are well aware of this issue. In 2007, the U.S. House of Representatives voted 235 to 184 to prohibit employment discrimination on the basis of sexual orientation. In 2013, the U.S. Senate voted 64 to 32 in favor of a similar ban. In 2019, the House again voted 236 to 173 to outlaw employment discrimination on the basis of sexual orientation. Although both the House and Senate have voted at different times to prohibit sexual orientation discrimination, the two Houses have not yet come together with the President to enact a bill into law.

The policy arguments for amending Title VII are very weighty. The Court has previously stated, and I fully agree, that gay and lesbian Americans "cannot be treated as social outcasts or as inferior in dignity and worth." *Masterpiece Cakeshop, Ltd. v. Colorado Civil Rights Comm'n*, 584 U.S. ____, ____, 138 S.Ct. 1719, 1727 (2018).

But we are judges, not Members of Congress. And in Alexander Hamilton's words, federal judges exercise "neither Force nor Will, but merely judgment." The Federalist No. 78. Under the Constitution's separation of powers, our role as judges is to interpret and follow the law as written, regardless of whether we like the result. Our role is not to make or amend the law. As written, Title VII does not prohibit employment discrimination because of sexual orientation [or gender identity]. . . .

For the sake of argument, I will assume that firing someone because of their sexual orientation may, as a very literal matter, entail making a distinction based on sex. But to prevail in this case with their literalist approach, the plaintiffs must *also* establish one of two other points. The plaintiffs must establish that courts, when interpreting a statute, adhere to literal meaning rather than ordinary meaning. Or alternatively, the plaintiffs must establish that the ordinary meaning of "discriminate because of sex" — not just the literal meaning — encompasses sexual orientation discrimination. The plaintiffs fall short on both counts.

First, courts must follow ordinary meaning, not literal meaning. And courts must adhere to the ordinary meaning of phrases, not just the meaning of the words in a phrase.

There is no serious debate about the foundational interpretive principle that courts adhere to ordinary meaning, not literal meaning, when interpreting statutes. As Justice Scalia explained, "the good textualist is not a literalist." A. Scalia, A Matter of Interpretation 24 (1997). . . .

Judges adhere to ordinary meaning for two main reasons: rule of law and democratic accountability. A society governed by the rule of law must have laws that are known and understandable to the citizenry. And judicial adherence to ordinary meaning facilitates the democratic accountability of America's elected representatives for the laws they enact. Citizens and legislators must be able to ascertain the law by reading the words of the statute. Both the rule of law and democratic accountability badly suffer when a court adopts a hidden or obscure interpretation of the law, and not its ordinary meaning.

Consider a simple example of how ordinary meaning differs from literal meaning. A statutory ban on "vehicles in the park" would literally encompass a baby stroller. But no good judge would interpret the statute that way because the word "vehicle," in its ordinary meaning, does not encompass baby strollers. . . .

Next is a critical point of emphasis in this case. The difference between literal and ordinary meaning becomes especially important when — as in this case — judges consider *phrases* in statutes. (Recall that the shorthand version of the phrase at issue here is "discriminate because of sex.") Courts must heed the ordinary meaning of the *phrase as a whole*, not just the meaning of the words in the phrase. That is because a phrase may have a more precise or confined meaning than the literal meaning of the individual words in the phrase. Examples abound. An "American flag" could literally encompass a flag made in America, but in common parlance it denotes the Stars and Stripes. A "three-pointer" could literally include a field goal in football, but in common parlance, it is a shot from behind the arc in basketball. A "cold war" could literally mean any wintertime war, but in common parlance it signifies a conflict short of open warfare. A "washing machine" could literally refer to any machine used for washing any item, but in everyday speech it means a machine for washing clothes. . . .

Second, in light of the bedrock principle that we must adhere to the ordinary meaning of a phrase, the question in this case boils down to the ordinary meaning of the phrase "discriminate because of sex." Does the ordinary meaning of that phrase encompass discrimination because of sexual orientation? The answer is plainly no.

On occasion, it can be difficult for judges to assess ordinary meaning. Not here. Both common parlance and common legal usage treat sex discrimination and sexual orientation discrimination as two distinct categories of discrimination — back in 1964 and still today. . . .

Consider the employer who has four employees but must fire two of them for financial reasons. Suppose the four employees are a straight man, a straight woman, a gay man, and a lesbian. The employer with animosity against women (animosity based on sex) will fire the two women. The employer with animosity against gays (animosity based on sexual orientation) will fire the gay man and the lesbian. Those are two distinct harms caused by two distinct biases that have two different outcomes. To treat one as a form of the other — as the majority opinion does — misapprehends common language, human psychology, and real life.

It also rewrites history. Seneca Falls was not Stonewall. The women's rights movement was not (and is not) the gay rights movement, although many people obviously support or participate in both. So to think that sexual orientation discrimination is just a form of sex discrimination is not just a mistake of language and psychology, but also a mistake of history and sociology.

Importantly, an overwhelming body of federal law reflects and reinforces the ordinary meaning and demonstrates that sexual orientation discrimination is distinct from, and not a form of, sex discrimination. Since enacting Title VII in 1964, Congress has *never* treated sexual orientation discrimination the same as, or as a form of, sex discrimination. Instead, Congress has consistently treated sex discrimination and sexual orientation discrimination as legally distinct categories of discrimination.

Many federal statutes prohibit sex discrimination, and many federal statutes also prohibit sexual orientation discrimination. But those sexual orientation statutes expressly prohibit sexual orientation discrimination in addition to expressly prohibiting sex discrimination. *Every single one.* To this day, Congress has never defined sex discrimination to encompass sexual orientation discrimination. Instead, when Congress wants to prohibit sexual orientation discrimination in addition to sex discrimination, Congress explicitly refers to sexual orientation discrimination.

That longstanding and widespread congressional practice matters. When interpreting statutes, as the Court has often said, we "usually presume differences in language" convey "differences in meaning." When Congress chooses distinct phrases to accomplish distinct purposes, and does so over and over again for decades, we may not lightly toss aside all of Congress's careful handiwork. . . .

As demonstrated by all of the statutes covering sexual orientation discrimination, Congress knows how to prohibit sexual orientation discrimination. So courts should not read that specific concept into the general words "discriminate because of sex." We cannot close our eyes to the indisputable fact that Congress — for several decades in a large number of statutes — has identified sex discrimination and sexual orientation discrimination as two distinct categories.

Where possible, we also strive to interpret statutes so as not to create undue surplusage. It is not uncommon to find some scattered redundancies in statutes. But reading sex discrimination to encompass sexual orientation discrimination would cast aside as surplusage the numerous references to sexual orientation discrimination sprinkled throughout the U.S. Code in laws enacted over the last 25 years.

In short, an extensive body of federal law both reflects and reinforces the widespread understanding that sexual orientation discrimination is distinct from, and not a form of, sex discrimination. . . .

In sum, all of the usual indicators of ordinary meaning — common parlance, common usage by Congress, the practice in the Executive Branch, the laws in the States, and the decisions of this Court — overwhelmingly establish that sexual orientation discrimination is distinct from, and not a form of, sex discrimination. The usage has been consistent across decades, in both the federal and state contexts.

Judge Sykes summarized the law and language this way: "To a fluent speaker of the English language — then and now — . . . discrimination 'because of sex' is not reasonably understood to include discrimination based on sexual orientation, a different immutable characteristic. Classifying people by sexual orientation is different than classifying them by sex. The two traits are categorically distinct and widely recognized as such. There is no ambiguity or vagueness here."

To tie it all together, the plaintiffs have only two routes to succeed here. Either they can say that literal meaning overrides ordinary meaning when the two conflict. Or they can say that the ordinary meaning of the phrase "discriminate because of sex" encompasses sexual orientation discrimination. But the first flouts long-settled principles of statutory interpretation. And the second contradicts the widespread ordinary use of the English language in America. . . .

Until the last few years, every U.S. Court of Appeals to address this question concluded that Title VII does not prohibit discrimination because of sexual orientation. . . . The unanimity of those 30 federal judges shows that the question as a matter of law, as compared to as a matter of policy, was not deemed close. Those 30 judges realized a seemingly obvious point: Title VII is not a general grant of authority for judges to fashion an evolving common law of equal treatment in the workplace. Rather, Title VII identifies certain specific categories of prohibited discrimination. And under the separation of powers, Congress — not the courts — possesses the authority to amend or update the law, as Congress has done with age discrimination and disability discrimination, for example.

So what changed from the situation only a few years ago when 30 out of 30 federal judges had agreed on this question? Not the text of Title VII. The law has not changed. Rather, the judges' decisions have evolved.

To be sure, the majority opinion today does not openly profess that it is judicially updating or amending Title VII. But the majority opinion achieves the same outcome by seizing on literal meaning and overlooking the ordinary meaning of the phrase "discriminate because of sex." . . .

The majority opinion [argues] that courts should base their interpretation of statutes on the text as written, not on the legislators' subjective intentions. Of course that is true. No one disagrees. It is "the provisions of our laws rather than the principal concerns of our legislators by which we are governed."

But in my respectful view, the majority opinion makes a fundamental mistake by confusing ordinary meaning with subjective intentions. To briefly explain: In the early years after Title VII was enacted, some may have wondered whether Title VII's prohibition on sex discrimination protected male employees. After all, covering male employees may not have been the intent of some who voted for the statute. Nonetheless, discrimination on the basis of sex against women and discrimination on the basis of sex against men are both understood as discrimination because of sex (back in 1964 and now) and are therefore encompassed within Title VII. So too, regardless of what the intentions of the drafters might have been, the ordinary meaning of the law demonstrates that harassing an employee because of her sex is discriminating against the employee because of her sex with respect to the "terms, conditions, or privileges of employment," as this Court rightly concluded. *Meritor Savings Bank, FSB v. Vinson*, 477 U.S. 57, 64 (1986) (internal quotation marks omitted).

By contrast, this case involves sexual orientation discrimination, which has long and widely been understood as distinct from, and not a form of, sex discrimination. Until now, federal law has always reflected that common usage and recognized that distinction between sex discrimination and sexual orientation discrimination. To fire one employee because she is a woman and another employee because he is gay implicates two distinct societal concerns, reveals two distinct biases, imposes two distinct harms, and falls within two distinct statutory prohibitions.

To be sure, as Judge Lynch appropriately recognized, it is "understandable" that those seeking legal protection for gay people "search for innovative arguments to classify workplace bias against gays as a form of discrimination that is already prohibited by federal law. But the arguments advanced by the majority ignore the evident meaning of the language of Title VII, the social realities that distinguish between the kinds of biases that the statute sought to exclude from the workplace from those it did not, and the distinctive nature of anti-gay prejudice."

The majority opinion insists that it is not rewriting or updating Title VII, but instead is just humbly reading the text of the statute as written. But that assertion is tough to accept. Most everyone familiar with the use of the English language in America understands that the ordinary meaning of sexual orientation discrimination is distinct from the ordinary meaning of sex discrimination. Federal law distinguishes the two. State law distinguishes the two. This Court's cases distinguish the two. Statistics on discrimination distinguish the two. History distinguishes the two. Psychology distinguishes the two. Sociology distinguishes the two. Human resources departments all over America distinguish the two. Sports leagues distinguish the two. Political groups distinguish the two. Advocacy groups distinguish the two. Common parlance distinguishes the two. Common sense distinguishes the two.

As a result, many Americans will not buy the novel interpretation unearthed and advanced by the Court today. Many will no doubt believe that the Court has unilaterally rewritten American vocabulary and American law — a "statutory amendment courtesy of unelected judges." Some will surmise that the Court succumbed to "the natural desire that beguiles judges along with other human beings into imposing their own views of goodness, truth, and justice upon others."

I have the greatest, and unyielding, respect for my colleagues and for their good faith. But when this Court usurps the role of Congress, as it does today, the public understandably becomes confused about who the policymakers really are in our system of separated powers, and inevitably becomes cynical about the oft-repeated aspiration that judges base their decisions on law rather than on personal preference. The best way for judges to demonstrate that we are deciding cases based on the ordinary meaning of the law is to walk the walk, even in the hard cases when we might prefer a different policy outcome.

In judicially rewriting Title VII, the Court today cashiers an ongoing legislative process, at a time when a new law to prohibit sexual orientation discrimination was probably close at hand. . . .

It is true that meaningful legislative action takes time — often too much time, especially in the unwieldy morass on Capitol Hill. But the Constitution does not put the Legislative Branch in the "position of a television quiz show contestant so that when a given period of time has elapsed and a problem remains unsolved by them, the federal judiciary may press a buzzer and take its turn at fashioning a solution." Rehnquist, The Notion of a Living Constitution, 54 Texas L. Rev. 693, 700 (1976). The proper role of the Judiciary in statutory interpretation cases is "to apply, not amend, the work of the People's representatives," even when the

judges might think that "Congress should reenter the field and alter the judgments it made in the past."

Instead of a hard-earned victory won through the democratic process, today's
victory is brought about by judicial dictate — judges latching on to a novel form
of living literalism to rewrite ordinary meaning and remake American law. Under
the Constitution and laws of the United States, this Court is the wrong body to
change American law in that way. The Court's ruling "comes at a great cost to
representative self-government." And the implications of this Court's usurpation
of the legislative process will likely reverberate in unpredictable ways for years
to come.

Notwithstanding my concern about the Court's transgression of the
Constitution's separation of powers, it is appropriate to acknowledge the
important victory achieved today by gay and lesbian Americans. Millions of
gay and lesbian Americans have worked hard for many decades to achieve
equal treatment in fact and in law. They have exhibited extraordinary vision,
tenacity, and grit — battling often steep odds in the legislative and judicial are-
nas, not to mention in their daily lives. They have advanced powerful policy arguments and can take pride in today's result. Under the Constitution's
separation of powers, however, I believe that it was Congress's role, not this
Court's, to amend Title VII. I therefore must respectfully dissent from the
Court's judgment.

Discussion

1. *The interaction of statutory and constitutional law.* This casebook concerns constitutional law, not legislation. However, we regularly pay attention
to the relationship between the development of constitutional norms and key
statutes, such as the Civil Rights Act of 1964. As noted in the casebook, federal courts interpreted Title VII and the Equal Protection Clause together until
Washington v. Davis in 1976. It is therefore worth asking what effect the Court's
interpretation of Title VII in *Bostock* will have on the Court's equal protection
jurisprudence.

There are two reasons this might happen. The first is external to legal doctrine: The general acceptance of equality rights for LGBTQ people in federal
and state statutes might encourage the Court to recognize discrimination against
sexual orientation minorities as a new suspect classification. The Court has not
recognized a new suspect classification since the 1970s. However, during this
period, the growth of statutory protections for sex equality led the Justices to
their 1970s sex equality jurisprudence.

The second reason is internal to legal doctrine: Justice Gorsuch adopts an
argument about the connection between sex discrimination and discrimination
against gays and against transgender people that might easily be adapted to the
Court's sex equality jurisprudence.

There are of course, differences between the text of Title VII and the language
of the Equal Protection Clause. Title VII speaks of "discriminat[ion]" against

"individuals" "because of" "sex." The Equal Protection Clause uses none of these words. However, equal protection jurisprudence, as it has developed since the 1970s, focuses on discrimination, emphasizes that the protection of individuals and not groups is its central concern, and recognizes sex as a quasi-suspect classification.

Finally, the argument made by the dissenters — that we should be bound by what the adopters of a law believed would be its effect — plays little role in sex equality jurisprudence. Were the Justices to argue that the adopters of the Fourteenth Amendment did not expect that it would protect gays or transgender people, they would have to deal with the problem that the same adopters did not think that the new amendment would protect equality (at least in our modern sense) for married women either.

2. *Discrimination "on the basis of" sex.* What do you make of Justice Gorsuch's argument that one cannot discriminate on the basis of sexual orientation or transgender status without discriminating on the basis of sex? Suppose an employer announces that he will not hire any homosexual or transgender people, sight unseen. Does this policy discriminate on the basis of sex, since presumably it applies to men and women alike?

Pointing to the text, Justice Gorsuch's responds that the policy discriminates against each affected *individual* — because for each individual, they could have been hired if their birth sex were the opposite. Thus, women who are sexually attracted to women could have been hired if they were men sexually attracted to women. Those born as women who now identify as men could have been hired if they were born as men and now identify as men. Do you agree with this argument?

Justice Gorsuch essentially adopts Andrew Koppelman's argument, made 25 years ago, that discrimination against gays and lesbians is sex discrimination, pure and simple. See Andrew Koppelman, Why Discrimination Against Lesbians and Gay Men Is Sex Discrimination, 69 N.Y.U. L. Rev. 197 (1994). An alternative view is that sexual orientation discrimination relies on similar mechanisms as sex discrimination — punishing those who do not conform to traditional gender roles and stereotypes — but is not the same thing. See the discussion in the casebook at pp. 1281-87.

3. *Bisexual erasure.* Does Gorsuch's argument work for bisexuals? Suppose an employer argues that gays, lesbians, and straights are perfectly fine, but not people attracted to *both* sexes. Does the employer discriminate against each individual bisexual applicant on the basis of their sex? Presumably if the applicants were of the opposite sex, they would still be bisexual. What, if anything, does this example tell us about using sex discrimination law to prevent discrimination against sexual orientation minorities? Cf. Kenji Yoshino, The Epistemic Contract of Bisexual Erasure, 52 Stan. L. Rev. 353 (2000) (arguing that both gays and straights have reasons to forget about the existence of bisexuals in anti-discrimination law).

4. *Statutory versus constitutional interpretation — institutional considerations.* If Justice Gorsuch — and Chief Justice Roberts, who joined his opinion — are willing to accept that sexual orientation discrimination is sex

discrimination in interpreting a statute like Title VII, should they also accept it in interpreting the Equal Protection Clause? If they accept it as a constitutional matter, then a constitutional right to marriage equality becomes an easy case.

Note that Chief Justice Roberts dissented vigorously in *Obergefell v. Hodges*, arguing that the issue should have been left to the democratic process. Would he argue that interpreting Title VII is one thing, because Congress can change the statute if it does not like the Court's interpretation, but that interpreting the Constitution is a very different matter? Do you agree?

5. *Textualism and/or originalism.* The conservative Justices debate the role of "textualism" in statutory interpretation, each claiming the mantle of Justice Scalia, who championed this approach. Essentially, textualism in statutory inter-pretation argues that in interpreting a statute, the text is the primary consid-eration. Conversely, legislative history — in the sense of the intentions of the statute's adopters — should play no role, and cannot counteract the meaning of the text. Instead, interpreters should use various canons of construction to clarify the text where it is ambiguous or unclear.

As the opinions of Justices Gorsuch, Alito, and Kavanaugh make clear, there are many different ways to be a textualist. In the hands of Alito and Kavanaugh, textualism starts to look very much like an inquiry into the understandings of the adopters, although both insist that they are only interested in the original mean-ing of the words of the statute in 1964. Gorsuch argues that their textualism is precisely the sort of inquiry into the adopters' expectations that Justice Scalia foreswore. They respond that Gorsuch's textualism has been cut loose from the adopters' meanings to reach radical results, with Alito even comparing it to a pirate ship flying under a false flag.

One can make a similar point about the different ways of doing originalism. Whereas textualism argues that the central concern of interpretation should be the text, originalism argues that interpretation should be bound by what has been fixed at the time of adoption, whether that thing is original intentions, original understanding, or original meaning. According to the most widely adopted ver-sion of originalism these days, original public meaning originalism, constitutional interpreters should be bound by the meaning the text had to the public at the time of adoption, but not the secret intentions of any of its drafters or adopters.

In theory, original public meaning originalism could reach very liberal results, including constitutional protections for LGBTQ people. That is because the orig-inal public meaning of "equal protection of the laws" is the same today as it was in 1868 when the Fourteenth Amendment was adopted. See Jack M. Balkin, Living Originalism (2011). The proper question is whether today's laws give LGBTQ people the "equal protection of the laws." If they do not, then it does not matter that most people in 1868 would likely have disagreed.

In practice, however, conservative originalists tend to focus on how lawyers would have construed the text at the time of adoption. This focus on original legal meaning generally produces results that resemble what the adopting gener-ation would have expected the text to do. Justice Thomas's opinions offer many examples of this approach.

Justice Gorsuch's opinion in *Bostock* has led to a reassessment of whether the conservative legal movement's embrace of textualism and originalism continues to make sense if it is going to produce such unexpected results. For examples of this debate, see Senator Josh Hawley, Was It All for This? The Failure of the Conservative Legal Movement, *Public Discourse*, June 16, 2020, https://www.thepublicdiscourse.com/2020/06/65043/; Jesse Merriam, Legal Conservatism after *Bostock*, *Law and Liberty*, June 29, 2020, https://lawliberty.org/legal-conservatism-after-bostock/.

Insert at the end of p. 1610:

SOUTH BAY UNITED PENTECOSTAL CHURCH v. NEWSOM
140 S.Ct. 1613 (2020)

ON APPLICATION FOR INJUNCTIVE RELIEF

The application for injunctive relief presented to Justice KAGAN and by her referred to the Court is denied.

Justice THOMAS, Justice ALITO, Justice GORSUCH, and Justice KAVANAUGH would grant the application.

CHIEF JUSTICE ROBERTS, concurring in denial of application for injunctive relief.

The Governor of California's Executive Order aims to limit the spread of COVID-19, a novel severe acute respiratory illness that has killed thousands of people in California and more than 100,000 nationwide. At this time, there is no known cure, no effective treatment, and no vaccine. Because people may be infected but asymptomatic, they may unwittingly infect others. The Order places temporary numerical restrictions on public gatherings to address this extraordinary health emergency. State guidelines currently limit attendance at places of worship to 25% of building capacity or a maximum of 100 attendees.

Applicants seek to enjoin enforcement of the Order. "Such a request demands a significantly higher justification than a request for a stay because, unlike a stay, an injunction does not simply suspend judicial alteration of the status quo but grants judicial intervention that has been withheld by lower courts." This power is used where "the legal rights at issue are indisputably clear" and, even then, "sparingly and only in the most critical and exigent circumstances."

Although California's guidelines place restrictions on places of worship, those restrictions appear consistent with the Free Exercise Clause of the First Amendment. Similar or more severe restrictions apply to comparable secular gatherings, including lectures, concerts, movie showings, spectator sports, and theatrical performances, where large groups of people gather in close proximity for extended periods of time. And the Order exempts or treats more leniently only dissimilar activities, such as operating grocery stores, banks, and laundromats, in which people neither congregate in large groups nor remain in close proximity for extended periods.

The precise question of when restrictions on particular social activities should be lifted during the pandemic is a dynamic and fact-intensive matter subject to reasonable disagreement. Our Constitution principally entrusts "[t]he safety and the health of the people" to the politically accountable officials of the States "to guard and protect." *Jacobson v. Massachusetts*, 197 U.S. 11, 38 (1905). When those officials "undertake[] to act in areas fraught with medical and scientific uncertainties," their latitude "must be especially broad." *Marshall v. United States*, 414 U.S. 417, 427 (1974). Where those broad limits are not exceeded, they should not be subject to second-guessing by an "unelected federal judiciary," which lacks the background, competence, and expertise to assess public health and is not accountable to the people. See *Garcia v. San Antonio Metropolitan Transit Authority*, 469 U.S. 528, 545 (1985).

That is especially true where, as here, a party seeks emergency relief in an interlocutory posture, while local officials are actively shaping their response to changing facts on the ground. The notion that it is "indisputably clear" that the Government's limitations are unconstitutional seems quite improbable.

Justice KAVANAUGH, with whom Justice THOMAS and Justice GORSUCH join, dissenting from denial of application for injunctive relief.

I would grant the Church's requested temporary injunction because California's latest safety guidelines discriminate against places of worship and in favor of comparable secular businesses. Such discrimination violates the First Amendment.

In response to the COVID-19 health crisis, California has now limited attendance at religious worship services to 25% of building capacity or 100 attendees, whichever is lower. The basic constitutional problem is that comparable secular businesses are not subject to a 25% occupancy cap, including factories, offices, supermarkets, restaurants, retail stores, pharmacies, shopping malls, pet grooming shops, bookstores, florists, hair salons, and cannabis dispensaries.

South Bay United Pentecostal Church has applied for temporary injunctive relief from California's 25% occupancy cap on religious worship services. Importantly, the Church is willing to abide by the State's rules that apply to comparable secular businesses, including the rules regarding social distancing and hygiene. But the Church objects to a 25% occupancy cap that is imposed on religious worship services but not imposed on those comparable secular businesses.

In my view, California's discrimination against religious worship services contravenes the Constitution. As a general matter, the "government may not use religion as a basis of classification for the imposition of duties, penalties, privileges or benefits." This Court has stated that discrimination against religion is "odious to our Constitution." *Trinity Lutheran Church of Columbia, Inc. v. Comer*, 582 U.S. ____, ____, 137 S.Ct. 2012, 2025 (2017).

To justify its discriminatory treatment of religious worship services, California must show that its rules are "justified by a compelling governmental interest" and "narrowly tailored to advance that interest." *Church of Lukumi Babalu Aye, Inc. v. Hialeah*, 508 U.S. 520, 531-532 (1993). California undoubtedly has a compelling interest in combating the spread of COVID-19 and protecting the health of its citizens. But "restrictions inexplicably applied to one group and exempted from another do little to further these goals and do much to burden religious freedom." What California needs is a compelling justification for distinguishing between (i) religious worship services and (ii) the litany of other secular businesses that are not subject to an occupancy cap.

California has not shown such a justification. The Church has agreed to abide by the State's rules that apply to comparable secular businesses. That raises important questions: "Assuming all of the same precautions are taken, why can someone safely walk down a grocery store aisle but not a pew? And why can someone safely interact with a brave deliverywoman but not with a stoic minister?"

The Church and its congregants simply want to be treated equally to comparable secular businesses. California already trusts its residents and any number of businesses to adhere to proper social distancing and hygiene practices. The State cannot "assume the worst when people go to worship but assume the best when people go to work or go about the rest of their daily lives in permitted social settings."

California has ample options that would allow it to combat the spread of COVID-19 without discriminating against religion. The State could "insist that the congregants adhere to social-distancing and other health requirements and leave it at that—just as the Governor has done for comparable secular activities." Or alternatively, the State could impose reasonable occupancy caps across the board. But absent a compelling justification (which the State has not offered), the State may not take a looser approach with, say, supermarkets, restaurants, factories, and offices while imposing stricter requirements on places of worship.

The State also has substantial room to draw lines, especially in an emergency. But as relevant here, the Constitution imposes one key restriction on that line-drawing: The State may not discriminate against religion.

In sum, California's 25% occupancy cap on religious worship services indisputably discriminates against religion, and such discrimination violates the First Amendment. The Church would suffer irreparable harm from not being able to hold services on Pentecost Sunday in a way that comparable secular businesses and persons can conduct their activities. I would therefore grant the Church's request for a temporary injunction. I respectfully dissent.

Discussion:

1. The central question in *South Bay United Pentecostal Church* is how to tell whether there has been discrimination against religion, which in this context would mean treating religious activities differently from comparable secular activities. What factors make religious and secular activities similar or different?

With respect to the danger of spreading COVID-19, are religious services more like grocery stores, banks, and laundromats, or more like lectures, concerts, movie showings, spectator sports, and theatrical performances? California argued that religious services are not like grocery stories, banks, and laundromats because people do not crowd together in grocery stores, banks, or laundromats to speak, chant, and sing. These latter activities are more likely to spread the virus widely. Therefore, California argued, by treating religious services differently, and more like concerts and spectator sports, it was not discriminating against religion. Does it matter which kind of religion is involved and which kind of religious ritual is being practiced?

2. Should churches be required to change their normal practices — for example, by offering more services per day with fewer people more widely spread apart? Or is the burden on government to accommodate the practices that adherents feel are required by their religion? If religion is the most important thing in people's lives, why shouldn't religious services take precedence over virtually any secular businesses? What role should effects on innocent third parties play in answering this question?

3. While this case was developing in the spring of 2020, the country experienced weeks of sustained outdoor protests against police racism following the killing of George Floyd. These protests involved large crowds, chanting, and singing. Should California have shut down or limited these protests in the interests of public health? (Note that California's treatment of these protests was not before the Court in this case.) Are outdoor protests different from indoor church services? From outdoor church services? Does it matter if protesters wear masks? If people at religious services wear masks?

4. This case is in an unusual procedural posture because it is a petition for an emergency injunction without time for a full hearing, during a period in which the state was rolling out its reopening plan in phases. Chief Justice Roberts argued that under the circumstances, courts should defer to local officials who best understand the relevant dangers, costs, and benefits, while Justice Kavanaugh argued that where there was a clear violation of the Free Exercise Clause, the Court should step in to protect constitutional liberties. Roberts responded that the constitutional violation was anything but clear. In these circumstances, what should the Court have done?